YUKIO MISHIMA

LITERATURE AND LIFE: WORLD WRITERS

Complete list of titles in the series available from the publisher on request.

YUKIO MISHIMA

Peter Wolfe

A Frederick Ungar Book
CONTINUUM · NEW YORK

To
Tommy Kneitel,
a free son
who has always known the difference between
a Guido and a Gomez
and also between a Hruba and a Hrichman

1989

The Continuum Publishing Company
370 Lexington Avenue
New York, NY 10017

Printed in the United States of America

Library of Congress Cataloging-in-Publication Data

Wolfe, Peter, 1933–
  Yukio Mishima / Peter Wolfe.
      p.   cm. — (Literature and life. World writers)
  "A Frederick Ungar book."
  Bibliography: p.
  Includes index.
  ISBN 0-8264-0443-X
  1. Mishima, Yukio, 1925–1970—Criticism and interpretation.
I. Title. II. Series.
PL833.I7Z926 1989
895.6'35—dc20   89-7739
                                                                      CIP

Contents

Acknowledgments

The author wishes to thank those whose time, expertise, and energy went into the preparation of this book: Marla Schorr, who typed and edited the manuscript; Richard H. Mitchell, Terence S. Martin, and Herman W. Smith, who supplied important background information; Costa Haddad and Terry Jones of the University of Missouri-St. Louis Arts and Sciences College, who both organized a grant that sped the book's completion.

The combined help of the following people amounts to a major contribution: Robert Des Verney, Ronald G. Hetrick, Yoshino Sato, German Padilla, Vernon Dent, Anita Hamilton, Spero Manilatos, Juliet Lowenstein, Mateo Cefalu, and Ken Post.

Chronology

1925   Kimitake Hiraoka born, 14 January, in Tokyo.

1928   Birth of Kimitake's sister, Mitsuko.

1929   Kimitake becomes so sick with auto-intoxication that he nearly dies; the debilitating effects of the attack linger into his adulthood.

1931   Enrolls as a student at the Gakushuin (Peers School).

1937   Begins studying at the Gakushuin's middle school; leaves the home of his grandparents to live with his mother.

1939   Death of Natsuko, his tyrannical grandmother.

1941   Publishes his first long work, "The Forest in Full Bloom," in the school magazine; takes the pen name of Yukio Mishima.

1942   Enters the senior school at the Gakushuin, where he will distinguish himself as both a student and a writer.

1944   Graduates from the Gakushuin first in his class and gets, as his prize, a silver watch from the emperor; passes his army physical, but, after being skipped over in the draft, begins studying at Tokyo Imperial University; *The Forest in Full Bloom* is published as a book.

1945   Removed by the War Ministry from the university and assigned to work in an airplane factory; encourages the misdiagnosis of an inexperienced doctor to avoid military service; death of Mitsuko.

1946   Studies German law at Tokyo University; continues to write fiction.

1947   Discontinues his studies to take a job at the Ministry of Finance.

1948   Enjoys enough success as a short-story writer to leave the ministry in order to write full time.

1949   Publication of *Confessions of a Mask,* which becomes a big hit in Japan; appearance of his first play, *Fire House.*

1950   A second successful novel, *Thirst for Love,* is published; uses his royalties to move himself and his parents into a fashionable suburban home just outside of Tokyo.

1951   Publication of the highly controversial *Forbidden Colors;* sails for the United States in December aboard the *President Wilson.*

1952   Travels in the United States, Brazil, Europe, and Greece.

1954   Publishes *The Sound of Waves* and sells the movie rights of the book to Toho, an important Japanese film company.

1955   Begins bodybuilding and weight lifting to overcome his puniness.

1956   Publishes *The Temple of the Golden Pavilion; The Sound of Waves* and *Five Modern No Plays* appear in English translation in the United States.

1957   Spends six months in the U.S., his visit highlighted by his impressive progress as both a bodybuilder and a speaker of English.

1958   Becomes engaged but has his engagement broken; rebounds from disappointment to marry twenty-one-year-old Yoko Sugiyama.

1959   Moves into an expensive new modern home with Yoko, the home practically adjoining one he built for his parents; his daughter Noriko is born; starts to learn kendo (dueling with bamboo staves).

1961   Birth of his son, Ichiro.

1963   Publication of *The Sailor Who Fell from Grace with the Sea.*

1966   Completes *Spring Snow* and begins *Runaway Horses;* poses for the notorious photograph of himself as St. Sebastian.

1967   Founds the Tatenokai, or Shield Society, his private army.

1968   Finishes *Runaway Horses* and begins *The Temple of Dawn; Spring Snow* is published.

1969   Publication of *Runaway Horses;* his ultranationalism has hurt his literary reputation.

1970   Publication of *The Temple of Dawn;* finishes *The Decay of the Angel,* the last installment of his *Sea of Fertility* cycle and delivers it to his publisher; the same day, 25 November, commits ritual suicide together with a favorite from the Shield Society.

1971   Publication of *The Decay of the Angel.*
1973   Publication of his collected work in Japanese in thirty-six volumes.
1974   Appearance of the only two English-language biographies of Mishima to date, Henry Scott-Stokes, *The Life and Death of Yukio Mishima,* and John Nathan, *Mishima: A Biography.*

1

The Point of Action

Why should this book be read? How much can be gained from it? Luis Canales, guest editor of the special Yukio Mishima issue of *Kaleidoscope Kyoto* (April 1985), explains that Mishima wrote "40 novels, 33 plays, a travel book, more than 80 short stories, and a large number of essays."[1] Of this huge output, which came out in thirty-six chunky volumes in Japan after Mishima's death, less than a third has appeared in English translation. How can this fraction of Mishima's published output enable the English-language reader to take hold of him? Why should you bother reading my book?

The answer stems from Mishima (who was born Kimitake Hiraoka) himself. Supporting Graham Greene's belief that every creative writer worth considering works from an obsession,[2] Mishima writes from his darkest self. So clearly does he lay his cards on the table, in fact, that they cover it. His life and work both spring from the same set of impulses, and we are not allowed to forget it. The persistence and depth of these impulses—conflicts he never resolved—make him a suitable subject for a full, accurate study in English. As in so much of Freud, linear development cannot describe Mishima's psyche. Patterns from his earlier work recur in the last things he wrote. This recurrence of incidents, images, and ideas shows his ahistorical unconscious pushing into the historical layers of his mind. The self in Yukio Mishima (1925–70) is one, not many. A biographer, Henry Scott-Stokes, points out that the work known in English as *The Forest in Full Bloom,* published when Mishima was sixteen, ends in a way similar to *The Decay of the Angel* (1971; English translation, 1974), his last work, written thirty years later. Mishima's first novel, *Thieves* (1948), another biographer, John Nathan, says, contains a love suicide[3]—a motif that would be re-

11

peated in Mishima's most famous work, "Patriotism" (1960, 1966) and implied in the late *Temple of Dawn* (1970, 1973).

But it is time to change our approach. If we do not have to read Mishima's whole corpus in order to know him, we do need to know about the culture from which the corpus springs: Japan's customs, beliefs, and notions of right and wrong. These differ widely from the realities we take for granted in the West. The enormous changes thundering through Japan in the last century enforced, rather than weakened, traditional Japanese values; in times of sweeping change, nations, like people, cling to what is stable and familiar in order to preserve their identity. Developments beginning early in the Meiji era (1868–1912) show clearly why the Japanese sense of self has felt so menaced in the past hundred years. The third quarter of the nineteenth century in Japan saw the fall of feudalism, a new tolerance toward foreigners, and, as a by-product of this nonexclusion policy, great advances in machine production. Buttressing this industrial growth were military gains, against China (in 1894–95) and Russia (1904–5). These successes and others like them brought about the annexation of Formosa (1895), Sakhalin (1905), and Korea (1910), and also the 1914 expulsion of Germany from the Shantung peninsula. In the years from 1945–70 Japan enjoyed outstanding prosperity, strength, and confidence. Her optimism had a solid base. Unprecedented economic advances, caused in part by new developments in shipping and heavy industry, raised living standards to new heights. Yet few Japanese could forget that this bonanza stemmed from the ravages of the Pacific War of 1941–45. Nor was the bonanza distributed equally. Edwin O. Reischauer shows postwar Japan suffering from poor roads and housing, water pollution, and a serious food deficit (in the late 1960s Japan was still importing 20 percent of her food supply).[4] There were also complaints of spiritual vacuity. Ivan Morris's thoughtful book on heroism in Japan, *The Nobility of Failure* (1975), quotes Mishima's lament that Japan's postwar boom has crushed her spirit; the "overwhelming importance" the Japanese people have attached to "security and material ease," Mishima groaned, has obscured "what is unique and most precious in their country's heritage."[5]

Others have spoken of Japan's singularity in different terms. In *Behind the Mask*, first published as *A Japanese Mirror* (1983), Ian

Buruma claims that it has made Japan an oddity even among her Asian neighbors: "Japan is in many respects the loneliest, most isolated member of the modern world. If we in the West . . . often find the Japanese odd, so do most Asians."[6] Much of Japan's mystery comes from two sources—her isolation and her overpopulation. Politeness has been Japan's customary response to the tensions felt by unequals occupying a common living space. The same people who fight furiously abroad are courteous and docile at home. The constraints caused by overcrowding give them no other choice. Because Japan is a small island nation with many large cities, people keep meeting all the time. The world-celebrated Japanese politeness rises from an awareness of the interdependency caused by this frequency of contact. A person who wins a job, a contract, or a place on a team that many others have strived for unsuccessfully will not want to feel guilty about his victory any more than he will want to incur the resentment of these others, particularly if some of them are neighbors, friends, and family. Because he cannot escape or hide from them, he derides his victory. He may also take the derision to heart, a practice sanctioned by Japanese tradition. He may even become civic minded, in a process that resembles what often happens with successful American capitalists. Whereas the American business tycoon may crown a career of high-volume swindling by becoming a benefactor and philanthropist, the Japanese super-achiever will more likely spurn both worldly goods and the tactics used to win them; Heihachiro Oshio (1793–1838), a hero of Mishima's, gave up his job as a police inspector, sold his vast library, and burned his home to protest political corruption in Osaka at age thirty-seven.[7]

Most Japanese today would shrink from Oshio's extremism. Instead, they would probably stave off the psychological stresses of success in two ways—by expressing faith in order and hierarchy and by rating the group over the individual. The title of the third chapter of Ruth Benedict's classic *The Chrysanthemum and the Sword* (1946), "Taking One's Proper Station," refers to the problems of the Japanese who wants to excel in a nation traditionally pledged to self-restraint. Benedict's chapter[8] discusses the Japanese preference for harmony and selflessness over egotism and self-interest. Strength in Japan lies in conformity, not rebellion, a fact that explains why the

Japanese cultivate strong ties within the family, the military, and the corporation. They will even suffer in order to meet their group obligations because group membership confers important compensatory benefits. Serving the commonweal can ease the pain of knowing that one's place in a tiny, congested nation is distressingly small. Although the Japanese may forfeit mobility and assertiveness, at least they know the boundaries of their freedom, and they can be reasonably sure that these boundaries are secure.

On the other hand, many believe that the Japanese have paid too much to define the limits of their lives. The pressure to conform finds expression in the proverb, "The nail that sticks out, must be hammered in." Benedict has tallied the psychological damage incurred by the rigidness of this public morality:

Social pressures in Japan, no matter how voluntarily embraced, ask too much of the individual. They require him to conceal his emotions, to give up his desires, and to stand as the exposed representative of a family, an organization, or a nation. The Japanese have shown that they can take all the self-discipline such a course requires. But the weight upon them is extremely heavy. They have to repress too much for their own good.[9]

1

Mishima dodged the stresses of nonconformism by adopting the stance of the superpatriot. In 1967 he founded the Tatenokai, or Shield Society, a private army dedicated to restoring the prestige of his defeated nation and reinfusing it with its old imperial glory. A brace of posthumously published essays (in the Winter 1971 issue of *The Japanese Interpreter*) conveys the urgency of his belief in the revival of militarism: "We have seen postwar Japan stumble into a spiritual vacuum, preoccupied only with its economic prosperity, unmindful of its national foundations, losing its national spirit, seeking trivialities without looking to fundamentals, and falling into makeshift expediency and hypocrisy."[10] He then compares Japan's alleged spiritual decay with that of ancient Greece, as formulated in Arnold Toynbee's *Hellenism*. Japan, claims Mishima, is languishing since having adopted Western humanism and democracy. Industrial urban Japan has paid too much for its largesse. For one thing, she has severed her traditional tie with her rural roots, a source of ancient wisdom and piety.[11] For another, the psychological stagnancy bred by consumerism has destroyed "the vitality of living in danger"[12] that fosters heroism; the plenty the Japanese have amassed has made them slow and sluggish besides taming their blood.

Mishima also sidestepped the guilt of the nonconformist by claiming that not he, but postwar Japan, by embracing the false American gods of materialism and equality, had lost touch with the nation's cultural identity. He saw in the ancient samurai tradition, with its emphasis upon male beauty, loyalty, and discipline, a wisdom that had almost disappeared. The sword represented for him the same promise of strength and renewal that the Aztec worship did in D. H. Lawrence's *Plumed Serpent* (1926). By using feudalism to check his country's westward drift, he showed his reverence for ancient law. His Shield Society only defied authority in the name of a greater, more potent, authority.

Today, this martial ethos sounds like drum-and-bugle music from a bygone age. It also invokes values not merely outmoded but also repugnant. Mishima's imperialism rests on a low view of mankind: Serving the throne is good because it will distract people from their selfish interests in the name of a grand ideal. Honoring the emperor's divinity will also dislodge the gods of postwar Japan—greed, materialism, and the private self; the Japanese fetish for American music, clothing styles, and social attitudes will yield to an awareness of Japan's noble origins. But will it? Mishima's devotion to a remote elitist past sounds pagan, strident, and suicidal. It also clashes with the conformism that was drilled into him from childhood. He retained more of this conformism than its categories. The guilty knowledge, however unconfessed, that his samurai worship flouted strict norms of behavior exhausted him. Exhaustion and guilt explain why he, the few Tatenokai members who had not abandoned him, and the neo-samurai in his fiction all fall short of their goals. Exhaustion and guilt explain, too, why these men act like guilty little boys punishing themselves for making a mess; the nail that sticks up gets hit. Were they more mature and social-minded, purpose would not drain out of them so quickly. They would be less vulnerable to guilt and better equipped to serve the community.

Rather than promoting slum clearance, clean air, or educational reform, Mishima disemboweled himself within an hour after subduing the commandant of Japan's Self-Defense Force.

Both his suicide and the rearguard warrior code that prompted it have hurt Japan at home and abroad. The West's knowledge of the warrior tradition comes, unfortunately, from the tradition's two great distorters—Mishima and the brilliant film director, Akira Kurosawa. Blood-splashed films like *Seven Samurai* and *Yojimbo* have created Japanified versions of American cowboy stories; such films feature duty- and death-ridden heroes who love their swords more than themselves. Although young renegades like the ones in Mishima's *Runaway Horses* (1969, 1973) have always held a place in Japan's samurai tradition, that place has been marginal. Samurai for centuries, going back to the Middle Ages, have cultivated self-improvement, usually by studying medicine, theater, languages, literature, or calligraphy. The raging drive to self-destruction that Mishima writes about moved very few of them, even the most warlike.

What is more, the imperial glory that he wanted to revive may have never existed except in his mind. Alex Shishin, writing for the *Japan Times* in December 1985, uses inequities in taxation during the long Tokugawa era (1603–1867), Japan's enslavement of Korea in the Meiji era, and the wartime atrocities committed by Japanese soldiers in both China and Indonesia during the Showa period (1926–89) to lay bare Mishima's ignorance of history. "There is always something bogus, or at least self-deceptive, about the sort of obsessions Mishima had about national purity,"[13] Shishin concludes. Obsession certainly fogged Mishima's view of Emperor Hirohito, whom the author continued to worship as a symbol of divine authority even after he denied his divinity. Mishima always ignored the emperor's pleasure. At least twice, Hirohito rejected the emperor-centered mysticism invoked by extremists to justify rebellion and slaughter. Nathan has discussed the first of these two incidents, the notorious Army Rebellion of 1936, which underlay Mishima's "Patriotism": "Emperor Hirohito . . . when he learned of the uprising, demanded angrily that the officers who had risen in his name be punished as 'mutineers.' "[14] Ten years later, in January 1946, besides telling his people that he was a person, not a god,

Hirohito denounced his divinity as "an imaginary and harmful notion."[15] Undaunted, Mishima denounced this denunciation (the *ningen sengen*); Hirohito's rejection of godhood angers the spirits of both the young rebel officers of 1936 and the kamikaze flyers of the Pacific War in Mishima's "Voice of the Hero Spirits" (1966). This (untranslated) semifictional work prefigured Mishima's political activism: Whether the emperor liked it or not, the uplift of Japanese culture depended upon the performance of violent acts in his serene name.[16]

Mishima should have been looking elsewhere if he wanted to improve his country's well-being. For instance, the ugliness resulting from postwar industrialism needed to be set right. Speaking of the urban sprawl that includes greater Tokyo, Osaka, Kyoto, Nagoya, and Kobe, Robert C. Christopher notes "factories built without the slightest concession to architectural aesthetics, warehouses that look . . . afflicted with giantism, enormous boxlike apartment buildings, and interminable clusters of shabby-looking shops, auto-repair establishments, and other small enterprises."[17] But, whereas Mishima couldn't have enjoyed this squalor any more than Christopher, he was hunting bigger game; the zealot cares less about instituting economic or social reforms than about redeeming souls. His cries usually vanish in the wilderness, too, because most people find them irrelevant. Edwin Reischauer claims that Mishima's pleas for martial valor and national pride did not affect the mood of affluence and optimism of the late 1960s, when Japan (though as ugly as Christopher claimed) had become the world's third richest country:

Support for the constitution [which removed Hirohito's political power and made him a symbol of the nation] . . . remained overwhelming, and there was still strong abhorrence of past policies of . . . authoritarianism at home. Rightists of the prewar variety constituted no more than a tiny disreputable fringe on the political scene.[18]

Did Mishima seek out this shabby, lonely fringe? His having founded the Shield Society to defend to the point of death an emperor who did not want or need defending shows the dangers of confusing politics with aesthetics. In his confusion, Mishima directed neither the patriotic nor the artistic impulse back toward everyday life. More's the pity, because to do so might have influenced the way his fellows saw and enjoyed life.

Ian Buruma noted correctly of him in the *New York Review of Books* in October 1985, "He wanted to believe in a mythical Japanese past when spirits were pure and values unsullied."[19] Mishima invented a local legend, called it history, and then acted on it as if it were real. His revivalism has an intriguing, if dangerous, allure. Like Hemingway, he valued bravery as the defining male experience; only through acts of courage can maleness be known and lived. The code of the warrior does for Mishima what bullfighting gave Hemingway; it provides a touchstone and a ruling metaphor. Like the bullring in Hemingway's Spain, Mishima's warrior code furnishes both a set of rituals and a moral proving ground. The purity of the samurai's commitment gauges his moral worth. He is both a competitor and a companion.

But the Shield Society had purposes other than cleansing and purifying. Many have accused Mishima of using military discipline to further his erotic fantasies. So unfeasible was his goal of imperial restoration that it remained permanently out of reach. Emperor worship legitimized Mishima's quest for the warrior's death of seppuku, or self-disembowelment. Buruma's calling him "an extreme mythomaniac" who was "obsessed and driven by sex"[20] refers to a politicized aesthetic that fused sex, violence, and martial courage with fanatical loyalty to the emperor. The aesthetic outlined each of the steps Mishima was to take to his death. And he loved these means to his end as much as he did the agonizing end itself. An insight into his motives comes from Christopher's statement, "Guilt is . . . the single most potent lever in personal relationships in Japan."[21] The statement can be supported empirically. Japan's smallness personalizes many of the casual bonds formed within her borders; the need for cooperation among strangers living in a tight, crowded space where the family serves as a model for behavior rules out the casual tie. Buruma's warning, "Mishima was in almost every respect an oddity, and it is dangerous to see him as typical of anything,"[22] raises questions that must have occurred to Mishima himself. Although his ultranationalism clarified the deep sources of political fervor, it did not link that fervor to judgment and responsibility. The courage and devotion of the Shield Society contained no plan for Japan's future, nor did it set forth a public policy based on freedom and justice.

Mishima wanted to build a new Japanese empire, using ancient symbols of power, external show, and angry patriotic rhetoric. But he had no agenda or program. He could not probe the coils of political negotiation and compromise. He wanted national glory but not the toil, the training, and the orderly implementation of an effective economy. He never addressed the practicalities of progress and reform. Reasoning from its lack of a political foundation, one may assume that Mishima knew his militarism to be unworthy of both him and his genius. The bogus romantic concept of destiny attracted him more than dialogue. In both *Runaway Horses* and *The Way of the Samurai* (1967, 1977), death is both the Japanese warrior's punishment and his reward. It may have been Mishima's, too. Not only did it fulfill his erotic obsessions; chances are that it also assuaged the guilt he felt over politicizing his private fantasies. By dying for a cause ludicrously at odds with the ruling consumerist creed of his day, Mishima conquered Japan so he could submit to it. He was too caught up in his private struggles to take part in those of his homeland. To impress himself, he pretended to be participating in an important political drama. Behind his growling and sword brandishing may have been a sincerely humble Japanese who wanted to say he was sorry for misleading his followers.

His plight resembles that of the aristocratic rebel as defined in Bertrand Russell's *History of Western Philosophy:* "The aristocratic rebel, since he has enough to eat, must have other causes of discontent."[23] The peace and prosperity enjoyed by Japan from 1950–70 ruled out wide-scale political extremism. Not only Mishima but also those to whom he preached had full bellies. Thus he peddled his psychosexual fantasies in military garb. His alienation deepened. The trouble with his loyalist orthodoxy is not that he comes down on the wrong side but that he misunderstood the arguments and repercussions it called forth. The same confusion occurs in his fiction. Mishima may be the worst possible subject for Marxist literary criticism, in view of Marxism's passion for linking cultural, social, and economic events. No irrelevancy, this point also serves as a caution to democratic readers, since the cultivation of self bypasses society in Mishima. He disregards issues related to improving either

the standard or the quality of life. Though he takes risks, he lacks a
social conscience. Rarely will he confirm the continuity between
people, as did the great English Victorians. Nor will he debate the
nature of the good society. And he also ignores the effect of self-
improvement upon social institutions. The motives and goals of his
characters are almost always personal. The sword counts more for
him than trying to improve a reality everybody shares.

In this regard, Mishima is typical; heroic effort in Japanese literature would not be heroic if it succeeded. Only the callous, the
greedy, and the calculating succeed in Japanese literature. Improving
society counts less than savoring the impulses made in our hearts by
a hero who dies serving justice or beauty. Ivan Morris explains this
preference for failure over success: "The Japanese veneration of the
hero as a demigod who is defeated by the world's impurity reinforces
the emotional and aesthetic appeal of *mono no aware* ('the pathos of
things')."[24] To add that failure is more beautiful when crowned by
the courageous, poignant death of a young man at the height of his
glory is to shed revealing light on Mishima. Fictional heroes and
heroines in Japan are slaves to duty; duty outpaces both self-fulfillment and personal welfare for them. Thus self-restraint counts as
much in Japan as freedom does in the United States. The best love
remains undeclared, said Jocho Yamamoto in *Hagakure*, subject of
Mishima's *Way of the Samurai*. Denial floods Japan's national ethic
and character. The strength of will that renounces not only pleasure
but also instinct ranks topmost among all virtues. Ruth Benedict
shows how this self-abnegation colors literature. Because sexual love
in Japanese literature often seeks no outlets, it bypasses the Western
virtues of mutuality and reciprocity. It also foils the Western reader's
expectations. Undeclared love provides no dynamic to build upon or
develop through. Thus motivation, dramatic conflict, and character
development all occur in surprising ways. A literary work built
around the ideal of purity—which usually denies enactment—can't
declare itself in the same way as one actuated by the Western ideal of
bonding:

It is consistent with this Japanese position that the "happy ending" is so
rare in their novels and plays. . . . There need be no happy ending. Pity and
sympathy for the self-sacrificing hero and heroine has full right of way. Their

suffering is no judgment of God. . . . It shows that they fulfilled their duty at all costs and allowed nothing—not abandonment or sickness or death—to divert them from the true path.[25]

2

Mishima did not write cozy, chatty books peopled by characters who ramble about themselves with quaint humor. To put his characters in Western garb and to give them Western values takes away the qualities that make them themselves. Mishima was not rational, and he did not intend his people to act in reasonable, Western ways. To try to rationalize either him or his work is pointless. The compelling, obsessional flow of his art registers the convulsions of breakdown. Acting without any positive expectations, his recklessly distraught people plunge into trauma. Four of Japan's great novelists of the century—Mishima, Shimazaki Toson (1872–1943), Junichiro Tanizaki (1886–1965), and Yasunari Kawabata (1899–1972)—addressed the dark side of eroticism; Toson's masterpiece, *A New Life* (1919), treats incest. In all four writers, sex is doomed, demonic, and perverse. Its compulsions recall the obsessive sexuality of that most hypocritical of eras, Victorian England. (In *The French Lieutenant's Woman*, John Fowles says that Victorian London had a thousand times as many brothels as the London of 1969.) A similar prudery has ruled Japan for centuries. Predictably, it has had the same wild effects; the more an impulse is suppressed, the more thunderous will be its release.

In their repression, Mishima's people resemble Victorians like Bill Sikes and Heathcliff. Living in a society that bottles up their feelings has made them neurotic and destructive. Like Edgar Allan Poe before him, Mishima is fascinated by the destructiveness of love. *The Sound of Waves* (1954, 1956) is his only novel translated into English that ends with a pair of young lovers marrying. Everywhere else, love is a matter of will and nerves, a disintegrative impulse and a bitter doom. His people reject what is kind and gentle. In *Spring Snow* (1968, 1972), he refers to "this instinctive rejection of anyone who showed him [the book's hero] affection" as "a kind of tumor." Kiyoaki Matsugae's failure to receive or return love (a failure also attributed to Mishima) stems from self-contempt. He has learned too well the Japanese lesson of humility. Despising himself, he automatically spurns his admirers. Late in the book, "kindness ruined the moment" of his first sexual encounter. The scenario he had planned as a rape turns out to be one of tenderness. By "gently" helping him enter her, Satoko Ayakura subdues the violence he had always identified with sex. Mishima hints that Kiyo punishes her for bursting his adolescent sex fantasy by climaxing immediately ("it all ended abruptly"). Such moments typify Mishima. He has both the decency and the intellectual clarity to condemn Kiyo's heartlessness. On the other hand, his humanity will dim in the blaze of the samurai ethic. Kiyo interests him more than Satoko despite her greater warmth and maturity. *Spring Snow* is Kiyo's book. Here and elsewhere, Mishima will give center stage to destructive characters (a woman joins sex to pain and death in *Thirst for Love* [1950, 1959]). It is as if the demonic impulses he invites from a safe distance invade and finally overtake his moral judgment as his stories unfold; the detachment of the objective observer curdles into obsession.

His allowing himself to ride hot waves of emotion divides him internally. As he did with the ultranationalism whose lurid gleams he could not resist, he adopted attitudes as a writer that he disapproved of intellectually. This self-division dwarfed his art just as it shortened his life. Perhaps Kawamura Jiro and Gore Vidal both judged well to call him a minor writer because his only subject was himself. This self intrigues him more than it does us. The world he writes about, both men agree, stands far from the one most of us know.[26] He follows the great European novelists of the century, Marcel Proust and James Joyce, in conveying the intense subjectivity of his heroes. But, unlike them, he sets up no creative tension between his heroes and the palpable world. To his credit, he begins with real people, and he believes that life counts more than art. To him, character is the essence of literature. But his allegiance to a defunct military code shrinks and dries his world, despite its surges of vitality.

Both the man and the book who influenced him most ignored the merits of communication and social bonding. "Jocho's teachings . . . emphasize . . . the man of action rather than the external fact of the action itself," says Mishima in *Way of the Samurai*. And self-realization is just as insular and antisocial in Mishima's fiction as in

Jocho's *Hagakure*. Both writers perceive action from the standpoint of the agent; in both, action disappoints. Fueling the oft-made argument that Mishima aestheticized his politics is the resemblance between his actionism and the doctrine of art for art's sake. Both systems of thought encourage elitism; both disdain social relevance. As has been seen, Mishima's love ethic rules out the enactment leading to the formation of family values. Mishima paraphrases Jocho in *Way of the Samurai* when he says, "Once love has been confessed, it shrinks in stature" and "One must die for love." These glosses approve of the young warrior's killing himself at the peak of manhood rather than propagating and thus strengthening the community. Jocho's pronouncement later in the book (p. 145), "Human beings must be overflowing with vitality," also earns Mishima's approval. The contempt for prudency and calculation implied by the pronouncement channels into his admiration for the fanatical Heihachiro Oshio, the rebel who died trying to overthrow vested power in Osaka in 1838. The passionate single-mindedness with which Oshio barged into public life impressed Mishima. Oshio's actionism, like that of Jocho before him and Mishima after him, rested on the belief that intellectual truth had to be acted on. It is not enough to perceive and reflect. But did Oshio forget that reflection and insight cannot be thrown out altogether? Inspiration divorced from good sense will always run to waste. Ivan Morris calls him "an absurdly poor planner" shackled by "poor organization" and "little grasp of practical detail."[27]

One need not be a Westerner to see the potential damage inhering in the samurai ethic. In his 1952 book, *The Lost Japan,* Hasegawa Nyozekan attacks his countrymen's tendency to rate intuition over intellect. The refusal to infer effects from causes, he argues, distorts objective reality and thus enshrines false gods:

Japanese religious and academic culture have . . . tended to be governed by primitive mysticism and illogicality. The war started as the result of a mistaken intuitive "calculation" which transcended mathematics. We believed with a blind fervor that we could triumph over scientific weapons and tactics by means of our mystic will.[28]

Mystical certainties rampage through Mishima's fiction as they do through his politics, his writing being ruled by instinct, not logic.

Because the stakes are always high, his art does not engage issues, inclining, instead, toward monologue. This singularity of point of view first denies joy and then ushers in disarray and disaster. The physical gratification that he prizes sours quickly, lacking a basis in psychic stability. At issue is not Mishima's belief that feverish irrationality perceives truths which transcend puny reason; the visionary always sees past the moment. Under question are the energies Mishima's perceptions set into motion. Can these energies free the soul from constraint and lead it to a higher level? Literature is supposed to say something about what it means to be human. Mishima sometimes neglects this obligation because he has forgotten that one of his goals is providing some integrated, holistic picture of human nature.

Although his works cried to be written, their power and flow are both blocked by an aloofness from the human condition. He is an original creative artist with little reverence for or delight in life. As in D. H. Lawrence, who also wrote about power and vitality, the release of energy in his work promotes little joy. But Lawrence hated because he first loved. Mishima, unlike him, does not ask if there is something grand and mysterious about the human personality. A person's thoughts, secret emotions, and the way his psyche works on what he sees—these processes *are* the person. But instead of rousing wonder in Mishima, they run in the same grooves. Rather than glorying in the strength, dignity, and mystery of simple people, he prepares his heroes for death. Nor does he sympathize with them, despite their agonies. Very few of them are kind and warm; hardly any fight the good fight. Locked in their lonely isolation, they ignore each other. Mishima does not use his artistry to defend them, but to belittle, attack, and kill them. Their deaths are thus robbed of import. Their last stands portray the deadness, not the vitality, of the imperial ideal.

Escape and confrontation will only struggle briefly in the psyches of Mishima's heroes. These men usually withdraw from the arena of shared feelings. Their attempts to connect to one another or to some living body of values have failed. They end up lonelier than they were at the start and perhaps a little wiser. What has gone wrong for them stems from their author's preference for separation over closure, for anger over love, and, probably, for death over life. Mishima's people are a wretched, unfulfilled lot, suffering emotional and moral disconnection in a world that has been kind to them materially. Few would want to trade places with any of them. Even the celebrated, accomplished ones, like the famous novelist Shunsuke, in *Forbidden Colors* (1951, 1968), dwell in gloom. Like those of Dostoevsky, who supplied the epigraph for *Confessions of a Mask* (1949, 1958), his people live on the edge; their outlook is bleak, and they have heavy emotional burdens. Many of them clash, too, with demons of their own devising. A puritanical university student in *Spring Snow* wants to have sex in the corner of a room closest to some "dirty gray snow he had seen shoveled into piles along the outside wall." Though he pities Mine, his sexual partner, he cannot resist degrading her. He is driven to soil both her and the act that joins him to her (Mishima's women usually accept sex more cheerfully and good-naturedly than his men). The following simile conveys the harshness of his lovemaking: "Lying there in the dark, Mine suddenly felt the cold like a sword thrust under . . . her kimono."

Such moments illuminate the dark corners of human life. The feelings Mishima dredges up from deep inside his characters show how fragile people are. But these dredging operations occur too rarely. Mine is a minor figure whose consciousness Mishima seldom enters. Like that of Satoko Ayakura in the same book, her normality is little more than a technical device. Structurally, it contrasts with the emotional instability and morbid self-immersion of her lover (later her husband), Iinuma, whose right-wing extremism and self-hatred both make him a more important character than she. This prominence explains why Mishima often borders on being a one-note writer. Seconding Kawamura and Vidal, Mamoru Iga said in 1986, "Mishima was at his best when he wrote in the first person. . . . However, he was rather poor at placing himself in the minds of others and observing an event from their point of view."[29] Therefore, the point of view Mishima favors often bores and disgusts us. Perhaps more importantly, it is too confining and limited to matter as much as Mishima thinks. We do see ourselves in his isolatoes. And the recognition occurs because they *are* ourselves; we have all visited the nightmare country of the human soul where loss of control encroaches upon hysteria and, perhaps, even madness.

But we all try to recover our grip. Mishima's people surrender to compulsion and call it destiny. As a result, they are beautiful but, alas, damned. Indulging their anarchic impulses stops them from living within normal limits.

Usually, they do not try. Etsuko, the main character in *Thirst for Love* (1950, 1969), dismisses Osaka as a "city of merchant princes, hoboes, industrialists, stockbrokers, whores, opium pushers . . . bar girls, shoeshine boys." This slur exemplifies her. In his introduction to the novel, Donald Keene mentions "her revulsion when suddenly she feels she is loved." Such revulsion occurs often in Mishima; love in the Mishima canon leads to the wish to inflict pain. Yuchan, or Yuichi, the main character in *Forbidden Colors*, does not identify love with shelter, nurture, or help any more than Etsuko did in *Thirst for Love*. All through the novel people buy him presents and give him money both to win his favor and to pay tribute to his beauty. These acts of homage bring out the worst in him—his vanity, his tendency to reduce all to sensation, and his distrust of his inner self. No wonder he resents his admirers. Having become the favorite in a cult of phallic worship, he tries to break away: "I am not at all happy to be called beautiful," he protests; "I would be much happier to have everybody call me that nice, interesting fellow Yuchan."

He also notes the devastation caused by his good looks on his admirers, who, being older and more experienced, should know better. He watches "three mature adults . . . blithely veer from the beaten path of common sense on his account, and in doing so . . . completely . . . disregard . . . him." Love has gone a-hunting and then denied the object of its quest. It is also spreading like a cancer. His admirers encourage Yuchan's narcissism, the element in his personality that stifles the courage he needs to resist them. In so doing, they guarantee their own grief along with his. The last page of the book finds him alone, uneasy with "a nameless freedom" that hangs "heavily in his chest." Because he has never been taught living values, he remains unmoved by the suicide of the man he called "a second father." Nothing else matters much to him, either. He dismisses the ten million yen he has inherited from his "second father's" death as quickly as he did the death itself. All the attention lavished by others on his good looks has starved his inner being. The last sentence of the novel shows this moral void getting ready to have his shoes shined. He has forgotten the wife anxiously awaiting him at home together with their baby.

Lovers remain apart in most of Mishima; death divides them in *Thirst for Love* and *Runaway Horses;* they are separated by convent walls in *Spring Snow; After the Banquet* (1960, 1963) ends with a divorce. In all cases, communication has failed. Sometimes, the frustration caused by the failure to connect is symbolized by an artifact that does not perform its intended function. In *The Damask Drum*, Mishima's 1951 adaptation of a fifteenth-century No play, a beaten drum remains silent. Expectations are thwarted again in the No play, *Hanjo* (1958), when a woman waiting for her long-absent beloved cannot, or will not, recognize him when he returns to her. The title character of the play, *Madame de Sade* (1965) enters a convent the same day her husband comes home after a long jail term: "the best love is undeclared." But what happens when love *is* declared and consummated? *The Temple of Dawn* (1970, 1973) ends with a fire. As in Dickens's *Great Expectations* (1860–61) and Patrick White's *Tree of Man* (1955), the fire stems dramatically from long-standing rottenness and decay. In Mishima's book, the corruption is sexual. Two couples (one lesbian) are having sex in the summerhouse they have visited for a weekend. It is as if the heat given out by their groping ignited the bedclothes nearby and spread through the house. The same sex that makes Mishima's people feel intensely and gloriously alive brings destruction and death.

Death pervades everything in Mishima. Just as Gustave Flaubert and Henry James both connected sexual love to money, Mishima yokes eros and death. Anxiety in his work is exacerbated, not exorcised, by sex. A thirty-eight-year-old judge in *Runaway Horses* remarks inwardly, "Just as he had never contracted venereal disease, neither had he ever experienced emotional arousal." The implied connection between sexual excitement and venereal disease, a small but a telling touch, carries forward the argument that sex costs heavily in Mishima. Some parallels with Western writers clarify Mishima's stand. In Thomas Mann, for instance, one of Mishima's favorites, sexual love invites disaster. Particularly vulnerable are Mann's artists. Artists suffer heavily for love in "Death in Venice" and *Dr. Faustus*. They fare just as badly in Mishima. Shunsuke, the famous writer in *Forbidden Colors,* joins the walking dead after discovering his wife's disloyalty. But the artist can be crushed without falling in love. The same power that gives the title figure of "The Boy Who Wrote Poetry" his poetic genius also decrees his early death. (Fittingly, the story includes Oscar Wilde's sonnet, "The Grave of Keats.") Common sense explains very little about motives in Mishima. What makes him unusual is his belief that anything of value exists in close proximity to death. Satoko tells Kiyo in a letter in *Spring Snow* that she thinks of him as "the spirit of snow." The end of her letter clinches the identification, so prevalent in Western writers, of snow and death: "To feel myself dissolve into your beauty and freeze to death in the snow—no fate could be sweeter," she writes. Her connecting love, snow, and death is prophetic. While trying to find her, Kiyo later catches a fatal chill.

Does he regret dying for love? Mishima's people feel responsible to their uniqueness. They want to find out who they are and what they stand for. Often their quests for self-definition bring pain. Etsuko of *Thirst for Love* calls her craving for Saburo "evidence of the limitlessness of the human passion for self-torture." She and Saburo offer each other nothing. He is the wrong age; he occupies a much lower social and educational level; he is already intimate with a local woman who shares his background and values. But Etsuko's obsession drives her on. After clawing his naked back during the milling and shoving of a street festival, she lifts a bloodstained fingernail to her lips "almost unconsciously." From this point forward, her passion rules her; the taste of blood has intoxicated her. Her last-chapter murder of Saburo—an unusually bloody and brutal one—surprises nobody. She is striking out at herself as much as at him. A man in love with a woman whose name he does not know in *Damask Drum* claims that unrequited love is bitter. Using *Thirst for Love* and *Spring Snow* as touchstones, he is wrong. When love is requited, thoughts of death start stirring. Besides, unrequited love can be controlled. It extrudes variables; it does not clamor for recognition; it makes no financial or temporal demands. But it also blocks the flow of oxygen. Logic thus decrees that the distant and the unattainable should entice Mishima's immature egoists.

Lawrence, another writer famous for his driven, headstrong characters, links potency and virility to death in works like "The

Ladybird" and "The Captain's Doll." But the unleashing of the dark, primitive forces of destruction in Mishima lacks Lawrence's creative potential. In chapter 5 of *The Temple of the Golden Pavilion* (1956, 1959), a beautiful young woman kisses the misshapen feet of a clubfoot. Her conduct describes the mystery and madness dwelling in the normal. It also foreshadows a remark made in act 3 of *Madame de Sade:* "I have come little by little to realize that when you run up against the thing you thought you wanted least in the world it generally proves in reality what you unconsciously most craved." Quickly and effectively, Mishima appears to have spoken a profound truth: that accepting the ugly, the despised, and the forbidden can refresh and uplift us because it answers a deep, unspoken need. The title figure of Mann's *Dr. Faustus* has sex with a syphilitic prostitute in order to free his soul from the shackles of prudency and send it out into the open. No such daring occurs in *Temple of the Golden Pavilion.* The debutante kisses the clubfeet of the seminarian because Mishima wants to humiliate her. Perhaps he even envies her beauty. If the seminarian's clubfeet point the way to freedom and power, Mishima never lets on.

Perhaps he would have kept silent in any case, since his politics reject negotiation and continuity. He founded the Shield Society in order to restore the sword to its rightful place in Japan. He believed that Benedict's *Chrysanthemum and Sword* magnified the arts of peace at the expense of those of war in describing the Japanese psyche. Yet the Shield Society was dismissed as either a joke or a homosexual club. And its preachments about the holiness of war did little to win public sympathy. Although pledged to restoring national pride, its members said nothing about controlling crime, relieving sickness, or feeding the poor. Japanese scholars have indicted Mishima for the Society's ignorance of reform and growth. In 1984, Noguchi Takehiho insisted that Mishima's emperor worship lacked social or political content. He saw Mishima, in his "haughty disdain," "almost totally indifferent to the poverty of the farming villages" that helped bring about the May 1932 uprising, one of the century's most shocking in Japan. Ten years before Noguchi's disclaimer, Masao Miyoshi attacked Mishima for failing "to set out a coherent politics." The attack sharpens: "Even in his [Mishima's] proposals for the reconstitution of Japan, he is indifferent to the economics either of wealth or of power."[31] This same aloofness to real issues makes *Forbidden Colors* a different novel from what we today might expect. Although homosexual or bisexual himself, Mishima, neither here nor elsewhere, tries to create public sympathy for homosexuals or depict the social values that put them at risk.

3

The virtues Mishima most admires—strength, control, and indifference to pain—describe the warrior, not the reformer or the negotiator. Were he a Westerner, he might be bracketed intellectually with writers like Flaubert, Henry James, and W. H. Auden, all of whom disclaimed the social utility of literature. One can still appreciate him for the reasons one finds *them* so valuable. Perhaps his greatest gift is a sensitivity to experience that transcends intellect. Mishima's genius lay not in having second sight, but first sight, a total immersion in actuality. He's extraordinarily sensitive to natural phenomena, their variety and abundance, beauty and pain. Unlike Sartre, he is not nauseated by the boundlessness of things. His energy verges on the exhausting; his curiosity includes a staggering range. *Confessions of a Mask* and *Forbidden Colors* both center on urban gays. Unfolding on the ragged fringe of bomb-ravaged Osaka, *Thirst for Love* has as its main character a woman who is sleeping with her dead husband's father. *The Sound of Waves* (1954, 1956) deals with boy-girl love on a small island. In *After the Banquet,* the main figures are a heterosexual Tokyo couple of fifty-five and seventy. The recording consciousness for much of *The Sailor Who Fell from Grace with the Sea* (1963, 1965) is a boy of thirteen. All of these works show Mishima writing with an unabashed sensuality; he knows the rewards love brings even when it is causing pain. This knowledge makes his people more existential than literary. His extravagant, exuberant prose captures the passion of his characters and communicates it with immediacy. "Patriotism" (1960, 1966), for instance, traces the growth of passion with great precision and fidelity to motives. Even though the death of the two main characters is reported in the story's first two sentences, what follows imparts such lunge and ferocity that one stays spellbound.

This concentration invokes human values. Mishima opposes the modern ethos that rates pleasure and personal fulfillment over duty and responsibility. He knows that, as human beings, people are capable of more than self-aggrandizement. Perhaps even today's Japanese could give him a cautious hearing, as the following statement from a 1985 issue of *The Economist* implies: "For the past 40 years Japan's approach to the world—its over-emphasis on exports, its under-emphasis on defense—has been based on a narrow calculation of immediate self-interest."[32] However glaring Mishima's faults, they exclude greed. The lyric surrender to the crown he envisioned makes the industrial moguls who have survived him look mean and calculating. If he sometimes confuses good and bad, he commits himself fully to his beliefs. And, unlike his foolish prognoses, his diagnoses inspire trust. This stranger to happiness knows that happiness cannot rest on material possessions. He also knows that looking abroad for inspiration can weaken a nation's self-image along with its moral fiber. Although his great courage sought deathly outlets, it had its roots in a noble premise—that life's meaning bypasses getting and spending. Our hearts go out grudgingly to this man and his gaudy protest. Eleven years after the publication of his 1974 biography of Mishima, Henry Scott-Stokes wrote an article for *Harper's* endorsing many of the same notions Mishima fought and died for: "The Japanese have built one of the richest and most productive nations on earth. But the cost has been high: they have had to set aside their ancient culture and shatter their country's ecology."[33]

Nobody lamented this loss more than Mishima. His fiction will often equate the process of Westernization with physical and moral breakdown. This process began long before Japan's 1945 surrender to the United States. In *Spring Snow,* which opens in 1913, an exercise hall once used for judo and fencing no longer stands. It has given way to a luxurious Western-style ballroom where lavish parties are held. A protest in the same vein, Mishima's grousing in *Runaway Horses* over an 1876 law forbidding both the traditional samurai hairstyle and the wearing of swords sounds churlish and inconsequential. But before discounting his grievance, it must be remembered that the practices being outlawed had descended from antiquity. Their continuance fostered an ideal combining religious worship and government. Dostoevsky championed this same ideal;

it dominates the first half of *The Brothers Karamazov*, which includes the Grand Inquisitor episode. Yet his theocratic ideal is usually admired, whereas Mishima's is mocked. It might surprise us to know how many of Mishima's detractors admire Dostoevsky, who endorsed some of the same principles. An accurate survey could say something useful about intellectual consistency in academe.

The comparison between Mishima and Dostoevsky need not be dropped. Intuitive and intense, both writers portray both the enchantment and the atrocity of their nations' psyches. In both, the portrayal hinges on high-strung, emotional characters struggling with a reality that threatens to crush them. Both share an instinct for the incongruous, the bizarre, and the uncanny. Their sharp, nerve-juddering images reveal a fascination for the repellent. The anti-social, the offbeat, and even the perverse can also lead to wisdom in both writers. *Runaway Horses* tells about thirty-five Bible students in Kumamoto in 1876 who tried to Christianize Japan. The incident is scarcely more than an anecdote. But its treatment shows that the small touches of important writers can also be telling touches. Although Mishima censures the Kumamoto band for being "eccentric and unrealistic," he praises their purity of resolve. The intensity of their commitment outshines their goal, which he recognizes as naive and impractical. The tensions of living in Japan have always invited such acts of extremism.

But the need to maintain social harmony decrees that extremist acts must be quickly crushed. Perhaps speed is necessary because the extremism that threatens to rip the social fabric also touches the Japanese soul. Later in *Runaway Horses,* a young terrorist organizes a rebellion to protest the government's handling of problems like unemployment and bad harvests (the year is 1931). The judge pronounces Isao Iinuma guilty; but, admiring his sincerity, suspends Isao's sentence. This act of clemency does not quiet Isao's patriotic fervor. He will die to end his countrymen's suffering, if he must. That he murders a rich tycoon who he believes is profiting from Japan's economic woes and kills himself straightaway adds an important humanizing touch. Yes, this carnage invites the boring interpretation that Isao's purity of resolve was too beautiful for our sordid world. Yet it also implies that Mishima was disturbed about his own extremism, especially the part connected with his suicide, which took place a year after *Runaway Horse*'s publication.

The impulse to aestheticize experience that led to his suicide rises from a profoundly Japanese context. Anglophones can recognize the impulse: the best English-language poet of the century, W. B. Yeats, posited an aesthetic of destruction based on the beauty and purity of violence. The American scholar, David Pollack, writing in the Tokyo-based journal, *Monumenta Nipponica* in 1985, links the Japanese infatuation with destruction to European existentialism. Both impulses feature *l'acte gratuit;* Dostoevsky's Raskolnikov in *Crime and Punishment* and Camus's Meursault in *The Stranger* commit motiveless murders in order tó affirm their own existence. Pollack argues that the gratuitous act of destruction in Japanese literature is usually directed to the perpetrator; the violence that ratifies the self also annihilates the self.[34] The rebel in Mishima will defeat the enemy in order to submit to him and the evil he stands for. The arsonist-acolyte in *The Temple of the Golden Pavilion,* the subject of Pollack's essay, calls his burning of the beautiful temple in Kyoto "a perfect and isolated deed." Later he claims, "I must do the deed precisely because it was so futile." This nihilism rests on a moral insight that Mishima rarely gets credit for making—the ability to see things whole. The acolyte's act of arson is so futile and trite because it cannot dent the ideal of architectual splendor that both inspired it and has moved so many viewers over the centuries.

Such insights temper Mishima's destruction-as-creation aesthetic. Perhaps he is most valuable when he writes, as he does in *Temple,* about life's absurdity, complexity, and sweetness. Coded emotional messages testifying to this rich variety recur often. A successful businesswoman on the brink of a major triumph in *After the Banquet* meets a shabby ex-lover whose blackmailing motives are as squalid as his looks. In both *The Temple of Dawn* (1970, 1973) and *The Decay of the Angel* (1971, 1974), the last two volumes in the *Sea of Fertility* tetralogy, a skinny, truckling lowlife claims acquaintance with the aristocratic judge Honda. The twenty years dividing the two meetings cannot hide the acquaintance or what it is based on. Both men are voyeurs; both patrol the same haunts to watch couples having sex. Like Kazu in *After the Banquet,* Honda cannot

escape his guilty past; sex is still the great democratizer. Also symbolizing the pull of the past is the sexual tie in which the woman is
older than the man (*Confessions of a Mask, Thirst for Love,
Forbidden Colors,* the one-act play *Dojoji, Spring Snow, Runaway
Horses,* and *The Decay of the Angel* all include this dynamic). The
symbol covers a wide sweep. Besides touching on Oedipal guilt, it
also alludes to the difficulty of communication between the sexes.
These two motifs refer tellingly to Mishima's homosexuality.

The self that emerges from his writing continues to fascinate.
Mishima probes hidden corners of consciousness to convey those
wayward but intimate perceptions that, though familiar, rarely get
expressed. Far from being tranced out on emperor worship, he has a
lively sense of the ridiculous. A quartet of middle-aged adults in
Spring Snow argue about the kind of wig needed to cover the shorn
pate of a young novice who will never leave her convent. Mishima's
appreciation of the incongruous also shows in the many other
instances where the imponderables of life mock our most careful
plans and wreck our hopes. As befits his highly erotic imagination, a
"forbidden" scroll of drawings in *Spring Snow* depicts a group of
men who gang-rape a woman and then get their penises torn out
and carried away in a boat while they howl in pain on the seashore.
Other scenes in Mishima reveal different novelistic energies. Earlier
in *Spring Snow,* Kiyo sends Satoko an angry letter and then, his
heart having softened, begs her to destroy it unopened. In *Forbidden
Colors,* a young woman goes to sleep alongside a youth of twenty-
three and wakes up next to an elder of sixty-five. The clean, raw
horror of her awakening recalls the power enjoyed by irrationality in
Gothic fiction. Elsewhere, too, Mishima will use incongruity to
endow events with importance. This importance can stem from the
accumulation of psychic tensions. The superior of a monastic order
in *Temple* turns up nattily garbed while stepping out with an Osaka
geisha. Yet our last glimpse of him shows him back in the seminary,
praying in abject humility. A character in *After the Banquet* insists
that he once saw Field Marshal Hermann Goering wearing work-
man's clothes and talking to a young beauty on the Berlin metro.

Then a hospital visitor in the play, *The Lady Aoi* (1956), announces that she has come to plague, rather than comfort, the
patient she is to see. The heroic knight that the young narrator of

Confessions of a Mask (1949, 1954) admires and wants to emulate turns out to be—Joan of Arc, a woman. The story "Three Million Yen" (1960) follows the movements of a prudent young Tokyo couple who discuss matters like the price of cucumbers and powdered milk. At story's end, these careful planners and budgeters reveal themselves to be professional exhibitionists. This revelation teaches the importance of being on guard. Mishima writes about forces that can tear apart the fabric of society and crush people. He also shows these forces from uncommon, unexpected angles. The new possibilities revealed by this strategy extend the emotional boundaries of what we know. Geoffrey Bownas, Mishima's collaborator for the 1972 anthology, *New Writing in Japan,* says in his "Translator's Preface," that Mishima would have won the Nobel Prize had he lived longer.[35] On the basis of Mishima's ability to conjure up excitement, Bownas may have been right.

The intensity of Mishima's commitment to his materials made his books social documents, psychological revelations, and confessions all at once. Contemplative and violent, cerebral and erotic, he arranges his materials into patterns that reveal selection and control. The force generated by these patterns takes his descriptions beyond photographic realism. He can also create dialogue that is sharp, accurate, and often funny. Yes, the undue emphasis he puts on pain, bloodshed, and death can repel and sicken. But his work is built on a core set of unifying ideas; it has a coherence and a consistency; it puts forth a philosophy, a vision, and a set of values. And without dismissing his offensiveness, it should be pointed out that there never was an important writer who did not challenge and disturb.

2

Cables of Discipline

Mishima's tendency to write from his private needs imparts the feeling that the child is still alive inside the man. This freshness and purity is enhanced by the confessional mode, the staple of Japanese fiction and the strongest single technical influence on his art. His rampaging descriptive zeal, his brilliantly realized scenes, and the passion with which his characters try to infuse their lives with meaning in an unforgiving environment all have the plangency of youth. By writing from his intimate self, Mishima also gives his work the hard-focus intimacy of a nightmare. Only a small hurt is needed to convulse a child's small world. But Mishima treats these shock waves differently from a Dickens or a J. D. Salinger. His people are not so much innocent or deluded as self-destructive. A novel like *The Temple of the Golden Pavilion* will probe neurosis and then describe it from the standpoint of the neurotic himself. Is this technique a product of Mishima's alleged masochism? He is excessively drawn to antisocial, even pathological, behavior. But he is also so absorbed in his own angst that he withholds sympathy; his self-absorption makes him indifferent to the underdog. Much that he writes about resonates in the readers' deep psyches. But this penetration does curiously little to edge the reader further along the road to self-knowledge. Preferring to exploit or indulge rather than understand, he has slighted the tie joining man's mutually shared world with the mysterious subjectivity underlying it. This dark private realm makes all people different. In Mishima, though, it similarizes; characters in his work who are deeply stirred act alike—they look for things and people to slice and smash.

It is the ease with which they yield to this destructiveness that tries the reader's patience. They have not worked hard enough to establish the truth; neither have they shown the reader that they know the difference between good and evil. And because they do not appreciate goodness, they also lack faith. This shortcoming leads to others. Since their instincts always push them in the direction of death, they overlook the power of the unconscious to heal the rifts in their waking lives. Nerve-worn and wide-awake, Mishima prefers fighting to healing. But his self-consciousness makes the fighting look like shadowboxing. His people crave naked combat, but then back away from it with great gobbets of sentimentality and myth mongering. Death for an alleged heroic ideal in Mishima looks more like self-betrayal than self-fulfillment. The first sentence of *Sun and Steel* (1968, 1970) shows him looking to express himself in a mode that transcends linguistic constraints; he wants to probe truths beyond the arbitrary formulas of language. Or so he claims. In reality, he does not write as fearlessly as he pretends. His splendid scenic effects, piercing insights, and throat-catching incongruities often subserve foreordained attitudes. Events and motifs pile up impressively, but usually add up to answers worked out long before.

1

Most of the answers pertain to the flesh. Flesh in Mishima is dynamic, spontaneous, and self-regulating. It also has a will of its own, which affirms itself in an estrangement from both spirit and spirit's corrosive handmaiden, language. Mishima's introduction to *Young Samurai* (published in Japan as *Taido*), a photo album of Japanese bodybuilders, declares that a strong body provides a better moral foundation than ideologies and concepts. It also tells why his declaration will win few friends in Japan. The notion of "the spiritual worth of the body" opposes the "dark, ancient Confucianistic contempt for the flesh" that has ruled Japan for centuries. This tyranny needs to be overturned, he continues. An appreciation of the vigor and the discipline that builds muscle and brawn must end this national devaluation of the physical.[1] *Sun and Steel* did more than complain about this supposed distortion of values. It also tried to correct it. The body rules in *Sun and Steel*, as Vidal said: "In *Sun and Steel* Mishima describes . . . his gradual realization that flesh is all."[2] But to be all, the flesh must first be young, bronzed, and muscular. In a 1964 article for *Life,* Mishima said that the Japanese worship youth as much as the Americans do; the alleged Japanese reverence for age, he added, "does not correspond to reality."[3]

His reading of postwar Japanese reality is probably accurate. Japan's Westernization since 1945 does include an appreciation of youthful vitality at the expense of the mature. For one thing, the mature have been squeezed out of the work force to make room for the young; for another, the Western music and clothing styles that have won such favor in Japan aim at a young consumership. Mishima's writing reflects this trend. Rather than infusing his books with wisdom and benevolence, old age in Mishima represents a loss of vitality, stamina, and even the basic decencies. Shunsuke in *Forbidden Colors,* Noguchi in *After the Banquet,* and Honda in *The Decay of the Angel* all support their withered, sagging flesh on creaking joints; their voices are clogged with phlegm; their dim, rheumy eyes seek out what is perverse. Honda's voyeurism brings him social disgrace. Going to the opposite extreme, the prudish Noguchi beats his wife and throws her out for committing what others may see as a small infraction. Before killing himself, Shunsuke, the voyeuristic author, gives up writing to avenge himself on the female sex. Together with Mishima's suicide at age forty-five, the nastiness of the elderly implies that either survival into old age is ugly and/or only the ugly survive.

In view of his poor self-control, he deserves credit for recognizing and trying to escape the snares of eros. Nor should he be attacked for pointing out the devastation attending sexual love. No wonder he wore a mask. He needed his military uniforms, loud Hawaiian shirts, and bodybuilders' loincloths to hide his true self. These protective interfaces distracted him from what he was. Unfortunately, he felt his pain to be past help. Anyone who plays a role, or wears a mask long enough will forfeit his identity, not knowing where the self ends and the charade begins. Also, nobody trusts a mask, least of all its wearer; a truth sayer evades no one's eye. Mishima wore himself out by sidestepping and then indulging the riot in his soul. His incarnations as writer, actor, dandy, warrior, clown, and gangster (he wrote gangster, or *yakuza,* novels and acted in *yakuza* films) fused his destructive demons and his creative angels. And he could not have banished one set of impulses without driving out the other, too.

According to the autobiographical *Confessions of a Mask,* the pattern took definite shape when the twelve-year-old Kimitake Hiraoka looked at Guido Reni's painting of the martyrdom of St. Sebastian and had his first orgasm. The memory of this excitement stayed with him. In 1966, he posed for a photograph in which he appeared as Reni's St. Sebastian, tied to a tree, his arms in the same position and the arrows piercing his flesh in the same places as in the Renaissance original. The front inside cover of the special Mishima number of *Kaleidoscope Kyoto* (April 1985) reproduces the Reni portrait alongside two St. Sebastian poems, "For Yukio Mishima," by the English poet James Kirkup. This prominence is justified. Scott-Stokes argues that Mishima's first look at the Reni St. Sebastian might have been the key event of his life:

> The beauty of the violent or excruciatingly painful death of a handsome youth was to be a theme of many of his novels. . . . Mishima thought the more violent, the more agonizing a death, the more beautiful it was; he made a cult of a Christian martyr, St. Sebastian, and he invested the ancient samurai rite of disembowelment, hara-kiri, with supreme beauty.[4]

Reni's St. Sebastian was to anchor Mishima's other erotic fantasies. Along with these fantasies, the portrait forms a chart of his wildest desires. Gwenn Boardman Petersen accurately calls this tracery of repeated symbols the record of an "obsessive . . . psychopathology": "Mishima's oddly self-conscious fascination with the flesh," says Petersen, asserts itself in an attraction to the "smells of zoos, bodies, toilets. . . . At some point in every narrative, at least one of Mishima's characters is beaded, or pearled, or just plain dripping with sweat."[5] This sweat usually coats rippling muscles. The Mishima St. Sebastian (reproduced by Nathan in the photo album following page 140 and by Scott-Stokes after page 172) shows sweat, running blood, pubic and armpit hair, and a stricken face. That of Reni (1575–1642) exudes spiritual content, and no blood runs from its dry hairless torso. The male body in anguish did focus Mishima's sexuality early in life. But Mishima added his own obsessive touches to the St. Sebastian paradigm before making it his own. Body hair, sweat, odor, and bloodshed lend poignancy to martyrdom. The tie-in with sex and religion creates a further heightening. The erect phallus of a man in *The Sailor Who Fell from Grace with the Sea* (1963, 1965) appears as a "lustrous temple tower"; using one's knowledge of Mishima's personal symbolism, one can predict the man's violent death.

Others will follow him. The beautiful die young in Mishima. In fact, the inevitability—perhaps even the necessity—of early death enhances their beauty. Reason and conscience cannot check this drive, regardless of what the laws of civilization may claim. Mishima says of a man in *Spring Snow*, "The coolness of reason had evaporated like cool sweat from his brow"; once passion is ignited, it resists controls. People are ruled by impulse and instinct, not by morality. And these first movers are always edged in red. Noriko Mizuta Lippit properly calls Mishima's "central theme" "the life whose beauty and brilliance are supported by impending annihilation."[6] Annihilation always sends out gleams. In chapter 28 of *The Decay of the Angel* Mishima says, "The essence of the flesh was decay." And in *Sun and Steel*, he speaks of "the special quality of muscles whereby self-endorsement inevitably meant self-destruction." Pride in one's own rippling muscles impinges on the truth that the muscles must shrivel and sag.

But the process of normal deterioration is too slow for Mishima. He prefers annihilation to be volcanic. The attainment of destiny for him always includes violence. Love clamors for destruction, not just destructibility. A character in *Sailor* who sees in "the dark rapture" of sex "something directly linked to death" defines the norm. He is not merely saying that sexual love is all the more precious because it must end. He has also intuited the tie between Eros and Thanatos. Referring to the St. Sebastian portrait, Mishima says in chapter 19 of *Spring Snow*, about Satoko's verbal attack on Kiyo, "She had marshaled just those words that were calculated to wound him most deeply, *like arrows aimed at his weakest points*" (emphasis added). Later, the seed of Kiyo's that takes life within Satoko will also cause death, the title of *Spring Snow* fusing death and renewal just as that of *Runaway Horses* alludes to emotions that have gotten out of control.

"Once love has been confessed, it shrinks in stature," says Mishima in *The Way of the Samurai,* adding that "men must have in a separate place the sacrificial object with which to satisfy their carnal desires." Here is Mishima at perhaps his worst. The severing of sex from love reduces sex to a mechanical, recreational exercise. The erotic tie exists only for itself; it is a release of animal energies that denies emotional or social bonding. Who wants to form a close tie with a "sacrificial object," anyway? And who wants to play sacrificial object to another's lust, particularly if one sees oneself in heroic terms? "How alike were the voices of pleasure and death!" Honda exclaims inwardly in *The Temple of Dawn.* To the sadomasochist Mishima, these two voices have chimed all along. Death is a superior consummation, the ultimate punishment to the masochist, whose chief thrill consists of being punished. "His eyes no longer saw his wife," says Mishima of the lieutenant preparing to kill himself in "Patriotism." The lieutenant is fixated by "the five or six inches of naked steel" protruding from the cloth-wrapped sword he has chosen to kill himself with.

Mishima is right there with him; narrating self and perceiving self have joined. Holding before him a lethal sword of penis length, the lieutenant feels a greater attraction than any his wife could exert, beautiful though she is. Death outranks life, and the lure of the penis exceeds that of the vagina. Besides, he has already had sex with her; it is time to move on to something more important, dying. Faced by what really counts, he assumes the submissive, or passive role. His death parodies sex, a "tremendous spurt of blood" shooting from his throat as it is pierced by the phallic blade. The last section of the story describes his young widow's suicide. Before dying, she kisses her husband's corpse, after which she licks the knife she plans to drive into her throat. She belongs utterly to death: her husband got a kiss, but the fatal knife receives a more intimate caress. She licks the knife because she loves it more; it also has the advantage over her husband of being able to enter her. Without doubt, she will keep her promise to her husband by following him immediately to the grave; lacking free-standing reality, she obeys his every wish. She cannot defy him any more than the lieutenant can defy Mishima. The three figures are dancing the same deathly step. This extraordinarily bloody story's last sentence, "She gathered her strength and plunged the point of the blade deep into her throat," reenacts her husband's death blow. The homosexual's erotic fulfillment coincides with his death. The self-hater clamoring inside the homosexual has been appeased; the story's closing pages contain enough blood, gore, and pain to please the most thoroughgoing masochist. Mishima's literary rehearsal for his suicide ten years hence couldn't have gone better.

One reason for its success is its extrusion of vitality. The story ends in a moral vacuum. The blood strewn everywhere and the "raw smell" of vomit and entrails filling the death room inspire the editorial comment, "It would be difficult to imagine a more heroic sight than this." Although one applauds Mishima's genius in making carnage so horridly vivid, one also finds the carnage more disgusting than heroic. Bloodletting both describes and defines death in Mishima. One of the subsections in the "League of Divine Wind" section of *Runaway Horses,* an account of samurai rebellion in the late nineteenth century, ends thus:

Morishita, Gigoro Tashiro, and Shigetaka Sakomoto committed seppuku in turn. Finally, Gitaro Tashiro and Kagami, performing the ritual together, cut open their stomachs and thrust their blades into their own throats.

Two paragraphs later Mishima writes, "the corpses of the . . . patriots lay slumped forward in perfect fulfillment of the ritual." This static formality conveys the similarizing power of death. Death erases those differences caused by the surge and rough anarchy of life. The suicides performed by the League members recall a Busby Berkeley dance routine, where all the carefully choreographed steps occur right on cue. Such formality opposes spontaneous life. Like the snow blanketing Ireland in James Joyce's "The Dead," the blood spilled in Mishima destroys individuality; even the face of the brave lieutenant in his death throes in "Patriotism" isn't "the face of a living man."

2

Robert Jay Lifton, Suichi Kato, and Michael R. Reich judged well to call their chapter on Mishima (pp. 231–74) in *Six Lives Six Deaths* "The Man Who Loved Death." Also germane is the statement from

Mishima's mother that they quote: "His death was the only thing he ever did that he really wanted to do."[7] If Mishima's mother was right about her son, then it follows that he relished every step on the way to his suicide, including having played the role of the lieutenant in the screen version of "Patriotism." (And he was also human enough to know that relishing the means to his agonizing end both delayed and distracted him from this final horror.) Speaking of the author of *Hagakure,* the subject of *The Way of the Samurai,* he says, "Death for Jocho has the strange, clear, fresh brightness of blue sky between the clouds." Much of this allure comes from death's absoluteness. Mishima doesn't see the soul facing eternal rebirth in its effort to attain its preordained destiny, or dharma; no Buddhist he. His habit of linking death to images of sunrise and sea posits a context of purity, beauty, and infinite wonder. This rhapsodizing may have been part of an extended pep talk. *Sun and Steel* presents death as the supreme synthesis; only death can bridge the gulf between thought and action, language and muscle, spirit and flesh. To achieve this synthesis is ennobling and uplifting. Certain members of the League of the Divine Wind carry out "their ritual suicides with extraordinary grace"; others "slew themselves heroically"; a youth who cuts himself open brings his life "to a brave conclusion." He has plenty of company. This part of *Runaway Horses* bristles with self-sacrifices like his.

Luis Canales's reading of Mishima's value system combines these two ideas: "Mishima was not a rightist or any other political 'ist.' He was most of all a narcissist and a masochist."[8] All love is suspect to Mishima because it diverts attention from the self. One reason that he and Jocho tolerated homosexuality was because it sidesteps the man-woman biological polarity and thus preserves maleness at the heart of the sword ethic.

His failure to work free of himself deepens the trauma that Canales alludes to. Trauma can be neutralized. Dickens pondered the cultural and spiritual malaise of Victorian England as much as Mishima did that of postwar Japan. But he also celebrated romantic and family love. His social conscience and his fondness for his characters both confirmed his belief that the world could be improved. Mishima has some of Dickens's vitality. But unlike those of Dickens, his people are not joined by benign affections or loyalties.

This literary genius who called Jocho's *Hagakure* "The One and Only Book for Me" is never so fully alive as when, like his mentor, he is writing about death. Ironically, this is where his Dickensian vigor trips him up. He often writes so urgently that he overlooks those annoying qualifications that fairness always demands. Thus his dark potency lacks intellectual balance. Because he is not anxious enough about the boundaries of what he knows, he does not dispense his judgments thoughtfully. He has construed reality destructively rather than compassionately.

Perhaps he is most himself in the nonfictional *Sun and Steel* (1968, 1970), where he can bypass the rigors of characterization and plot structure. Marguerite Yourcenar is right on target when she calls this short polemic "almost delirious."[9] Cool and precise this philosophical ramble is *not*. Mishima's dualisms are varnished words without insides. Ingenuity replaces moral complexity and logical consistency. This headstrong, soggy work that ends with Mishima's death in the clouds neither freshens nor expands our perspective. The solo kamikaze flight forty thousand feet above sea level that ends the book has as its goal something Mishima could not find in the muddle and compromise of his earthly life—perfection. He already knew perfection to be an unfit goal for imperfect mortals; no effort can be pure or intense enough to put man on a footing with God. But from the start, Mishima equated death with the divine attributes of purity, stability, and completeness. As a schoolboy, Kochan, the Mask, feels a compulsion toward suicide that joins with a craving for perfection. The "unconscious perfection" of Omi, the schoolmate the Mask loves, has no intellectual properties, a condition that excites the Mask, who favors "sheer animal flesh unspoiled by intellect." Omi relates to the world physically, and, partly because of him, the Mask believes that "a precise definition of the perfection of life and manhood" can come from simply naming the parts of his beloved's body.

The Mask also connects sexual desire to the sea. The sea fascinates him because it can kill him; like Mishima, he cannot swim. Phrases like "the razor-keen blade of the sea's enormous ax" and the "dark-blue guillotine [of a wave] . . . sending up a white blood splash" equate the sea with malevolence and destruction. A deft pattern of cross-references keeps this evil within the sphere of sexuality. The phrase, "the sea's sensation of deep abundance," recalls Omi's "abundant" armpit hair together with "Sebastian's abundant beauty" in the Reni painting. The power of this abundance to choke, stifle, and crush reflects Mishima's understanding of the truth that more can be less; a yearning for the absolute loosens one's hold on the actual.

3

But was Mishima a persecutor or a victim, a tortured, driven artist or a slick cosmopolite who knew all the angles? Even if he fit all these definitions at different times, he also affected a facade to shock people. Why? Perhaps he enjoyed indulging his staggering range of energy and talent. Perhaps he wanted to impress people while also hiding from them. The challenge of such a double maneuver would have appealed to his pride and his virtuosity. This writer who faced his readers squarely, building an impressive oeuvre around a few core ideas, would use a persona in his social relationships. His elaborate stratagems were sometimes infuriating. Martin Seymour-Smith said he was "no more than a nasty little boy." To Buruma, he was ruled by inner conflict. Buruma said of him in October 1985, "Part of him wanted to be a samurai, part of him a pop star in a Hawaiian shirt." A month earlier in the *New York Review of Books,* Buruma yoked this division to Mishima's homosexuality— itself an ambivalent life mode in view of his wife and two children: "Mishima was like the Japanese society ladies who dress in evening gowns in Tokyo, but in kimonos abroad." Scott-Stokes wrings other meanings from Mishima's running costume changes, calling his man "an odd and bizarre character, part gentleman and part gangster," who "played the clown incessantly, appearing in nude reviews, acting in second-rate gangster movies."[10]

Some of his acting took on the dimension of reality. In a novel like *Humboldt's Gift* (1975), Saul Bellow's gangsters dine with intellectuals. The metaphors that Norman Mailer likes to draw from boxing and his hero worship of Muhammad Ali have joined pugilism to literature in a fresh, new way. But Mishima fused the merits of a well-trained body with those of a creative mind more impressively than Mailer. This wearer of aloha shirts and blue jeans

followed a strict routine of weight lifting, kendo, and military training. He posed for lurid photos.[11] He performed in a cabaret act, at
the end of which he and his partner, another man, kissed. At parties,
he vied for attention. Some of these parties, by the way, he hosted
himself at considerable cost. But after they were over, he would go to
his study and write for six or eight hours. And he wrote more than
the prolific Mailer. Once he settled on a writing career, he wrote
practically every night of his life; enough to fill thirty-six large
volumes by age forty-five. The quantity and quality of this output
sufficed his colleague and mentor, the Nobel Prize winner Yasunari
Kawabata, to say that a writer of Mishima's importance only appears once every five hundred years.[12]

The flawless calculation that forsook the human displayed itself
most dramatically in his suicide. Scott-Stokes explains:

Mishima . . . stuck rigidly to his schedule. He had calculated that at the end
of November he would deliver the final section of *The Decay of the Angel*
. . . to the magazine *Shincho*. The magazine was publishing the work in
installments. . . . Mishima had in fact completed the final part by August
1970. . . . Thus Mishima could plan far ahead so that his death would
coincide with his handing over the conclusion of his last book, and his
literature would officially end on the same day as his life. It is typical of
Mishima that he controlled his last actions to the last detail.[13]

Others have noted that Mishima planned his death so thoroughly
that the morning of 25 November 1970 he told various members of
the Tokyo media corps exactly where and when he would die. Forget
for the moment his heartlessness in orchestrating a suicide down to
the last detail; forget, too, his telling TV and radio journalists about
his plans but remaining silent with his family. Look instead at the
suicide itself, which Jiro referred to correctly as a "bizarre, disgusting death."[14] What is most abhorrent about it was the planning that
went into it. Had Mishima forgotten that all through *The Way of
the Samurai* he condemned calculation in favor of spontaneity? His
suicide expressed his self-alienation more accurately than he knew.
An act so inhuman belongs to no Japanese tradition. So besotted
was he on dying that his *seppuku* mocked both the culture and the

ideology it was meant to vindicate. Mishima's exhibitionism
smirched the purity of the code he died for.

His death, a logical product of his having confused life and art,
has come to rival his books as his claim to fame. Scott-Stokes
asserts, "Mishima's suicide ranks to this day as the single most
startling news event in the postwar history of Japan."[15] Junro
Fukashiro, in an article called "Post-mortem" that ran in the *Japan
Quarterly* for Spring 1971, discussed some of the reasons given for
the suicide. These included the insanity theory, the aesthetic theory,
the exhausted talent theory, the patriotic theory, and the love-suicide
theory (some have said that beefy young Masakatsu Morita, who
immediately followed Mishima to death, was also his lover).[16] Opin-
ions about the "incident" have varied greatly. Henry Miller praised it
as a great service to Japan; Robert Scalpino, in disagreement,
scorned it as a *dis*service.[17] But as controversial an issue as it
remains, most of us today would agree that the incident has received
too much attention. It begins the Mishima chapters in both of the
Mishima-centered books in which Robert Jay Lifton had a hand.
Petersen and Yamanouchi also use the incident to start *their* chapter-
length discussions of Mishima.[18] Scott-Stokes and Nathan begin the
only two English-language biographies of Mishima to date in the
same way.

The events comprising the incident are ludicrous enough to have
embarrassed Mishima's own countrymen into silence. Buruma calls
him "a nonsubject in Japan," adding, "Not much is written about
him any more. Few people talk about him." Also writing in 1985,
Scott-Stokes said that no biography of Mishima had been published
in Japan.[19] Some may argue that Mishima is Japan's most important
writer of the century. Few would shrink from calling him the most
notorious. The process by which he has become a national liability
in many Japanese eyes can be charted. Without doubt, he knew
enough to forecast the failure of his prospective junta. Momentum
had been building against it. His attempt to win recruits for the
Shield Society from Waseda University in 1967 had failed. Two years
later, the society still lacked an identity, a role, and a clear sense of
purpose; in military as well as civilian circles, it was either despised
or ignored. The frustrated members bickered among themselves.

Some even resigned. Mishima's rebellion was doomed long before it happened.

Did he know how dismally he would fail? His earlier remark, "I came out on the stage, longing to make people weep, and instead they burst into loud laughter,"[20] applies more strictly to the incident than to any other event he ever staged. Here is what happened. On 25 November 1970, he and four other members of the Shield Society used a well-rehearsed dodge to capture the commanding officer of Japan's Self-Defense Force in downtown Tokyo. He gave the senior officers who tried to rescue their chief an ultimatum: that unless he were permitted to address the eight hundred troops stationed in the garrison, the chief would die. After some angry words, threats, and even bloodshed, the rescuing officers relented, and Mishima walked out to the parapet of the balcony adjoining the commandant's office. Then he began a patriotic harangue lamenting the degradation of postwar Japan. But his impassioned words went unheard. Those that did not disappear in the hoots, hisses, and jeers of the troops thirty feet below were swallowed by the racket made by three helicopters circling above. Seven minutes into a speech planned for a half hour, he stopped talking, went back indoors, and killed himself.

"Most Japanese are right in regarding Mishima's *seppuku* as little more than the pathetic act of a very gifted buffoon," said Buruma about the incident's climax,[21] and it is hard to refute him. Mishima had always confused life and art. His having dedicated his art to irrelevant, wicked ideologies culminated in the sweeping of his last public performance into a void. He could not complain about the tornado of noise that drowned him out. His returning indoors less then a quarter of the way into his speech signaled his acceptance of the bathos and absurdity of his grand scheme. He had gotten the angry rejection he both deserved and secretly craved. The impending disintegration of death, foreshadowed by the racket outside the Headquarters Building, had mocked his long, futile struggle for order and coherence. Life had avenged itself on him. This exhibitionist who loved pain was not worried that he had forfeited the sympathy that usually goes out to martyrs and underdogs. Showing off to himself as always, he staged his last clown act as a media event and accepted the consequences. The exercise of will always appealed to him more than the exercise of options. Dying in screaming pain among friends was the only part of the incident that had happened as planned. The shock registered over the littleness of his three surviving colleagues by those attending their trail would not have fazed him. Under his big, shapely muscles lurked the tiny, delicate boy who was barred from playing sports at school. Considering his storyteller's instinct for inevitability, the gasps heard in the court-room might have even drawn from him a wry smile.

Yet this neurotic misfit also wrote brilliant books. If they have achieved a worldwide readership despite his infamy, more power to them. Buruma's calling him "the most translated Japanese author and certainly the best known"[22] implies that the books *did* make their own way. Others would endorse this view. Pollack admires him as "one of the finest craftsmen of language in the world,"[23] and, as has been noted, Kawabata said that a writer of his mettle only comes along once in five centuries. Such accolades sound wrongheaded; Mishima based much of his work on ideas and attitudes that repel most decent people—both in and out of Japan. But Milton proved with his anti-Catholicism, Céline and T. S. Eliot with their dislike of Jews, and Edward Albee with his woman baiting that a writer who harbors repellent values can still enlarge and refresh us. The beautiful books that Mishima wrote about terrible things can enrich us, too.

3

A Boy's Own Stories
Confessions of a Mask
Thirst for Love

What is fascinating about Mishima is what is taken for granted, which always holds true when a fresh, exciting world is brought to light. In his case, that world is the product of a dark, nearly despairing vision; according to Gwenn Petersen, the heterosexual ties in his work are as "sick, sterile, and mutually destructive" as the homosexual ones[1]—an important truth because most of Mishima's people, particularly in the early work, are driven by sex. Petersen's truth suggests others. The sexual dynamic in the early Mishima endorses the samurai belief that the best love is undeclared. However sharp and dizzy the joys of erotic love, they also bring, in their wake, pain and guilt so overwhelming that all sensual delight is negated. The rich, dark glint given off by *Confessions of a Mask* (1949) and *Thirst for Love* (1950) conveys this isolation. Wit and irony do not describe the early Mishima's style—cool charm, polish, and composure being the gifts of the social comedian, a role his self-absorption rules out. Not surprisingly, he also lacks the detachment for paradox. Thus his confessional mood seldom shifts, his attitude to his people stays fixed, and he rarely develops character.

What he does instead occurs often, as Henry Miller has said: "To open most any one of his books one senses immediately the pattern of his life and his inevitable doom. He repeats the three motifs, youth, beauty, death, over and over again."[2] These motifs push to the fore of *Confessions of a Mask,* an autobiographical work of baroque pressure and convolution and also a big commercial hit in Japan. To indict the Mishima of *Confessions* for writing without affection for people is to miss the mark, even though the non-Japanese reader might be puzzled to find all the characters except the narrator so distant and dim. *Confessions* channels the three motifs Miller lists into the genre of the I-Novel *(Shishosetsu)*, the dominant fictional form of the century in Japan. This popular mode of confessional writing helped the fledgling Mishima express his deepest sense of life. Led by intimate, often unconscious impulses, he always wrote allegories of his private experience. *Confessions* could be the most brutally private and probing of them all. Describing it in the same vein as other critics have described Lawrence's *Sons and Lovers* (1913), Nathan shrewdly calls it "a book Mishima felt certain he must write in order, quite literally, to survive."[3] The wild fantasies recounted in the book reflect his knowledge that he was a person before he was a writer and that he had to face his private impulses before transmuting them into art. *Confessions* represents his coming to terms with himself. If it probes psychic realities that seem pathological, it also conducts its probing operations with unforgiving candor.

The book's title, admittedly, calls this candor into question. How credible is the confession of a mask? Why does Mishima wear a mask if he is speaking plainly and honestly? He uses a protective interface again in his next novel to appear in English, *Thirst for Love*, in which the person who identifies sexual love with bloodshed is a woman. Offsetting this evidence is the personal record; the biographies of Nathan and Scott-Stokes, both of which rely on interviews with Mishima and his circle, show that Mishima lived through the crises recounted in *Confessions*. Like other artists, he used his chosen medium to explore, but not tame, his ambiguity, absurdity, and anxiety. Like Lawrence before him, he had to sort out the sources of both his grief and his joy before he could function as a person, let alone as a writer. He knew that his psyche differed sharply from those of most people, and, rather than denying or downgrading this truth, he felt responsible to it. He is not indulging his ego so much in *Confessions*—which came out when he was four years younger than Lawrence was at the publication of *Sons and Lovers*—as affirming both the pain and the joy of its wild outlaw energy. Keene sees his main goal in *Confessions* as a confrontation with his dark side, "the monsters in his inner heart."[4] Had he been content with either romanticizing these monsters or sanitizing them, he would have only cheated himself. And he knew it. At age twenty-three, he had to face the truth, having just left the Finance Ministry in order to write full time. No psychological dead end or shadow game, the book reveals the same sincerity found chiefly in homosexual writers in the West, like Isherwood, Tennessee Williams, Joseph Hansen, and, perhaps, Lawrence himself.

1

Nathan says of the author of *Confessions*, "What he hoped to find was the source of his fascination with death. . . . What he discovered was his homosexuality."[5] Perhaps Nathan's dichotomy is too sharp; Mishima's erotic drive always impinged heavily on death, as his magnetic response to Guido Reni's St. Sebastian portrait showed. But Nathan is right to point out that the novel outgrew Mishima's original intent. *Confessions* deals less with the formation of a self than with the recognition and perhaps acceptance of a self that has already been formed. Kochan, or the Mask, Mishima's stand-in, knows enough about himself at age fourteen to confront his sexuality. But his sexuality also makes him flinch, and his belief that everyone else's is smooth and simple delays his self-confrontation. He remains torn between the messages his psyche is putting out and the sexual values he has gleaned from his family and schoolmates. Much of the book shows him oscillating between a lyrical surrender to impulse and the resolve to conform. Condemning *Confessions* as a one-man show, Miyoshi finds this oscillation annoying, disproportionate, and preemptive: "Throughout the book, there is only the 'I' who feels and does not feel, thinking about himself, looking at himself. This 'I' fills the whole story, leaving no room for anybody else."[6]

Miyoshi's disclaimer neglects the truth that people see each other's problems much more clearly than their own. The Mask's sexual preferences declare themselves before the Mask is five years old. But they frighten and repel him, and he spends the next eighteen years testing alternatives. He deserves credit, not blame, for accepting himself at this point. This pale weakling who has often been accused (sometimes by himself) of indecisiveness has discovered who he is and what he wants by age twenty-three. How many people can claim the same? What Miyoshi condemns as a fault should perhaps be praised as a virtue. *Confessions* extends both the tonal peculiarities and the emotional boundaries of the I-novel. In chapter 2, Mishima says of Tokyo in the 1930s, "The snow seemed like a dirty bandage hiding the open wounds of the city, hiding those irregular gashes of haphazard streets and tortuous alleys . . . that form . . . the panorama of our cities." This description of Tokyo is the book's longest; the city that surrounds and feeds the Mask discloses itself more as a mood than as a solid presence. The novel has intentionally omitted the material spectacle of life provided by Western city writers like Dickens and Georges Simenon. Nor will wartime Tokyo have any special character; when mentioned at all, crises like food shortage, bomb damage, and low morale flicker briefly across the page. The war is treated casually and intermittently throughout. Keeping his social foreground sketchy, the Mask also says little about his wartime job "at the N airplane factory, near the city of M." The following description of an air raid in which many died reflects Mishima's knowledge that the public and the private spheres collide destructively in wartime. More central to the art of the novel is his preference to summarize this destruction from a distance rather than dramatize it:

In the fire these miserable ones had witnessed the total destruction of every evidence that they had existed as human beings. Before their eyes they had seen human relationships, loves and hatreds, reason, property, all go up in flame.

Miyoshi's observation that Mishima loved his sister "almost incomprehensibly"[7] shows again the severity of control monitoring *Confessions*. The first page of chapter 4 devotes only two short sentences to this beloved sister's death. Even she must pass before the reader unnamed and nearly unnoticed if she and her sad early death clash with Mishima's artistic intent. The sensibility pervading the book is always Mishima's, but only as it captures the monumental sexual foreboding of Kochan the Mask. Western readers may complain that, for all the red-hot emotion crashing through the book, the book's tone is distant and pallid. But Kochan's self-absorption diminishes the reality of substances he can push against. To change the metaphor, the way the scenes neither build nor blend—no technical flaw—shows the disconnectedness of Kochan's life. So knotted is his psyche that any straightforward naturalistic rendering of places or people would falsify his perceptual anxiety. Sense data only reach us after they are filtered through his consciousness. But this process does not make the book the one-man show that Miyoshi alleges. Sometimes, the data reach us with great suddenness and sharpness, particularly when Kochan becomes inflamed by another boy. In these cases, the detailing grows nearly pornographic, and the sentence rhythms take on a heavy, sensuous cadence. Also given prominence is the figure of Hirschfield, whom Kochan reads avidly and names twice. Heretofore unidentified by English-language critics of the novel, Magnus Hirschfield was a Jewish sociologist, homosexual, and operator of Berlin's Institute of Sexual Science, which Nazi thugs destroyed in 1935.[8]

Drawn to other notable gays from the West, like Whitman, Wilde, and Proust, Kochan finds in Hirschfield's writing a discussion of his own erotic profile—the fusion of homosexuality and sadism. For most of the way, he ignores Hirschfield's fusion; he is not ready to apply it to himself. This reluctance characterizes the book. Befitting his grudging integration, the book is largely episodic. It becomes more dramatic and consecutive when it shows Kochan at school. But even this continuity will break down in the interest of maintaining his freedom from narrative logic. His perceptions always direct the book's flow along with his reluctance to face what he is. For this reason, he wastes a great deal of effort hiding from himself. For this reason, too, time may shift in tandem with what looks like a digression. Near the start of chapter 3, he cites "a passage from something I wrote at the age of fifteen." Yet seven pages later, he recalls an incident that occurred when he was "about thirteen or fourteen." Though not climactic, this later-reported incident means more to him than the more recent one cited earlier in the chapter. This disjuncture of time again focuses the book's main business—Kochan's self-recognition. To sharpen the finale, Mishima selects carefully and omits ruthlessly. Less than fifteen pages from the end, he writes:

> A year passed before Sonoko and I awakened. I had been successful in the civil-service examinations, graduated from the university, and had an administrative job in one of the ministries. During that year we managed to meet several times.

This focusing recalls that of James Joyce's *A Portrait of the Artist as a Young Man,* another random-looking but highly selective novel that extrudes all events but those that contribute to its young hero's development in one particular area. A comparison between the two short novels invokes others. Both works begin with their heroes' earliest memories; Kochan is the same age as Joyce's Stephen Dedalus at both the start and the end of *Confessions;* he lives on an island nation; like Stephen, he also rejects his inherited background, and his energies culminate in a recognition of what he must do, rather than in a resolve to do it. The book that ends with his recognition contains one less chapter but almost exactly the same number of pages as its magnificent prototype. Finally, Mishima was ten years younger when *Confessions* broke into print than was the thirty-four-year-old Joyce in 1916, the publication date of *A Portrait.*

One justification for the running comparison between Joyce and Mishima comes at the close of chapter 2, the critical halfway marker of the four-chapter *Confessions.* Kochan asks in the chapter's last paragraph, "I was feeling the urge to begin living. To begin living my true life?" What prompts this urge? One of his schoolmates has just died of TB—a disease that afflicted both Kochan and Mishima in childhood. Another schoolmate, whom Kochan loves unrequitedly, has just revealed himself as sexually straight and thus out of Kochan's reach. Frustrated, confused, and lonely, Kochan *must* look at himself closely if he is to gain self-acceptance. But his chapter-ending question invites one with prior claim. By starting anew, will he be scrapping his past and rebuilding his life on a fresh set of realities? Or will he accept the life he has been furtively leading as truly his own?

Choosing between these alternatives terrifies him. Part of his panic comes from not knowing how to present himself to others. According to Keene, he wears a mask because his discovery that he differs from most people forces him "to protect himself from their attacks."[9] But the psychological outweighs the social imperative in *Confessions;* Kochan must be something before he can become part of something else. Even though this priority resembles a spectrum more than it does a split, Mishima describes Kochan alone much more than with others. Being alone shows Kochan the futility of wearing a mask. The mask he puts on to simplify his life only creates new problems. Rather than easing him into reality, it has taken on a reality of its own, confusing, in his mind, the actual and the sham. Overhanging his search for identity is the metaphor from Shakespeare's *As You Like It,* "All the world's a stage." Kochan slips in and out of roles dictated either by the needs of a given moment or by his self-image. As the book's narrator, he also speaks at two levels. Often, the narrating self and the perceiving self will merge, and he will include his emotional responses to an event he is describing. Occasionally, he will step back from the narration in order to give his adult reactions to his adolescent behavior. But because he is writing his memoir at age twenty-three, he cannot step back very far. Though Mishima's first-person technique resembles that found in Dickens's *Great Expectations* (1860–61) and John Fowles's *The Magus* (1965), it lacks the irony found in these English novels.

The hard, relentless focus resulting from this lack of comic distance can make *Confessions* a rough read. Kochan's tortuous examination of his heart includes thoughts about his possible impairment, his laziness, his evil. At times he worries whether only the high drama of war will give him the resolve he cannot supply from within. Then he will experience an other-directed feeling but analyze it away rather than act on it. Such moments find him reproaching himself for failing to trust his heart. At more barren times, he tries to replace apathy with conviction or cleverness. As early as age fifteen, he discovers an apparent advantage he enjoys over his fellows. Because girls his age do not move him erotically, he can deal with them coolly and candidly. But this poise will shatter quickly. He will attack himself for a quality—like being emotionally immune to girls—he had previously praised. Then he will pass into a black mood. This morbid self-scrutiny can immobilize him. The allegedly "simple and abstract curiosity" he refers to at the start of chapter 4 is neither abstract nor simple. His misjudgment of it also follows one of his best insights. A person who inspects his feelings as closely as Kochan, one might object, should read them more accurately. But his wants are so submerged and smoldering that he misreads them, his evasiveness having blocked the natural flow and growth of his emotions. So contorted is his psyche that he cannot define his best interests most of the way, let alone act on them.

Though he reads and quotes Nietzsche, his constant self-questioning shows that he lacks the Nietzschean will to power. Both love's consummation and its failure stir in him thoughts of death. A love letter sent him by a young woman makes him envious (and not jealous, as the book's translator, Meredith Weatherby, in a rare but recurring error, claims). Seeing in Sonoko's letter an unguarded spontaneity he could never match, he feels reproached. This proof that he cannot invest his heart makes him long for death. Here is another Nietzschean echo—that of the transvaluation of values. Rather than inspiring him to climb to a higher psychic level, Sonoko's declaration of love shames him so badly that he wants to slink away and die. He knows that she deserves more from a man than he can give.

The moments that do bring him to erotic life he places between brackets; they can be enjoyed because they exist apart from anything that matters. His denying these soul-juddering moments any connection with his everyday being puts him at cross-purposes with himself. The same carnality that dwarfs everything else gets dismissed as a trifle. How can Kochan find his bearings? This aspiring writer quickly loses the patience to distinguish degrees or gradations of truth. All too willing to don the mask, he watches his feelings coarsen and warp. He even hides from himself. "Use can almost change the stamp of Nature," said Shakespeare (*Hamlet*, 3.4.168). Thus Kochan will devise smoke screens and ruses to extend his masquerade. Going against his instincts, this runt plays the roughneck with a couple of girls. His inverted sense of duty and propriety also sets in motion a psychological whirligig that defies both common sense and clarity. Lacking a stable selfhood, he does not know when he is following his heart, trying to prove something, or just showing off to himself. A simple act like putting his arm around a girl's waist incites a series of mental acrobatics so tortuous that he questions his heart's questionings and doubts his own doubts about his reservations.

2

The reader's own doubts surface very early, with the novel's epigraph from Dostoevsky's *Brothers Karamazov:* "Beauty is a terrible and awful thing. . . . God sets us nothing but riddles. . . . The man with . . . Sodom in his soul does not renounce . . . the Madonna." Mishima is flattering himself by asking us to apply this ambiguity to him and to Kochan. Virtue and vice do not blur in the novel; neither does the action rise to the supernatural. Kochan's sexuality asserts itself at age four or so, which is as early as any Freudian could wish, and it remains unchanged. The only ambiguities it stirs come from Kochan's uneasiness with it. At the start of chapter 3, a fourteen-year-old Kochan says that bus conductresses have sex appeal because of the tightness of their uniforms. His remark refers to an impression that has been lodging in his psyche for ten years. At the age of four, he saw a night-soil gatherer, "a young man . . . with handsome, ruddy cheeks and shining eyes," carrying a bucket of excrement on each shoulder. What made Kochan's earliest memory so erotic were the close-fitting trousers worn by the night-soil man. The sharp, provocative outline created by these "thigh pullers" gave Kochan "a presentiment . . . that there is in this world a kind of desire like stinging pain." This excitement comes from the coincidence of male beauty with waste and decay. But the coincidence is not intrinsic. Kochan imagines it, embellishes it, and makes it a psychological necessity. Then he builds both a sociology and a system of aesthetics around it.

The slow decomposition symbolized by the night-soil man's burden soon gives way to the sudden, violent dissolution of manslaughter. Kochan edits the text of a Hungarian fairy tale to make it conform to his bloody fantasy. Then he changes the pictures in a boys' adventure magazine. Still later in his adolescence, after masturbating to the Reni St. Sebastian, he conjures up the idea of a murder theater, in which young Roman gladiators die to entertain him. But they are not shot to death; firearms are banned from the theater. The murder weapons used in Kochan's psychoerotic theater must draw blood on contact—from the belly, the place where the entry wound occurs in the act of *seppuku*. The knives, spears, and arrows aimed at the bellies of the victim-players did the same job as did sexual contact in the hard-core porn films that began appearing in Japan in the 1950s. They provide spurts of blood, just as the orgasm in X-rated American films like *The Devil in Miss Jones* and *Behind the Green Door* furnished the viewer with the visual spectacle of sperm. This parallel is prophetically apt. Kochan's murder fantasy reaches full expression in a daydream at the end of chapter 2. His hero, the school's best athlete, is choked to death, lashed naked to a large serving dish, and surrounded by a garnish of salad leaves. Then Kochan, after kissing him many times, jabs a fork into the dead athlete's heart and begins slicing his breast in preparation for a cannibal feast.

The anemic Kochan's wanting to eat the flesh of his beloved at age fourteen or fifteen refers again to the nightsoil man. "I want to *be* him," said Kochan, riveted by the man's clinging trousers. Here is no simple mystical merging of lover and beloved as is found in nineteenth-century Romantic poets like Shelley and Whitman. Even at the age of four, sexual attraction so overwhelms Kochan that it invades his social imagination. A countering mentality has overtaken him that he will never shed. This frail, delicate son of a highly educated civil servant wants to gate-crash the lower classes. After longing to be on a level with the night-soil man, he dreams about joining the enlisted ranks of the army. Even at school, eight or ten years later, he would trade his reputation as an honor student for that of a hoodlum. His heroes, no bookworms or even average scholars, come from the slums, fail their exams, and sport big muscles under cheap clothing. To Kochan, these surly, brainless louts enjoy a rich animal life both closed and forbidden to him.

The first representative of this gutter glamour to impress Kochan after his childhood is a muscular, athletic schoolmate a couple of years his elder named Omi. Kochan's attraction to Omi expresses itself erotically. Kochan mentions the different parts of Omi's body, fantasizes about his nakedness, and, for the first time with a boy, wants to have sex with him. Here is Miyoshi's summary of Omi's magnetic appeal for the Mask:

Omi is beautiful, strong, and rebellious. But his character qualities do not matter much; it is his appearance—his body—that arouses the nar-

rator. . . . If the "I's" passion here is genuine, it is also exclusively physical. . . . His expectations exclude all but the hardest sexual pleasures.[10]

Miyoshi's sharp assessment needs to be slightly modified. Kochan
opens himself to Omi to begin with because Omi represents the
forbidden lower depths that first moved Kochan in the excrement
bearer. A discipline problem at school, Omi was already denied
promotion two or three times before meeting Kochan; he has been
banned from the school dormitory; he may have even lost his
virginity.

Omi's notoriety, his anti-intellectualism, and his arrogance all
make him a perfect object for Kochan's lurid sexual fantasies. As
will be dramatized more vividly in *The Sailor Who Fell from Grace
with the Sea* (1963, 1965), amiability and gentleness violate the
rough, savage justice Mishima associates with male potency. No
sooner does Omi display a humorous streak than he shrinks in
Kochan's esteem. Civilized graces like humor can lead to reciprocity,
an ideal that clashes with Kochan's belief that heroic male beauty is
marked out for bloodshed and death. Unable to live within normal
limits, Kochan believes that the pounding, surging blood of a prince-
ly youth will burst the confines of his heart unless a knife relieves the
pressure. A nonintellectual with no social graces like Omi could
never cultivate mutuality, intuitive understanding, and similarity of
interests with Kochan. But it doesn't matter. Kochan does not want
to connect with Omi in this civilized, open-ended way. The reduc-
tive, simplistic nature of his love for Omi declares itself in the
statement, "My blind adoration of Omi was devoid of any element of
conscious criticism, and still less did I have anything like a moral
viewpoint where he was concerned." Omi's muscles, scowling
hauteur, and thuggish good looks have exempted him from ordinary
standards of judgment; morality has nothing to do with the fever he
has stirred in Kochan. His mind and spirit might even blunt
Kochan's intoxication with his animal force. No liability, Omi's
ignorance is prized by Kochan, whose ideal of erotic fulfillment
extrudes all contact other than physical. In chapter 2, he says that
full sexual satisfaction could only come to him in the embrace of a
foreigner whose language he did not know.

Though built on denial, this constricting view of sexual love can unleash surprising intensities. Kochan's love for Omi takes on a new power and definition when Omi exercises on the school gym's horizontal bar. Watching bold, sullen Omi perform his routines stirs Kochan more deeply than ever before. Immediately, Kochan pulsates with erotic desire. The anchors he fantasizes tattooing on Omi's muscle-knotted arms represent a male adventurousness equated with sailors, stevedores, and roustabouts—lonely men lacking in formal education and refinement. Kochan's imagination is set racing still more by Omi's sweating body. The sight and particularly the smell of male sweat excited Kochan when, as a youngster, he would observe a platoon of soldiers walk past his home following drill. He has remained indirectly aware of this memory for over a decade. His subconscious has also embellished it. The product of effort and straining, sometimes even of violence and pain, sweat moves him all the more when it glistens and drips from an unclad, muscular youth. Enhancing this excitement, he discovers to his wild glee, is the hair growing profusely out of Omi's armpits. Omi's deep armpit hair has swept Kochan into an ecstasy, in which visions of bloodshed and death stir dizzy sexual vibrations.

Confessions introduces still other sexually related motifs that will recur in Mishima's later work. An amorous young couple will part dramatically at a train station again in *Spring Snow,* and a youth fretting over a young woman will deliver a package to a relative she lives with in *Runaway Horses.* But perhaps the motif first seen in *Confessions* that will later become a staple of the Mishima canon consists of the festival or procession. A sexually inflamed woman hides behind the anonymity of a street parade to claw the naked back of the man who inflames her in *Thirst for Love.* An aging unmarried couple sleep together for the first time in *After the Banquet* after watching a religious ceremony shatters their inhibitions. *Confessions* also contains a religious procession that smashes civilized restraints. To hint at the importance of the motif, Mishima places the procession at a strategic point—the end of chapter 1.

A mob of local firemen carrying a shrine blunder through the gates of the home of Kochan's parents. Amid bellows of noise, they trample the lawn and garden. Their destructive rapture shakes Kochan so deeply that he does not know if he is feeling joy or terror. The wantonness of the devastation, along with the looks worn by the stampeding firemen, "the most obscene and undisguised drunkenness in the world," has created an appalling purity of motive. Having shattered social constraints, the men are not negotiating for a commodity. John Nathan's biography reprints a 1956 photograph of Mishima having just finished a festival march. He is getting ready to lower the shrine he and some friends have been carrying, and his expression combines relief with gratification. He has broken through his reserves. In a group, people can act with a recklessness they would not risk when alone. But their frenzy will only live briefly, especially if they are Japanese and thus burdened by heavy social prohibitions. Mishima's people feel this pressure. They also lack the patience, gentleness, and self-regard to fulfill themselves in a close personal tie. But sooner or later, they forsake the false security represented by the group. It is then that motives of self-contempt and suicide flare forth.

These motives bedevil Kochan because he condemns intellectually what excites him sexually—beefy young hooligans from the lower social orders. His only serious attempt to close with a suitable young woman extends over a couple of years and centers on Sonoko, a sister of one of his schoolmates. Despite her "unusually graceful body" and "beautiful legs," Sonoko appeals more to Kochan's moral sense than to his instincts. If any woman could rouse his blood, it would be Sonoko, judging from his reluctance to part with her. The terror that accompanies sexual arousal in Mishima comes to him through her brother rather than through Sonoko herself. Though no love triangle is mooted, this hint of erotic attraction stays in our minds as Sonoko's bond with Kochan deepens and her hopes to marry him rise.

The conflict of interests emerges when Kochan and Sonoko visit her brother, Kusano, in an army post. This apparently innocent outing gives Kochan a shock of overwhelming self-insight. He discovers that the hand extending from Kusano's khaki uniform is chapped, shell-like, and heavily callused. Kusano's lobsterlike grasp conjures up those scaly-handed menials, fishermen, and athletes the younger Kochan wanted to be raped by and then kill; the roughness of such hands can scrape off the veneer of breeding and culture that passes for civilized behavior among the genteel, educated class that Kochan belongs to and hates. Kusano's abrasive hands and the riot they cause in Kochan's soul is one of several instances in which reality foils the Mask's expectations. The first occurred in early childhood, when his fantasies about a heroic young warrior whose picture he had been admiring ended with the discovery that the warrior was Joan of Arc, a woman. Life never organizes itself to satisfy his hopes and expectations. Years later, as an ephebe, his efforts to establish himself heterosexually meet sudden reversal when he fails with a prostitute and when, during a party game, he sees the gleaming, shapely thighs of a pretty coed and feels no sexual arousal.

None of these developments promise well for Sonoko, even though she is ignorant of them. Nor does his customary practice of analyzing every fluctuation of feeling she stirs in him improve her chances. After she and her family leave Tokyo, he takes the train to spend weekends with her. But he does not know whether the joy he feels at parting on Sunday evenings betokens relief to be away from her or gladness bred by the weekend's pleasure she gave him. Meanwhile, others are questioning his conduct and its meaning as closely as he. A moment that symbolizes his growing stress occurs when his sixteen-year-old sister teases him about marriage. His answer to her taunts—"If you don't leave in a hurry, I'll throw this ink bottle at you"—conveys his defensiveness. He has pitted the intellectualism he is accustomed to escaping into against the naked upsurge he finds so threatening. If he could ink over the doubt and discomfort quickened in him by Sonoko, he would do it immediately.

He will declare his love for her in his frequent letters. But he will also make excuses to cut short his visits to her. Finally, the refuge of letter writing is taken from him. Kusano writes him a friendly, unthreatening letter assuring him that he should not feel rushed into making any premature decision about marrying Sonoko. Kusano also assures him that a negative response would not hurt their friendship. The directness of this appeal rattles Kochan, whose courting style has consisted of mixed signals and shadow games. Straightaway, he takes the letter to his mother. So needful is he of her help that she assumes a surprising new attractiveness; he notices her strong white teeth, an attribute that the Mishima archetype will only find, as a rule, in the men he wants to have sex with. But the protection Kochan seeks from his mother is withheld. His mother does not support him in his evasiveness, as he had hoped. Her question, "Do you love her, or don't you?" has a simplicity and plainness that are alien to him. Her advice, "You'd better just send a plain answer," to Kusano, also presumes an honesty, decency, and uprightness beyond his powers. The answer he finally sends is indirect, ambiguous, and artificial.

In the following months, Sonoko gets over her disappointment, moves on, and continues to grow. A year or so after reading Kochan's weasel words, she marries. Another sign of her development comes in her increasing skill as a pianist. Kochan meets this transformed Sonoko accidentally on a Tokyo street soon after deciding that he cannot love a woman. Every warm impulse he ever felt for Sonoko revives in him—but only because, as a married woman, she cannot test his deepest loyalties. Lying about having rejected her two years before, he pleads to spend time with her. As usual, he tries to control the emotional atmosphere of the meetings she agrees to hold with him. Though feeling no sexual desire, he claims to prize their encounters. He asks her to keep seeing him. In other words, he is willing to leave matters between himself and Sonoko as shapeless, indefinite, and nondirectional as they were when he was courting her. His insisting that, by continuing to meet him, she is merely playing with water, not fire, as she alleges, voices his selfishness. Once again, a love triangle involving him, her, and a man close to her (here, her husband) sheds revealing light on Kochan's heart. The triangle is a formal, or technical, device rather than a dramatic issue. Sonoko would not leave her husband for Kochan even if given the chance. The Mask's eagerness to keep seeing her shows that he neither respects her feelings nor cares about her welfare; a Japanese wife seen frequently in public with a man other than her husband risks both her reputation and her marriage. He is just using her to fill in time until someone more exciting drifts his way.

When chance does float this person before him, he gives up Sonoko—but by default, not conviction. And in keeping with his indecisiveness, his breakup with her is not portrayed, but only conjectured. Conjecture and surmise envelop him throughout. Speaking of the book's final scene, Keene says, "The book ends with the implication that the narrator will throw off his mask of compliance to society and accept his perverse desires."[11] The book's closing actions justify this reading. With still half an hour left to them, Sonoko and Kochan drift into a dance hall. The following description portends the hell Kochan is about to relegate himself to. Note the denial of space and time characterizing the dense, airless, odious ballroom:

> The hall was crowded with office workers . . . extending their lunch hours to suit their own pleasure. A sultry heat struck us full in the face. Abetted by a defective ventilation system and heavy drapes that shut out the open air, the stifling fever-heat that stagnated within the place was raising a milky fog of dust-motes against the reflecting light. One did not need . . . smells of sweat and bad perfume and cheap pomade. I was sorry I had brought Sonoko.

Nothing natural, let alone healthy, could survive in this urban bog. Images of depression and letdown, like acned, sodden female skin running with mascara alternate with descriptions of artificial, out-of-season flowers. Logically enough, the tune played on the bandstand is too "overpowering" for dancing. The most normal person in sight, Sonoko, can hardly breathe, and it is a tribute to her normality that Kochan ignores her in the book's closing moments. She and Kochan leave the stifling, blaring dance hall for the adjoining courtyard. And here Kochan's blood takes fire. He sees a shirtless young hoodlum, his bulging muscles accented by both a sweaty waistband and armpits sprouting tufts of black hair. "A strange shudder ran through my heart," Kochan recalls, adding, "I could no longer take my eyes off of him." The sadomasochistic fantasy that attends all sexual desire for Kochan snaps into place; he imagines a dagger piercing the young tough's bellyband and blood spilling over his anguished supine body.

Though this vision depletes and depresses Kochan, the clamor it also creates in him tells him who he is and what he is made of. In the book's last sentence, he looks briefly away from Sonoko before leaving the shadeless courtyard with her, and he sees the following apparition: "Some sort of beverage had been spilled on the table top and was throwing back glittering reflections." This spilled drink might well be Coca-Cola; sticky-sweet Coca-Cola had just thickened Kochan's palate. Besides representing postwar Japanese sleaze, this dark, disturbing image carries forward the horrible portent created by the steamy, cloying ballroom itself. The life of shame and guilt that awaits him as an active consenting gay will not be described by Mishima till *Forbidden Colors* (1951). But clever Kochan intuits what awaits him. Perhaps he can also take some bleak satisfaction in knowing that gleams of gladness will sometimes brighten his pain and that, more importantly, this pain has been freely chosen—by his deepest, truest self. He has moved closer than ever before to an honest self-definition.

Although his practice of showing only a thin edge of himself disallows any equation of youth and happiness, it does not negate the importance of his breakthrough. Even life's worst trials can make us bigger by helping us cope with more and finally understand more. The reflection given back by the sticky pool of Coca-Cola led to the writing of *Confessions of a Mask*. As Nathan has shown, the book's first-person technique promoted greater self-insight and self-acceptance in Mishima, whose life coincides with Kochan's on most key points:

> Reliving his life in *Confessions of a Mask* through his first-person hero, Mishima drove himself remorselessly to the recognition that he was a latent homosexual and, worse, a man incapable of feeling passion or even alive except in sado-masochistic fantasies which reeked of blood and death.[12]

Kochan's situations look baroque, grandiose, and all the more perverse because of his mask. Yet they are also illuminated by passages of genius. *Confessions* has a power, economy, and beauty that forecast Mishima's eminence as a literary artist. Yourcenar's estimate of this early novel as "a short masterpiece on the theme of anguish and withdrawal" makes good sense. And while most might disagree with Scott-Stokes's opinion that it is also "the best of Mishima's works,"[13] few would deny it the virtues of vividness, honesty, and control. Still fewer would begrudge the acclaim with which it launched its young author into the global community of letters. *Confessions* makes its points obliquely; it never strays from its intriguing confusions; it avoids direct statement. Yet we are moved. Though sketchy, fragmentary, and puzzling, the work defies one to forget it. Because its quandaries and evasions capture so accurately the turmoil of its narrator's mind, it could not have been written otherwise.

3

Thirst for Love develops thematically but departs technically from *Confessions.* Published only a year after his more overtly auto-biographical novel, this 1950 work also gives an intimate look at Mishima. The intimacy stems in part from a new attentiveness to setting. If Kochan moved along a flat, monochromatic plane, Etsuko, the main figure of *Thirst,* feels the jar and jostle of *her* surroundings. These surroundings, moreover, jar and jostle each other in a way that gives the book a continuity and solidness of effect absent from *Confessions.* The detailed descriptions of both Osaka and Maidemmura, the town about an hour's train ride away where most of the action unfolds, foregrounds the domestic realism governing the action. As in Kochan's home, three generations occupy the Sugimoto household on Osaka's suburban fringe. But their representatives appear for longer stretches than did Kochan's relatives, and they serve the plot more effectively. Food is prepared, household chores are done, and crops are gathered in *Thirst.* Nor are the people performing these daily duties lightly sketched, Mishima giving background information on most of them and delving into their psyches. Useful from the standpoint of fleshing out Etsuko's living space, his new powers of characterization also deepen the reader's understanding of her. She lives more fully than Kochan partly because she is seen from different perspectives. To fend off a simplistic, one-dimensional response to her, Mishima will shift point of view to show how she and her problems look to others. These others must be credibly drawn if their reactions are to carry weight.

This sense of consequence declares itself immediately. Like Kochan before her, Etsuko enacts Mishima's belief that, for most of us, the enemy is within; we often hurt ourselves much worse than our rivals or our enemies can. This pain wears no disguises. Determined to confront himself directly, Mishima would not try to mask the sadomasochism goading him as duty, tradition, or social propriety. He says in chapter 3, "To some people living is extremely simple; to others it is extremely difficult." The novel's action bears out this editorial intrusion. Someone like Etsuko, who keeps stumbling over and recoiling from her emotions, finds everyday existence a quagmire. But she also makes existence boggy for those who once found it a breeze. Her outbursts denote frustration and helplessness, not heroism. So self-divided and self-defeating is she that she throws away the prize, the sexual favors of a young rustic she had pined, struggled, and degraded herself for. Anger rays out from her. Saburo, the gentle, bashful innocent of eighteen who inflames her, must die.

Mishima's matter-of-fact response to his death cannot be seen as a moral lapse. Mishima's not condoning her evil because she is just a woman and has thus forfeited his ire. *Thirst* is not sexist fiction. But the mistake of reading the work as a sexist tract does invite itself. Mishima does not usually develop his women as fully as his men. But he will give them enough presence to convey a sense of what they are. Though the women in *Thirst* lack the same rich dimensionality as the men, the book's main character is female. Called by Yourcenar "A young woman half mad from sexual frustration,"[14] Etsuko challenges Mishima more deeply than did his alter ego, Kochan. The sexual savagery fantasized about in *Confessions* gets acted upon in *Thirst;* in addition to being female in origin, Etsuko's passion is more sustained, more forbidden, and more active than Kochan's. Mishima's reference in chapter 3 to "the drunk who, fearing that if he takes another swig he will become sick, lifts the bottle again," alludes to her self-destructiveness. The allusion is apt; her self-destructiveness propels the action. Whereas Miyo, the "dull-witted country maiden" Saburo impregnates, tries to protect him when he is menaced, Etsuko, who may have also poisoned her husband, kills him. Anyone who deliberately hurts another person hurts herself, too. The book's closing sentences support this real-politik. "The crowing of roosters in the middle of the night" in which Saburo dies signals a false dawn. No illumination comes; Etsuko's problems remain unsolved, her pain persists, and Saburo lies in the earth. Awakening to darkness after the ordeal of committing murder had plunged her into sleep, she sees that she has betrayed herself.

Mishima devoted so much care to Etsuko because he poured so much of himself into her. Her problems mirror his; his own anguish informs the novel's deep structure masked as hers. Scott-Stokes believes that *Thirst* tells perhaps more about Mishima than the more apparently autobiographical *Confessions:*

As Flaubert was Madame Bovary, Mishima was Etsuko. He, too, felt a compulsion to love and to hurt the object of his love; he, too, was repelled when the other responded to his approaches. . . . To accept the love of another was the hardest thing that could be required of him.[15]

Mishima's failure to accept love also finds voice in Donald Keene's introduction to *Thirst*. Keene's mention of Etsuko's "revulsion when suddenly she feels she is loved" (p. vii) refers to Mishima's awareness of this problem in himself: a person must love himself before accepting the love of another. The self-tormented Etsuko spends more time in the novel with Maggie the family setter than she does with any person in the Sugimoto household. A dog demands less than a person, even one as rudimentary as grinning, inarticulate Saburo, who dooms himself the moment he returns Etsuko's ardor. Anyone as eaten up with self-contempt as Etsuko will equate love with devastation. The sweat and blood covering their bodies as she and Saburo struggle in the pampas grass at the end symbolize vitality for Mishima. The "bursting affection" she feels for Saburo in her semi-conscious erotic trance shows her gripped by this vitality, too. But self-contempt intrudes upon her ecstasy. Her wild screams chill his ardor; he recoils from her. But only briefly, to his confusion; so torn is her heart that, after repelling him, she clutches at him and begs him to wait.

Other parts of the action also show Mishima pouring as much dread into *Thirst* as he did into *Confessions*. The chance that Etsuko poisoned her husband recalls both Mishima's irrational fear of poison and his bent for self-destruction; her brother-in-law Kensuke's lying his way out of military service during the war invokes still-another authorial anxiety. More fully drawn than his wife Chieko, Kensuke justifies Keene's claim in the book's introduction (pp. v–vii) that *Thirst* develops its characters better than *Confessions* did. Kensuke, like Mishima, suffers from asthma. At different points of the action, Mishima calls him "a languid dilettante" and a "literary youth gone to seed" who suffers "a complete lack of self-sufficiency." He also justifies these indictments by denying Kensuke any free-standing adult life. Though married for five years (intriguingly, at the same age Mishima would be when *he* married eight years after the book's 1950 publication), the thirty-eight-year-old Kensuke lives in the home of a father he despises, and he lacks both a job and children.

This embodiment of Mishima's worst self-doubts would be hard pressed to find the energy for child rearing or work. He skulks around the house avoiding chores; the occasional household task he is shamed into performing he does slowly, poorly, and grudgingly. This ne'er-do-well would rather study Greek and Latin than work. Also indicative of his elitist's contempt for what is near is his love of French literature. At the start of chapter 5 he is reading Anatole France from a prone position. The first page of chapter 3 also showed him "sprawled out reading a book," and he prefers leaning against walls or furniture to standing straight. For a minor figure, he receives what may be a disproportionate amount of authorial scorn. His very tie with life is weak. His tactlessness, his boredom, his practice of being waited on, and the squeamishness that turns his head from a woman who has fainted all make him the ineffectual parasite that Mishima worked so hard to avoid becoming himself.

Mishima treats Kensuke's brother, Etsuko's husband, more briefly, since he died a year before the time of the novel. But despite this foreshortening, what he has to say about Ryosuke may reveal as much about him as did his more extended portrait of limp-wristed Kensuke. Mishima's calling Ryosuke a dandy calls to mind the occasions when the term was applied to him. Cousin to the masochist, the dandy subverts himself. Always trying both to shock others and to top his last turn, he puts incredible pressure on himself. Ryosuke's four female visitors to the hospital during his final overthrow imply this loss of self. Why should four women visit this married hospital patient in the first place? The aggressive sexuality that drew them to him conveys the dandy's need to be outrageous, even at the expense of his welfare. It probably also denotes the dandy's conventionality; the reactions of others count more with him than his own needs. Etsuko's belief that Ryosuke belonged to nobody alludes to his infidelity. It also refers more subtly to the elusiveness of the artist Mishima's persona, to the artist's compulsion to dramatize himself, and, finally, to his shaky self-image. These qualities underlie the book. Mishima's inflicting great pain on Ryosuke before letting him die in early manhood parallels the conduct of Etsuko, who, besides maybe killing him, insults his memory by sleeping with his father.

The oft-mentioned decrepitude of Yakichi, her aged lover, restores the familiar Mishima fusion of love and death. At one point, the fusion invokes higher purposes. "Is sickness perhaps, after all, only an acceleration of life?" Mishima asks in chapter 2 while a feverish, bedridden Ryosuke is undergoing a medical examination. Ryosuke's meandering thoughts recall Tolstoy's belief that imperfection is the best condition for self-improvement; stench, fever, and delirium can promote wisdom by taking us to the heart of things; Prince Andrew Bolkonski's idolatry of Napoleon in *War and Peace* shatters when, recovering consciousness, he sees his hero in person on the battlefield of Austerlitz. No such transcendence graces Mishima's people; being swept into the death drift rules out tragic elevation. The dying belong only to death. The idea that sex achieves its consummation in death comes forth during Ryosuke's final struggle. As he passes into delirium, he laughs wildly from a mouth dripping blood (the open mouth will later serve as a leitmotif in Saburo's death). Carrying forward the implications of this erotic image, he groans "like a bride" during his throes, while Etsuko calls the sixteen days he takes to die "the happiest" in her life, surpassing in joy the delights of her honeymoon.

Her wild heartbeat continues to disclose chaos and dread after Ryosuke's death. Not only does she allow creaking, rheumy Yakichi to perform his son's sexual office; the stuffy, fetid air of the Sugimoto home also resembles that of the hospital where Ryosuke died. This rankness has been spreading. The transfusion Ryosuke got in the hospital during his sad last days contained blood from the veins of a sickly lower-class man. Saburo, a menial, dies from a blow inflicted by a mattock first seen in his own hands.

But nobody in the book argues more forcibly that one's destructive demons lie within than the nerve-raddled Etsuko. Perhaps this insomniac and misfit descends from Henrik Ibsen's Hedda Gabler,

Strindberg's Miss Julia, and their many displaced, headstrong nieces and grandnieces (like Julia, Etsuke has a dead mother; like Hedda she's the only child of a general whose death predated the present-tense action of the work featuring her and who, presumably, left her little or no money). The alienation of this well-bred, refined Tokyoite may cut deeper than that of Kochan the Mask, whose parents and grandparents are all alive. Her elegant speech and manner both label her an outsider to her neighbors in the little community where she has come to live. The week her door calendar has fallen behind conveys again how out of joint she is with her surroundings. This estrangement makes itself felt straightaway. On her way back home from the train station in chapter 1, she prefers taking a roundabout path to shortcutting through a "squalid community" of government houses built right after the war, even though it is raining. But if this rain creates a meancing portent, it is also connected with growth. The acreage where childless Etsuko travesties marriage produces rich yields of vegetables and fruit.

Her barrenness flows from her nature. Her paramour, old Yakichi, is probably no longer fertile despite what his love of the soil implies. In her marriage to his son, she played the passive feminine role, but only in the physical sense. Mentally, she dominated. If she murdered Ryosuke, she also saw to it that the poison she fed him produced symptoms that would resemble those of typhoid fever. Because the boundary dividing mind and body cannot be known, her mental mastery of him pushed into the realm of the physical. She outlasted him. And she will also outlast Saburo, killing him within moments of their first sexual contact. She prefers death to life. Even before embracing nightly an elder who often seems more dead than alive, she relished her husband's final overthrow. She also preferred the chemical smell of Lysol emitted by the hospital where Ryosuke died to that of the fresh, wind-washed outdoors nearby.

She knows that the hospital atmosphere inhibits life. Both her loss of control and self-loathing spur her to commit acts that recoil destructively upon her. Only a masochist could insure her own misery as well as Etsuko. So spiteful is she that she endangers her fragile health by taking a bath and then pulling the plug in order to stop Saburo and Miyo from bathing together. Each of her plans to defeat Miyo, in fact, is wilder and more self-defeating than the one preceding it. When Miyo's pregnancy becomes known, she tries to force Saburo, the putative father, to marry Miyo. Her motives convey her deviousness. She wants to assert her power over Saburo. Also, in a maneuver that will recur in *Forbidden Colors,* she tries to punish him by forcing him to marry a woman he does not love. But she cannot enjoy the heady wine of malice. Lacking Etsuko's moral training, Saburo bestows little importance on marriage; whether or not he marries Miyo hardly matters to him. Meanwhile, Etsuko continues playing Br'er Rabbit to his impassive Tar Baby. This folly has not escaped her; neither has her obsessiveness drowned her conscience. She knows when she is sinning, and she punishes herself accordingly. Whenever she does the rustic lovers a nasty turn, she gets sick; her insomnia attacks worsen; literally, she burns her hand twice—once on a hot stove and once in an autumn bonfire.

It is always she who suffers agony and collapse, not Miyo or Saburo, whose innocence has put them beyond her snares. In chapter 4, the couple laugh and play while gathering persimmons. The branches of the tree that holds the fruit shake "in concert" with their frolic; nature is approving of their fun. But Etsuko disapproves; no green persimmons are needed to sour *her* expression. The easy joy of this "pair of puppy dogs" has tormented her. Although her efforts to divide them do not whet their zeal to be together, they do damage her already wounded self-esteem. She knows that apple-cheeked Saburo does not merit her malice and, moreover, that this malice falls below any standard of decency. Thus she makes sure that her schemes both to divide and to discredit the lovers all backfire. Using sex as leverage, she bullies Yakichi into banishing Miyo from the farm. But she wants more revenge. In a scene omitted from this spare, economical book, she also gives herself the fiendish satisfaction—and self-torment—of bundling the sobbing, pregnant Miyo into the departing train herself.

Whatever she wants from Saburo, it is worth maiming herself for, disrupting the routine of the family farm, and turning Miyo away. But the crisis she has fomented must play itself out, partly in public. Moral cowardice spurred her to get rid of Miyo during the days Saburo was away from the farm and thus could not protest. When he does return some days later, advisedly at sunset, he brings more darkness to Etsuko. Nothing she can do fazes him. He continues to

address her politely as "Ma'am" or "Madam," and he seems unmoved by Miyo's absence. Smiling and stolid, he cannot provide the
big dramatic scene she wants; her anxieties stay bottled up inside
her. Her mind races, she loses her bearings, and she wanders beyond
the point where she can recognize, let alone define, her best interests. Saburo has a great deal in common with Miyo; his prospects
for happiness with her surpass by light years his outlook with
Etsuko. Yet these realities do not matter. Etsuko never ponders a
future with him, and she has omitted the virtues of kindness and
reciprocity from any tie she envisions between Saburo and herself.
Why, then, her wildness? Did the envy of an unrequited lover
compel her to drive Miyo away? Or can all her attempts to close
with Saburo be explained by simple lust? Finally, in viewing him as a
sexual object, has she underrated him?

And has he resisted her perverse novelette out of dullness or
cleverness? As in Henry James, an inversion of values and standards
may have occurred. The rustic sees perhaps more clearly than the
cosmopolite, and simplicity might point the way to truth better than
sophistication. These possibilities fret the nerves of the complex
urbanite Etsuko. When Saburo finally makes the sexual advance she
has been debasing herself for, she resists "without knowing why."
She has brought him to the moment of sex, only to repel him. Death
is the only outcome for the internal struggles of this contrarian.
Ridden by guilt for subduing an uneducated farmboy to her obsession, she lashes out destructively. But guilt has not overwhelmed her.
Lacking the moral fiber to punish herself as she deserves, she flails
out at Saburo. Her braining him with a mattock, an attempted
beheading, expresses both sexual rage and sexual revenge. The
aptness of this symbolism cannot calm her, though. When asked
why she killed Saburo, she can only mutter feebly and inanely, "He
was making me suffer." The nocturnal crowing of some nearby
roosters that later awakens her shows her the futility of her mad
outbreak.

4

Saburo, the target of this outbreak, recalls Henry Fielding's Joseph
Andrews and Tom Jones. Keene views him correctly as an ordinary

fellow who gets into trouble: "Saburo is the strong, sunburned young man, devoid of any intellectual preoccupations, who would appear in many subsequent novels, a healthy young man who cannot fathom Etsuko's complex desires."[16] Though perceptive, Keene has exaggerated the contrast between Saburo's cheerful back-country indolence and the vexed striving of Etsuko. This collision of nerve-worn consciousness and opaque physicality attains subtleties beyond Keene's dichotomy. Yes, Etsuko does want to crush Saburo, whose healthy outdoors normality both attracts and intimidates her. Maggie, the setter she loves, shows this Japanese Li'l Abner an affection she withholds from her, and he can bury himself for hours in work that would only bore and alienate her. In fact, she is probably too neurotic to dedicate herself to any enterprise that is not destructive. Nor is Saburo a blameless victim. Like Joseph Andrews and Tom Jones before him, he would have avoided many serious problems by seasoning his virtue with prudency, particularly when the need arose. No special powers of intelligence would have been required of him to spot malignancy in Etsuko.

The instinctive contentment that first enriches him and then leads to his undoing comes quickly into view. This planter and harvester whose seed will later spring to life in the fertile field of Miyo's body first appears outdoors, as he will in most of his appearances in the book. The outdoors is his element. He returns home from a trip to his mother's in chapter 5 by walking through the teeming abundance of a rice field; besides feeling comfortable enough in a tree both to climb and frolic in it without falling, he identifies a wildflower whose name has eluded Etsuko. He even dies outdoors, but in a part of the Sugimoto property that calls attention to the wrongness of his death. He is killed in an area known as the grape field, even though no grapes have grown there for years. The peaches that now grow from trees planted in this rich soil and that fetch high market prices sustain the idea of fruitfulness, as does Saburo's burial in the grape field. The identification of Christ with gardening in the Gospels sets forth the simple goodness of the gardener Saburo as a source of transcendent values.

This thematic identification would please Mishima, whose inner strife resembles that of Etsuko, Saburo's killer. The gardener's ironic burial place discloses both the tormented creator in Mishima and

the cool, poised craftsman. Like the false dawn ending the book,
Saburo's murder denies promise and hope. But the fertility connected with his burial plot also implies renewal. Mishima's sugges-
tion that the false dawn will yield to the true and that loss will
promote gain only makes sense according to the mad nighttime
logic that caused the murder of this Hiroshima youth. The ambiguities surrounding Saburo's death also show in Mishima a tendency
to hedge his bets that will vanish with the years. He is using, in
Thirst, the consolations of literary convention to soften the harsh
doom he rains upon the book's male lead.

His irony works better when it is directed to Etsuko. Suitably, the
gardener first appears in daytime "lying on his back" in "a green
plot." He first becomes aware of Etsuko as a shadow falling between
him and the September sun. Her malignancy has been prefigured,
all the more neatly because Saburo's patch of green is situated in a
cemetery. But he is not sleeping when Etsuko's shadow blocks his
sunlight. He is reading. And Mishima's militarism, which had already made strong psychological inroads by 1950, prevents us from
discounting Saburo's samurai adventure story as commercial pap. In
fact, the heroism displayed in the story channels intriguingly into a
remark he prompts from one of the Sugimotos in chapter 2: "This
fellow acts as though he knows nothing, and he knows everything."

Both the extent and the value of this knowledge confound Etsuko.
When she tells him that she saw the socks she had given him in a
garbage can, he answers "without hesitation" that he threw them
there. She is unnerved; his answer is too direct and forthright for her
devious mind. Immediately, her vexation spreads, and it meets new
obstacles. Trying to protect Saburo, Miyo claims to have thrown
away the socks. Direct answers are still best. Miyo explains reasonably that she took the socks to begin with because she did not want
Saburo to feel obligated to Etsuko, their giver; then she disposed of
them because they did not fit her. "What she said made sense,"
Etsuko remarks inwardly of this explanation. But she still wants to
push pins into the lips of this "witless girl" who speaks the truth.
Saburo's making sure that Etsuko sees him wearing the gift socks
after a discreet interval of a few days only fuels this rancor. She goes
through his and Miyo's belongings when they leave the house, fully
mindful of the contempt she felt for Yakichi when she found him

spying on *her*. Instinctively, Mishima's simple people help each other, whereas the complex ones reach out to draw blood, to inflict pain, and to disclose guilt. This sharp moral contrast impresses itself upon Etsuko. Puzzled by the absence of incriminating evidence in the two lovers' rooms, she wonders, "Are they . . . being circumspect in avoiding my search . . . ? Or am I . . . missing what I seek because it is . . . in plain sight?" She has lost her way. Her obsession is making her fabricate cunning, complex meanings out of nothing.

Besides increasing her self-contempt, this obsessiveness wins her no advantage over Saburo, a willing singer of songs whose inner harmony she cannot discompose. When she accuses him of mistreating Miyo, he will not slink or cower. Instead, he looks straight at her and admits that he fathered the baby Miyo is carrying. The directness of both his speech and his eye confuses Etsuko. Having blitzed him with questions and accusations, she has expected him to quail. He keeps reversing her expectations and throwing her off stride. Later in the same confrontation, her failure to make him squirm induces a longing to be touched by him. She asks him to continue their walk, hoping that she will charm him into making a sexual pass. But he tells her instead that the hour is late. This pattern of advance and withdrawal recurs at the end. Again, she is fretful, quivering, and intense, while he is relaxed and composed. His calm maddens her. How can she move him? She lies; she pleads; torn between fading hope and guilt, she avoids his eye. Her psyche is so raw and convoluted that she rejects the truth when she hears it from him.

Their relationship is doomed because the hypertense fanatic from Tokyo and the simple, slow-pouring object of her fanaticism share nothing vital. Like Peter and Jerry in Edward Albee's *Zoo Story* (1958), they even lack a common linguistic base. Also, as with Peter and Jerry, words exaggerate the gulf dividing them. The love that Etsuko rhapsodizes about means nothing to him. To him, love is "a completely unnecessary concept" that has "no room in his life." Any link between love and sex or between love and marriage never occurred to him before she cornered him with her feverish talk. The closest he has ever come to love was the lust that flared out between him and Miyo, whom he scarcely knew before having sex with her. Although he still desires Miyo, he rarely thinks of her. The news of her departure from Maidemmura neither saddens him nor makes him happy. He acts from instinct, and he lives for the moment, unlike Etsuko, who worries every impulse to death. Their linguistic differences have prompted others. Saburo cannot understand why an aristocratic widow would buy him two pairs of socks, let alone want to have sex with him. It simply never occurs to him that "this ever-distant matron older than he" sees him as anything but a servant. He has no idea of the scheming and maneuvering she has undertaken to close with him.

Mishima's description of his downfall has the benefits of psychological insight, narrative tempo, and atmospheric effects that create a sense of crisis. The images and symbols enlivening the action were not inserted for decoration but for dramatic purposes. They flesh out character, add texture to setting, and sharpen the moral issues rising from the action. Especially noteworthy is the animal drive building from the book's aggressive sexual symbolism. Mishima's keen nose imparts some of this physicality. The smell of sweat and mold infuses that of face cream during one of Saburo's ruts with Miyo. Sustaining the equation of sex and death, Etsuko recalls her husband's slow death in the Hospital for Infectious Diseases as a series of smells. This symbolism expands rhythmically. After Miyo's pregnancy is announced, Etsuko chides her inwardly for not shaving her armpits. The previous sentence saw her noting Miyo's having, to date, escaped morning sickness. Could the rude peasant vigor that has kept Miyo hale and the aromatic tufts of hair budding from her armpits be related? Mishima's making Etsuko's observations of these phenomena follow consecutively implies a connection. And his connecting principle is barren Etsuko, who feels reproached and resentful over failing to attain Miyo's level of sensuality.

Her awareness of her lack of animal vigor had sharpened at the Autumn Festival that occurred in the previous chapter—i.e., midway through the book. As the rites began, she heard her brother-in-law Kensuke, the book's other avatar of cerebral sex, call sexual love a union of symbols and anonymities. Then she sees a shouting, wide-eyed Saburo pushing and milling in a procession of local youths. What grabs and holds her attention is his "sharp . . . white . . . shining . . . sparkling" teeth, always a mark of sexual radiance in Mishima. The impression holds. Later at the farm, the spectacle of

A Boy's Own Stories

these strong white teeth magnetizes her again. Perhaps their tearing, grinding action can inflict on her the punishment she knows she deserves for implicating Saburo in her wild fantasies. Perhaps she envisions their gleaming whiteness running with blood from the knife she would like to plunge into his throat (blood from Ryosuke's diseased gums mottled *his* teeth just before his death). Though she does not stab Saburo, she slashes his neck and then brains him. But this symbolic beheading has not slaked her lust. After burying Saburo, she treads the earth covering him—"as if she were walking on bare skin." Her lust would not run its full course until she has pushed him as deep as possible underground. Even in death, he exudes a boyish cheer and sexual charm she must crush. "From his mouth," she notes, "protruded a row of sharp white teeth. He almost seemed to be smiling." To hide this glancing whiteness, she sprinkles a handful of dirt into his mouth. This source of erotic excitement and dread has driven her to inflict pain, to kill, and, as a final insult or tribute, to stuff with dirt.

The scene where his teeth first compelled her, the orgiastic Autumn Festival in Tenri of chapter 3, surpasses by far the procession that ended chapter 1 of *Confessions*. For one thing, the festival, the book's longest scene, meshes more smoothly with the action than its earlier counterpart. The mob of locals that stormed into Kochan's garden was made up of nondescripts; the devastation they caused is not mentioned again after its occurrence; none of them reappear in the action. Saburo, on the other hand, the center of interest during the festival, had already asserted his thematic importance. Also, Etsuko, whose charged response to him had established this centricity, plays an active role in the festival, unlike Kochan, who was a four-year-old bystander when his family garden was trampled. Bolstering this thematic unity is the descriptive power of the festival scene. The booming drums, the sparks and gleams shooting from nearby bonfires, and the thronging and roiling of the hundred shouting processioners create a frenzy rivaling those found in E. M. Forster's *Passage to India* (1924) and L. P. Hartley's *Eustace and Hilda* (1947).

This excitement builds from Mishima's expert handling of his red-hot materials. The "swirling, needless waste of life's energies" overflowing from the extravaganza intoxicates Etsuko. Diving into the colliding, churning mob of half-naked processioners, she gouges Saburo's back. But this first physical contact with him—demented, destructive, and dictated by her—does not climax the chapter. The spotlight is stolen from her—and its theft tallies with the wild surge of energies the chapter had described. This brimming vitality did not run completely to waste. Symbolically, it has borne fruit. Caught up in the dementia, Miyo faints. The medical exam she is soon given reveals her to be pregnant. This announcement makes Etsuko feel small and cheap; she knows that the father must be Saburo, whose blood is still stinging her mouth. The direct and the natural have outpaced what is destructive and perverse. Her mad fantasies have come to naught. Once more, she is bested by the simple, the obvious, and the unassuming.

The book's shrewd organization lends impact to the festival scene and others like it. Rhythm and tension will sometimes build from sequencing or juxtaposition. Mishima's identification of love and death in Etsuko's psyche provides some good examples. As in *Confessions,* the people in *Thirst* exist on the plane of ordinary social interaction. But early on, the reader also sees them joined at some obscure, inner level. This deep bonding generates a hypnotic intensity when Etsuko's memory of first being moved by Saburo's muscular arms and strong young voice recalls her trip to Ryosuke's cremation site. Another moment of subliminal interweaving occurs in her recalling the shabby, sickly blood donor who helped prolong Ryosuke's wretched life. Having married into a farming family, she will not be able to escape the lower classes. The anonymous sufferer whose blood was transfused into Ryosuke's veins describes the unconscious process by which the unprivileged will insinuate themselves into her vital zones. Purebloods who go slumming get slummy, and the way is ever downwards.

Sustaining our interest in this drift is its setting forth. Mishima will recount Etsuko's torment from her point of view. Her inability to control her mad heartbeat soon alters the domestic routine of her household. To describe this alteration, Mishima will move to the point of view of a family member. Then he will add a dollop of intrigue by making his recording intelligence Saburo—who either does not know about the scheming he has incited or has transcended it. The novel's first sentence describes an effect of her obsession:

"That day Etsuko went to the Hankyo department store and bought two pairs of wool socks." Her buying Saburo socks rather than a hat or scarf imputes to him a "descendental," as opposed to transcendental, disposition. But who is doing the imputing? And whose disposition does Mishima have in mind? Etsuko bought Saburo the socks because she perceives him as a fleshly presence. Yet she is so disoriented by him that she spends half a day riding trains, fighting crowds, and trudging through rainy streets all for the sake of his feet. How reliable is her judgment? She is probably more aware of Saburo's feet than he is. This awareness amounts to nothing more than raw sexual hunger; as a mind or a spirit he does not exist for her. Pehaps he should be grateful. The truth that his spirit and mind both escape her destructive lust makes him her superior. His innocence defeats her. Although she kills him, she never corrupts him. His personality and his psyche both remain intact.

He also lies unmourned in the grape field. Mishima is too pessimistic to invoke sunshine without first throwing out some gloom. The gloom he introduces into *Thirst* brings rain. Rain falls in the ominous first scene and recurs on and off the rest of the way, perhaps most notably when Ryosuke goes to the hospital where he will soon die. The heavy rains that abet the fertility of the Sugimoto farm cannot keep this offshoot of the family tree alive. Ryosuke's death widens a family rift that declares itself as a travesty of the basic family tie, marriage. The death results most dramatically in his widow's sleeping with his widower-father. Meanwhile, Yakichi's son-in-law lives, but in distant Siberia, and he never writes home. Kensuke, Yakichi's jobless son, does live together with his wife, but their having had no children after five years of marriage suggests, along with his cynical ideas about sex, that he may be sterile or perhaps even impotent as well as asthmatic. When Etsuko changes her kimono after coming home in chapter 1, the silken sash howls "like the scream of a living thing." And why not? All the Sugimotos have burdens heavy enough to make them want to howl. They are all badgered, and they all live on the edge. In his brilliant description of both their disquiet and its contagion, the twenty-five-year-old Mishima served notice to readers everywhere that his apprenticeship was finished.

4

Narcissus Bound
Forbidden Colors

Mishima's tone fills out in *Forbidden Colors* (1951). The book's wealth of detail, density of texture, and spread of character types all develop a rich vibrato absent from both *Confessions* and *Thirst*. Part of this abundance comes from the book's length; *Colors* is longer than *Confessions* and *Thirst* combined. But part comes from maturity of vision. Lunging into the savage complexity of life, the Mishima of *Colors* envelops us in thickets of almost mythic meaning. His dark, tightly coiled images will crowd us. At times, his caddish brilliance will degenerate into a schoolboy's desire to shock, as in his reference to a mere walk-on as "a counterintelligence man who liked to wear women's clothing." But little is lost by these rare touches of poor taste. His more discreet moments will reveal an exquisite perceptiveness to changes in both social behavior and psychological response. His relentlessly compulsive style also relaxes in his disquisitions on subjects like sex, beauty, and the reconciliation of spirit and flesh.

This polyphony directs itself to the pain and disequilibrium of postwar Japan. Along with the book's length (403 pages), the vocal range of *Colors* addresses the problems of dispersal and dislocation often referred to as the crisis of modernity. The Tokyo of *Colors* brims with contradictions, inviting at one moment and threatening the next. A murderous passion coexists with the civility rising from Japan's tradition of politeness and good breeding. This ambiguity creates a tallying response in Mishima. *Colors* portrays postwar Japan in such disturbing detail because he both relishes and recoils from its baroque exuberance—its arrogance, energy, and upbeat tempo. Images of urban squalor abound. In chapter 24, a moving train runs past "ill-humored blocks of gray buildings" and "cloudy, black factory landscapes" that include dark abandoned plants disfigured by peeling, sun-blistered paint, broken windows, and advertisements touting the products of a materialist, consumer culture. But the battle lines are smudged. Although a Japanese woman sleeps with an American soldier for material gain (an event that will recur in *The Temple of the Golden Pavilion* and *The Temple of Dawn*), Mishima treats her rut too casually to give it much importance in postwar Japan's cultural warfare. Accomplished, well-bred Japanese both distract and harm the book's twenty-two-year-old main character more than any number of foreigners. This baleful influence prevents one from viewing young Yuichi (or Yuchan) Minami as a person trapped between a vanishing and an emerging ethical system.

At times, the book describes cultural and spiritual alienation as a function of being gay, some of its descriptions of gays unleashing both pathos and force; like some Russian novelists, Mishima can strip his characters bare. Defined as "that endlessly tiresome principle of majority rule," heterosexuality asserts itself most dramatically on Sundays. Because Sunday belongs to the established order of the heterosexual family, gays have nowhere to go. "A homosexual's Sunday is pitiful," one reads in chapter 15, which is appropriately entitled "Blue Sunday." Gays feel most lonely, excluded, and depressed moving in the daytime world of parents and children enjoying one another's company at the zoo, on the beach, or around the picnic table. But homosexuality was not imported from the West. For decades, Tokyo has abounded with gay trysting places where a Western face will not be seen for months at a time. What is more, if gays grieve on Sundays, Mishima sometimes indicates that they deserve no better. Looking foward to the militarism that would overtake him in the 1960s, he says that the samurai and the homosexual both prize male beauty. Yet he also shows this same male beauty causing depression and despair.

He makes this disturbing point by returning to the Tokyo and the homosexuality that dominated *Confessions*. As has been seen, *Color's* added length provides a richness, a heft, and a shading missing from the earlier book. Resonance and complexity also stem from Yuchan. Not only does he appear before us for longer spells than Kochan the Mask; he also carries forward from Kochan by moving from latent to active homosexuality: he acts on the self-truths that Kochan was just starting to accept. In adddition, he is a newlywed and, by turns, a new father. This complication varies and enriches the domestic realism so central to *Thirst*. More thematically, perhaps, it gives Mishima the chance to lecture on the virtues and drawbacks of gay fatherhood. Here and elsewhere, the gay must practice self-denial; whatever satisfaction parenting gives him comes at the high cost of a "frightful self-desecration." He must pay. Throughout the book, his search for both context and continuity will come to grief. An ex-count of forty-two who has had a thousand male lovers goes to pieces when his wife leaves him, even though he has not had sex with her for a decade. Gay love in Count Kaburagi's circle will also invade the worlds of high finance and national security without adding a jot to Japan's store of comfort, wealth, or fun. As Yuichi's new marriage shows, no institution can escape the snares of gay sex; Count Kaburagi's wife bolted, in fact, because she caught the count having sex with Yuichi.

From the start, Mishima's descriptions of gays generate revulsion. In chapter 4, Yuichi takes a trolley ride during which he overhears the conversation of two gays en route to a popular cruising area called (in English) the "Park." The greasy hair, pale cheeks, and effeminacy of the speakers all make the embryonic gay Yuichi see himself for the first time as ugly. What happens when he follows his older counterparts into the "Park" only deepens his self-disgust. His search for self-being finds him stumbling and reeling. This searcher for freedom and spontaneity finds the fellowship of gays ruled by pettiness, calculation, and affectation. Whereas he sought elegance and refinement, he discovers the rudimentary. Likened to "creatures native to the depths of the sea," the denizens of the Park move "like a clump of seaweed untangling slowly from the water." This water stagnates even as it flows. Its symbolic wellspring, the epicenter of Tokyo's gay world, is the foul-smelling men's room of the Park. Called simply "the office," this pickup place observes a strict protocol. As the following passage indicates, the formalities of gay solicitation are all the more rigid and elaborate for resting on what is unsaid: "It was an office where the tacit office procedure is based on winks instead of documents, tiny gestures instead of print, code communication in place of a telephone." But an effect cannot be more real than its cause. As Mishima's controlling metaphor of the workplace infers, the visitors to the office are negotiating for thrills. But their businesslike search occurs "under a cloud of evil odors." What they find will ultimately repel them. Appropriately, the stink uncoiling from the office drives Yuichi away before he gets past the doorway.

But can he flee from himself? The question carries into chapter 8, "The Jungle of Sentiment," which is largely a treatise on the gay subculture. Any prowler in this jungle becomes "a kind of unsightly monster"; nor can the monstrousness be redeemed. Preferring to be straight, the gays in *Colors* both despise each other and know they are despised by their fellows—a constant that accounts for the prominence of the mirror motif (chapter 2 is called "Mirror Contract"). One reason Yuichi has so many admirers inheres in his having appeared to defy this archetype by being married. Voicing an opinion (disguised as fact) that sounds ridiculous today, Mishima insists that gay males are "incapable of maintaining a home." But he is also an artist, albeit an angry or wrongheaded one; he respects the truth of the imagination too much to compromise it with a personal grudge. The fire engines that wail several times in the book symbolize a genuineness of emotion beyond the reach of the wallowers in self-reflexive gay sentiment. The garden adjoining a gay love nest in chapter 8, with its dried-up spring, leafless trees, and flourishing plants, exhibits different stages of growth and downfall. This defiance of natural process conveys the dangers of homosexuality. Even gardens can be swept into the jungle of sentiment and turned into "unsightly monsters."

The same contagion that infects gardens also corrupts the worlds of family, education, and business. It can even seep into the generation gap. Sometimes, the processes concur. No sooner does Nobutaka Kaburagi make love to Yuichi than he appoints the younger man his private secretary. The new year rung in at the start of chapter 14 begins with the count and his wife, who also lusts for Yuichi, visiting his home. The Kaburagis have poisoned the realities Yuichi lives by. In the next chapter, his turning up at a gay club is taken in stride by the other guests. His autonomy has already begun to erode. As soon as he began frequenting gay clubs, he forfeited his privacy. And the loss of privacy in this gossip-ridden world can also bring loss of self. So high does gossip run in Tokyo's gay set that a jealous shopkeeper learns enough about Yuichi within a couple of hours to fill up a poison-pen letter, copies of which he sends to Yuichi's family.

What sets the whole rancid process in motion is male beauty. Male beauty enshrines false values. Because the sixty-five-year-old writer Shunsuke Hinoki sees Yuichi as "the most beautiful youth in the world," he uses Yuichi to avenge himself on women, the source of his worst woes. And Yuichi's own woes? Yuichi's handsomeness has become a liability, most of his problems stemming from it. Shunsuke, one of many examples in recent fiction of the artist as troublemaker, worsens these problems. A week after being jilted by nineteen-year-old Yasuko, he follows her to a resort on the Izu Peninsula (site of another setback in Mishima's "Death in Midsummer"), where she is vacationing with Yuichi. The vacation has brought Yuichi little rest or fun; every night he lies alongside Yasuko without touching her, waiting for her to fall asleep while pondering the effect on her of his dispassion. Hearing the news of Yuichi's disquiet focuses Shunsuke's vengeance. He gives Yuichi 500,000 yen to marry Yasuko, presumably sealing her gloom, since her nightly sexual craving for Yuichi will go unanswered. Or nearly unanswered; despite being gay, Yuichi can occasionally bed a woman. But the bedding must occur on his own strict terms. Even while fantasizing about other men, he can barely squeeze out an orgasm. He certainly cannot climax inside Yasuko wearing the condoms his avenging mentor Shunsuke gives him for his honeymoon. Not surprisingly, Yasuko becomes pregnant immediately, and Shunsuke's revenge plot goes awry.

The wild stories he later uses to justify new stratagems show Yuichi's beauty continuing to vex him. Not only Shunsuke but also three accomplished, refined middle-agers debase themselves to move close to Yuichi. Meanwhile, the corruption has infected its unwilling source. Yuichi's schoolwork slips; he spends less and less time at home; he stops having sex with Yasuko. To his credit, this loss stings him deeply. Having lived with his widowed mother for many years, he knows the burdens of womanhood. He now sees them aggravated in Yasuko because of his sexual rejection of her. This intimacy with women's problems makes the mincing effeminacy he finds in Tokyo's gay set particularly repulsive to him. And, of course, the mirror world the gay lives in sends this repulsion back to Yuichi himself.

In chapter 26, he observes that, whereas cosmetics enhance a woman, they degrade a man, making him both look and feel unnatural; the lotions, pomades, and creams that go into Count Kaburagi's careful grooming give the impression of "man-made filth." Reducing life to performance robs a man of his manliness. More is the pity, the novel argues, because gay males have already shut out so much of the world. The metaphor describing this self-negating is the mirror. Count Kaburagi gets Yuichi to sleep with him by presenting him with a mirror image of himself. "Desire mingled with desire; desire redoubled desire," Mishima says of the effect of the count's seduction technique: "Spirit dozed above spirit. Without any help from desire, Yuichi's forehead touched Yuichi's forehead." In view of the young man's beauty, whose forehead would be more exciting to touch, even for Yuichi himself? The count has won the day pandering to the younger man's narcissism. His verbal performance has passed into reality. He has tricked Yuichi into accepting as reality a mirror image or reflection.

This trickery breeds danger. The novel repeatedly claims that a mirror's flat, hard sheen promotes deathly values. The mirror is both a cage and a trap. Besides encouraging vanity, the superficial image it puts out restricts the vision. By contrast, the window, which provides access to the world beyond the self, fosters interchange. Rejecting the window for the mirror thus represents forsaking vibrancy, freedom, and breadth of outlook—all for the sake of a flat surface copy of oneself. Mirrors promote posturing. The gay will pose before the mirror because he values physical appearance over any indwelling virtues. But the self-absorption that slights deep truth and the rich outside world fosters passiveness, as well; posing rules out movement, change, and growth. Those who cultivate appearances lose the ability to judge, to choose, and to create. The owner of a gay bar on the Ginza spends two hours preparing his face each morning. Readers need not know how long he spends putting on his evening makeup to infer that anyone so self-obsessed could never free himself for productive activity. Nor is Rudy unusual for a member of the fellowship. Shunsuke will confirm the fellowship's twisted values by killing himself soon after discovering that he has fallen in love with Yuichi. Mishima's running comparison between those two outlaws, the artist and the gay, expresses its meaning in suicide.

1

But Mishima flinched from this meaning. The moral outlook of *Colors,* which ends right after Shunsuke's death, is both defensive and blurred. This confusion stems from Mishima's intellectual rejection of values he accepts emotionally and intuitively. For instance, he says derisively that women and male gays share the same greatest fear, old age. But then, after brilliantly describing the waste and pain caused by pursuing young flesh, he mocks the elderly. Old age in the novel is like a small scratch or cut he cannot stop fingering and soon infects. He cannot put Shunsuke on stage without referring to his wasted hands, his rheumy voice, or his tear-soaked eyes. Called a "fidgety, lonely old man" and "this pompous ancient man," Shunsuke enacts Mishima's belief that age does not bring wisdom or benevolence. He is as twisted within as he is without. The books that have made him rich and famous contain nothing of himself but his rhetorical craft. Bubbling over with kindness and cheer, they clash stridently with the hate-filled diaries that express his true self.

These, nobody sees. And his statement in chapter 24 that he hardly ever writes letters conveys again his reluctance to share anything vital with others, at least in writing. Shunsuke is Mishima's most deeply divided character to date. The writing that wins him worldly prizes also starves his spirit. The probability that Mishima poured as much of himself into Shunsuke as into Yuichi makes *Colors* a record of his deepest fears. And perhaps also a forecast of his suicide nineteen years later? Shunsuke's successful writing career sheds as much painful light on this speculation as does his suicide. His collected works are coming out in twenty handsome volumes, and his lectures can pull in two thousand listeners. But these achievements, besides screening the public from his real self, represent a loss of vitality, stamina, and, sometimes, decency. Perhaps his mother's rejection of him in childhood warped his heart; his chance for happiness may have been wrecked in the cradle. This idea, though treated briefly and casually, nevertheless explains his wretchedness. Convinced of his unworthiness, he chose a career in which success confirmed failure at a deeper level. Equally convinced that he never deserved love, he married three women he knew would let him down.

By the time he comes before the reader, his body has dried up as much as his poor psyche. Lacking the distinction of his attainments, he looks more like an alderman than an artist. He has lived in gloom for so long that happiness threatens him; the joy of other people throws his puniness and gall in his face. His perfectionism is "an illness like death" because, an evasion tactic, it serves inhuman ends. Even though he loves Yuichi, he cares nothing about his welfare. He will pull Yuichi out of school, make him miss his exams, and take him out of town for a night or two if, by so doing, he can embarrass, hurt, or avenge himself on others. Hatred moves him more than love.

Part of this malice stems from Mishima's chronic fear of age. Age is defined cruelly in the novel. Nearly every character over the age of thirty-five has a health problem; nearly every one is defeated or ill-tempered. A shopkeeper who is not yet forty dodders about like a graybeard. Old age is both an affliction and a judgment. Mishima's harshest pronouncement on a character consists of linking him/her sexually with an older person. People who have sex with the aging deserve only scorn; they are capable of any depravity. In fact, their being sexually drawn to older people identifies them as vicious and perverse. Mishima says of a young gay, "His twisted tendency among twisted tendencies led him to feel affection only for men who were sixty or older." Four chapters later, he seems shocked that a man in his sixties has a lover his own age. Has he forgotten that people feel more comfortable with their own kind? Would life improve if everybody was sexually fixated on youngsters in their twenties? His having invited this question shows him endorsing the same values he detests. No less than the dainty, primping customers at Rudon's Bar on the Ginza, he values physical beauty over all other manly attributes, and he believes all interpersonal attraction to be sexual. Though he knows that basing a close tie on looks bypasses important inner realities, he cannot put his knowledge to work. He writhes in his self-imposed chains. These struggles to convert preachment to practice create terrific narrative tension. By building his novel around Yuichi, Mishima has ushered in a self-defeating system of priorities. Like Shunsuke, both Kaburagis, and the automobile executive Yaichiro Kawada, he admires Yuichi more than he understands him. Like theirs, too, his judgment has been fogged by Yuichi's good looks. He would rather ogle Yuichi than try to know him.

Mishima's portrait of Yuichi also reflects his awareness of both his dark side and the dangers uncoiling from it. Physical in disposition, with his narrow hips, slender frame, and classic face, Yuichi balances the more cerebral Shunsuke. This difference shows each man serving a different warning to his author. Shunsuke voices Mishima's fear of becoming old and ugly, a lonely closet gay misunderstood by his readers and misrepresented by his publishers. Counterweighting his inner turmoil is Yuichi's inner calm, just as his advancing years counterweight Yuichi's youth. Whereas Shunsuke confirms and perhaps justifies his existence through activity, Yuichi is so passive that he is nearly static—Narcissus frozen in awe before the mirror. But the frenzy he incites in others nearly makes this unmoving mover a god figure, physical union with whom brings salvation. Mishima, who stood much closer in age to Yuichi than to his fellow writer Shunsuke at the time he was writing *Colors,* saw the pitfalls of this kind of power. Otherwise, he would not have used metaphysical symbolism to describe it. If he was worried that the years would turn him into a Shunsuke, he may have feared still more the immediate danger of becoming a Yuichi—the prototype of the handsome young gay who asks for nothing, gets everything without knowing its value, and unintentionally maddens everyone he moves.

This warning takes on added force at novel's end. Accepting the mind-body dualism that conditions his view of Yuichi, Shunsuke tells his young protégé in the last chapter, "There you are, beautiful nature. Here I am, ugly spirit." His saying, as well, "Spirit and body can never engage in dialogue," stands as a confession of defeat. He and Yuichi are joined again, but in the shadow of money, postwar Japan's idol, according to Mishima. Yuichi has visited Shunsuke to return his 500,000-yen wedding gift. But instead of returning money, he acquires more. Has he lost his freedom of will? After playing a game of chess with him, Shunsuke retires to the next room, presumably to nap. But he poisons himself instead, having first written a note directing Yuichi to his will, in which he left the young man his whole fortune of eleven million yen.

Does this bonanza confirm Yuichi's triumph? After breaking the hearts of three adults twice his age, he has won both Shunsuke's love and his purse. The recklessness with which these cosmopolites risk both reputation and security for him portrays their defenselessness in the presence of beauty. Without trying, Yuichi has reduced them to swine; in the next-to-last chapter, the Princeton-educated Kawada cancels an important business dinner to meet Yuichi—who stands him up. But the beauty that wrecks Kawada's peace also recoils upon itself. Yuichi would rather be known as a clever student or a good family man than a breaker of hearts. He would also like to bring out his intimates' best qualities. But he fares no better with the young than with his elders. As if the enjoyment of erotic pleasures entailed penalties, one young man shaves his head after sleeping with Yuichi. An innocent affair with another lurches into crime and then threatens Yuichi's family. Perverting romantic love, young Minoru steals 100,000 yen from the safe of his older lover because he wants to elope with Yuichi.

Mishima saves his final judgment of Yuichi's beauty for the end. Here is Yourcenar on the subject of the novel's finale: "The story has a happy ending at the appropriate level: Yuichi inherits a fortune and, elated, goes off to have his shoes polished."[1] Yourcenar has flubbed one fact. The news of his windfall does *not* elate Yuichi any more than the death of the man he called "a second father" saddens him. As will occur at the end of *The Temple of the Golden Pavilion* (1956), a heartless hero has learned little or nothing, and the same little or nothing is all the future holds in store for him. Yuichi's many admirers have distracted him so much from his inner self that he can only respond superficially; physical sensations are all he trusts. Unlike Kochan at the end of *Confessions,* he fails to recognize his best interests. And how does Mishima view it all? Sexual looseness has been rewarded: Yuichi's exchequer is bulging; his family is solid; his baby daughter is so strong and healthy that his sick mother can die content. But none of this matters much to him. And Mishima is too puzzled by his noncaring to moralize about it. Nor does he suggest that Yuichi will reform. His failure to resolve the book's tensions declares itself as nervousness, impatience, and disapproval. He seems annoyed at his own dithering.

Most of his annoyance stems from his muddled view of Yuichi. He tries at times to correct the false images of Yuichi set forth by his idolators. Mrs. Kaburagi likens him to a graceful young wolf; her husband sees him as youth incarnate; to Shunsuke he's radioactive material. Are any of these views correct? Has anyone perceived him clearly? Yasuko, his wife, knits him a winter jacket; maybe she does not trust him to keep warm in the winter on his own. But he first appears in the summer, and he is more heroic than helpless. Walking to shore from the ocean, this slender, graceful swimmer of twenty-two, his strong white teeth catching the sun, looks like a god from ancient myth. But the shorebound princess who loves him at first sight is Mishima's stand-in, Shunsuke. The long, highly graphic description of Yuichi emerging onto the beach from his swim has a breathless compulsiveness. That he is described rising triumphantly from the sea, an element Mishima always feared, shows the artist reacting to his artifact from deep sources. The intensity builds. Within hours after evoking comparisons with Greek heroic statuary, this "amazingly beautiful young man" reveals deep internal struggles. So pained is he over denying Yasuko sex that he wants to die. But if his failure to have sex incites the death wish, sex's actualization causes mischief of its own. And the same misery that dogs him when he is tense will disrupt his ease. A month after failing to please Yasuko, he drifts into midtown Tokyo "with no particular destination in mind." That same soft evening, he has his first sexual experience with another man.

Mishima seems puzzled by Yuichi's shattering of his inhibitions to become an active gay. His never calling Yuichi Minami (the initials of whose name he shares) Yuchan, his name in the Ginza's gay set, creates a false impression of authorial objectivity. Yuichi's aimlessness put him at the mercy of his instincts in chapter 2, where he drifted into the Park. His instincts seem to have betrayed him. Ten chapters and some three months later, he notes that the freedom he had sought as a married gay has wrecked his self-esteem. But his observation, "I'm not even faithful to myself, am I?" causes him little worry. Why does a spectacular-looking man like him need self-esteem? Just before making his observation, he heard one of his friends say of him that his eye was cloudy. He need not sharpen his vision. No internal demons are contending for *his* soul. Perhaps the demons are holding back until they can decide the value of this enigmatic prize. He baffles the reader, as well. Not content merely to show Kaburagi a love letter sent to him, Yuichi, by the count's wife, he also tells his love-besotted suitor that he will not sleep with him any more. Then he will act nobly. By returning the 100,000 yen Minoru had stolen from his foster father—lover, Yuichi extends compassion to a man who had wronged him; Fukujiro had told both Yuichi's mother and wife about Yuichi's homosexuality when Minoru and Yuichi began keeping company. But such acts of integrity are rare. Mishima may have only included Yuichi's interview with Fukujiro to create the illusion in Yuichi of a great emotional and moral range. All he has created, though, looking back to the interview with Kaburagi, is a pair of scenes in which Yuichi behaves inconsistently. No connective tissue has been filled in to make his conduct credible.

Rather than joining Yuichi's beauty to an adult sense of responsibility, Mishima goes soft on his man, letting him off too easily several times in the book. Yuichi, for instance, wants Yasuko to have an abortion because he knows that the demands of fatherhood may end the fun of the one-night stands he has been enjoying with men. Later, he believes himself in love with Mrs. Kaburagi, "who through absence had acquired a beauty unknown in the world." What he is feeling—a yearning for the remote—is sentimentality, not love, as Mishima well knows. But he neglects to say that love's true test comes in dealing every day with the pain of the beloved, like a pregnant wife's morning sickness. And it is on this important subject that he is annoyingly inconsistent. Whereas Yuichi ignores Yasuko during most of her pregnancy, the ordeal of childbirth brings out his humanity. Shunsuke had asked him to watch the birth of his baby because he assumed that seeing the squirming, wet membranes comprising Yasuko's "complicated crimson interior" would disgust Yuichi and turn him against the baby, a response that would pain Yasuko more than ever. Two other older people, his mother, and the attending physician, also know how repellent Yuichi could find the spectacle of Yasuko's raw, helpless flesh being invaded by gleaming steel knives. But he defies their warning to stay out of the delivery room. And his defiance pays off. Instead of being sickened by the gore and the screams, he humbles himself before the miracle of new life entering the world. His humility takes the form of self-negation. Accustomed to being seen, this neo-Narcissus glories in the act of seeing; the perceived has become the active perceiver, and the creator is created anew. The statements, "Narcissus had forgotten his own face" and "His eyes had another object than the mirror," infer that chapter 25, "The Turnabout," describes two births. Along with little Keiko, Yuichi comes to life amid the welter of the delivery room.

But his new life gutters quickly; Narcissus returns to the mirror. Less than two pages after Keiko is brought home, Yuichi resumes having sex with men. He cannot forget his face. His new inheritance of Shunsuke's eleven million yen will also aggravate his narcissism, a trait defined in 1986 by Anatole Broyard as "the modern art of the self, the confining of the self, and the loneliness and sadness of the self confronted by itself."[2] Yuichi is trapped inside a golden cage with mirrors on ceiling and floor. Perhaps he ponders getting his shoes shined in the book's last sentence because he wants to look down and see his face in them. This speculation tallies with Mishima's anger. He is punishing Yuichi for tempting him sexually. But he also has it in for Shunsuke for having fallen in love with Yuichi. His close resemblance to Shunsuke yields some painful, if predictable, results: despite all his learning, Shunsuke often looks ridiculous, he suffers a great deal, and he kills himself. The self-loathing Mishima inflicts this woe on Shunsuke because Shunsuke has failed him. And the failure is the same one that was already warping Mishima's heart and pushing him toward suicide in the early 1950s. Both Mishima and his neuralgic sixty-five-year-old stand-in miscue fatally in aestheticizing experience. The warning Mishima served himself through Shunsuke did not curb his death drift. Why shouldn't this unstable man transfer much of his self-disgust to Shunsuke? The older writer plays the role in Mishima's tortured psychodrama of the messenger who brings bad news to the palace. Mishima knew all this and he hated it. A comment

Yamanouchi made about him in 1978 applies just as strictly to Shunsuke in 1951: "He lived all along in a phantasy world, which could never be authentic except through serving the ultimate purpose of being transformed into an art form."[3]

Mishima's reading nourished his intuitive understanding that the running together of art and life brings disaster. One of his favorite writers, Thomas Mann, related artistic creativity to moral decay throughout his career; the more supernal the art, the more deadly its slamming recoil upon the artist. Shunsuke perverts his creativity by using it to punish Yasuko for having spurned him. The title of chapter 5, "Entrance to the Stage," alludes to his efforts to control Yuichi—by telling him when to sleep with his wife, when to stay away from home, and when to lead on would-be lovers, both male and female. This extended attempt to make Yuichi his puppet must fail. First, it ignores the realities of accident, growth, and human inconsistency. Life cannot be pushed into the aesthetic sphere, where everything clicks into its preordained place. Shunsuke's plans keep getting overturned. He should have taken his cue from the falseness he complains about in his fiction. Too much control kills. His books are dry and distant because he has denied the people populating them the freedom to surprise.

By also ignoring Yuichi's power to surprise, he undoes himself. In chapter 6 he orders Yuichi to dance (with a woman at a party). Yet this "perfect living doll" has already been stepping to his own tune. He defies not only Shunsuke, but also his other would-be manipulators, the Kaburagis. As with Saburo and the more seasoned Etsuko in *Thirst,* his youthful candor keeps throwing these sophisticates off stride. For his part, Shunsuke stumbles leaving the starting gate; he has overlooked completely the possibility of Yasuko's getting pregnant on her honeymoon. Besides, he can never slake his vengeance. After settling his score with Yasuko—which he never does, anyway—he has other offenders to get even with. But his worst victim is himself. Like Pygmalion, he came to love his creation. But like Mary Shelley's Dr. Frankenstein, he sees the creation resist him. His ensuing grief he accepts as punishment for having perverted his artistry. Even Mishima is so annoyed with him that he excludes him from the action for a hundred pages or more at a stretch.

Yuichi represents a last chance for Shunsuke. An artist at odds with his art, he has always sidestepped in his clever books the subject closest to him—the pain wrought by loving. His inability to write out, or even honestly examine, his sufferings has put him at their mercy. In a nice dovetailing of motifs in chapter 1, Mishima says of him that he "hated the naked truth." Why should he not? He has just seen his wife naked with another man. And why should he not strike out at Yasuko for having discarded him? Damaged people inflict damage—particularly on those who have damaged them. Yet what defeats him is his self-disapproval. He has done plenty to disapprove of. Not only does he resemble Dickens's Miss Havisham of *Great Expectations* in using an attractive younger person to avenge himself on the opposite sex; in his tormented pride, he also wants to create, in Yuichi, a perfect instrument of revenge. As has been noted, his spite trips him up from the start. Although he insists that women lack brains and souls, his ruling purpose becomes the savaging of them. Although he calls marriage a trifle, he gives Yuichi a 500,000-yen bribe to marry Yasuko. He has reduced himself to a cipher by novel's end. He has stopped writing. Neglecting home truths, he reads mostly European decadents like Joris-Karl Huysmans, Walter Pater, and Oscar Wilde. The little Japanese literature he reads consists mostly of homosexual tracts written 600–800 years ago; otherwise, he prefers poetry in which no people appear.

Lending momentum to his death drift is his increasing immersion in gay society; he spends more and more time in gay hangouts, learns the jargon of the gay subculture, and makes friends with gays. By the time this process ends, with his falling in love with Yuichi, little of him remains. His death in the book's last chapter generates no excitement. Nor did Mishima intend it to. A purveyor of dead values, Shunsuke has championed death from the start of the book. In chapter 11, while promoting the idea of an abortion for Yasuko, he is nervously fingering a book called *Texts on Death*. Yuichi describes him shrewdly to a friend in chapter 27 as "one you can kill and he won't die." The last chapter vindicates this view, describing him as a living corpse. He pours Yuichi a glass of wine and harangues him on meaningless abstractions. No more interested in the older man's wine than in his words, Yuichi neither says nor drinks anything during the harangue. He then beats Shunsuke at chess.

This is when Shunsuke poisons himself in his library. Fittingly, he dies among his books, those repositories of dead values printed on flat, dry membranes. How can Yuichi, or anybody else for that matter, mourn such a passing?

2

This painful book that tapers off to a quiet nihilistic ending has received some harsh criticism, much of which is directed to its structure. Yourcenar believes that *Colors* creaks "like the wheels of a badly greased vehicle," and Miyoshi condemns it as "one of the gaudiest and emptiest [books] Mishima ever wrote."[4] These attacks are partly justified. Like Shunsuke, Yasuko will disappear from the action for 100–150 pages at a time. What is worse, she will drop out for no good reason. Ponderous with background information, *Colors* also suffers from lack of distancing. First of all, Mishima talks too much instead of letting his characters direct the action. His treatises on homosexuality are excessive and disconcerting. Also, he shares the fears and hostilities of his people rather than showing, through dramatic incident, how these emotions came to be. Novelists whose psyches reflect those of their characters must show either why the characters hate and love or describe the forms their love and hatred take; they have to provide insight into emotion. This alchemy Mishima does not perform because he stands too close to the crises he is recounting.

Perhaps more artistically aware than Miyoshi or Yourcenar knows, Mishima uses other techniques to help the reader through the long, hard pull. The greater length of *Colors*, he believed, called for a greater technical and stylistic range. At times, he will intrude in order to hint at future developments. He will tease out intriguing meanings from the juxtaposition of scenes. Right after showing Yuichi in a flirtation with another man in chapter 3, he cuts to Yuichi's wedding. The young waiter Yuichi was flirting with next appears in the subchapter that opens just after the wedding. Yuichi's seeing him on the way out of his wedding reception serves as a portent; the waiter's face haunts Yuichi throughout the honeymoon. The portent releases the rest of its force in chapter 10. Unfolding in

October, a time of intense homosexual activity for Yuichi, the chapter ends with the revelation that Yasuko is pregnant.

This scenic cross-referencing augments other motifs and devices that Mishima uses to relax narrative pressure. Perhaps his favorite way of lightening the action comes from his use of conventions from the French well-made play. *Colors* contains many near misses and shocks (like Mrs. Kaburagi's finding her husband doing a love scene with Yuichi). In a complication worthy of Eugène Scribe or Victorien Sardou, both Kaburagis love the same man—a young husband and father-to-be. When, bound by their mutual shame, they track Yuichi to Kyoto, they maneuver elaborately—all the while denying the meaning of their maneuvers—to close with him. Another surprise that works well because of its consistency with what preceded it comes in chapter 29. This is where Mrs. Kaburagi convinces Yuichi's long-suffering mother and wife that he is not gay by announcing that he is her lover. Earlier, both mother and wife had arrived within five minutes of each other at the same gay nightclub for the same fraught reason—to see if the anonymous letters they have received citing Yuichi's homosexuality have any substance. Sometimes, though, the sudden turn of events can create horror, as in chapter 22 when a tipsy young woman reels into bed with Yuichi but wakes up alongside Shunsuke. Mishima's reasons for writing this scene into the novel go beyond shock effect. The horror generated by the scene impinges on the sad truth that Shunsuke can only lure a woman into bed by first getting her drunk and then taking another man's place next to her. Let the critics who have accused Mishima of flat-footedness or tunnel vision reread this scene. In a single stroke, the scene shows him both brightening and deepening his plot while sending shock waves through the whole narrative.

Adding further vigor to such scenes is the aggressive sexual symbolism carrying over from *Confessions* and *Thirst*. Yuichi's straight white teeth express his erotic radiance. Their nonappearance conveys his nonsexual moods. At a time when he is ignoring Yasuko, Mishima says of him, "He was becoming more silent; his white teeth were seldom shown." Yuichi's teeth continue to radiate sex. In chapter 20, his lips part, revealing his dazzling teeth, while he is reading a love letter. Immediately afterward, Shunsuke, who witnessed the letter reading, realizes that he is in love with Yuichi. But even Yuichi is not safe from strong, attacking teeth. On his way home from a gay party, he accepts a ride from a man who bites him so hard that he bleeds.

The animal hunger surging through *Colors* makes the book abrasive and alienating. It is a matter of temperament whether the reader will find the book profound and exalting or, more simply, irritating. Many will probably deem it an art curiosity. Its rich, morbid beauty does reward a close reading. But after a while Mishima's thinly veiled self-absorption grows as repressive as the gay subculture he depicts. The rhythm created by the fascination and revulsion awakened in him by homosexuality beats you down. Finishing the book can make you feel half dead.

But more comes across than gall and gloom. Though heavy with self-loathing and despair, *Colors* respects living values. It argues, mostly through Shunsuke, that all love is sexual, and it extends this disturbing argument by showing sex hewing to the curve of the family. Sexual love in the novel both evokes and rests upon the family tie (except where the tie is marriage). Shunsuke, for instance, falls in love with Yuichi within months of asking to become his spiritual father; one of Yuichi's other lovers always calls him "Nephew-San"; to the youth with whom he first experiences gay sex, he is known as "big brother"; the live-in lover of starry-eyed Minoru, whom Yuichi meets in chapter 27, is also the youth's foster father. These pairings suggest others. Yuichi's widowed mother is an invalid whom Yuichi, thanks to his good business sense, protects like a father or a husband. Yasuko, whom he marries in chapter 3, he treats more like a sister than a wife. Perhaps Mishima is showing, through these realignments of basic family roles, how modern life corrupts the family. His rich range of characters, both gay and straight, young and old, and the variety of indoor and outdoor settings in which they appear all justify this thematic sweep. *Colors* cannot be snubbed as a sick book. The dangers it sets forth shadow everyone; the warnings it voices deserve all our ears. By portraying brokenness and abnormality as everyday events in the postwar urban state, the book shows how we participate in each other. The interdependence implied by this mutuality also challenges us to inspect more closely the bonding points joining us to others. A novel that questions our root values with painful concentration, *Forbidden Colors* will compel all who are interested whence the postwar generations came and where they are heading.

5

Sundowners
The Sound of Waves
The Temple of the Golden Pavilion

1

A new direction for Mishima, *The Sound of Waves* (1954) takes place on the island of Uta-Jima. This tiny place has fourteen hundred inhabitants, most of whom live in its lone village and support themselves by fishing in the nearby Pacific. Mishima makes Uta-Jima, whose name in Japanese means Song Island, a living force. It has a topography, a system of animal and plant life, and several local landmarks, which have inspired legends, superstitions, and jokes. The islanders both know and value this lore. But they also face the great outside world. No narrow-minded churls, the islanders who worship the sea god will also use modern sailing and fishing techniques. A generator supplies their electrical power. During the course of the action, a group of high schoolers spends a week in Osaka and Kyoto, and a young student returns to the island for spring vacation from her college in Tokyo. What she comes home to is no backwater. The island has a Young Man's Association that publishes a mimeographed bulletin and also performs various civic works projects, like cleaning sewers, salvaging drowned ships, and killing rats. Meanwhile, the female counterparts of these youths attend classes in etiquette and homemaking, and women of all ages collect firewood, gather seaweed, and dive for abalone.

This richly detailed reality both surrounds and infuses a tale of boy-and-girl love, some of whose features come across in Petersen's excellent summary:

> Shinji, son of a poor-but-honest widow, experiences the hardships of a fisherman's life. Into his island world comes the beautiful fairy-tale princess [called Hatsue] . . . who is later locked up in her fairy-tale tower. . . . There is, of course, a wicked-prince figure. . . . There is even an ugly sister—a part given to the lighthouse keeper's jealous daughter.[1]

Love builds quickly between Hatsue and Shinji. Although both are islanders, they have never met, Hatsue having spent the last few years living with relatives on the mainland. Their first meeting, an accidental one, occurs, fittingly, at the island's highest point, an observation tower now being used for storage. At once, they form a bond. In order to prevent local gossip, they agree to keep silent about their chance meeting. By the time they speak again, their bond has strengthened, thanks to both their mutual attraction and the rumors each has heard about the other's being engaged to someone else. A mutual disavowal of these rumors lends comfort and brightens prospects—but not for everybody. Their would-be intended mates, Chiyoko (no last name given) and Yasuo Kawomoto both try to prise them apart. In line with this traditional comic function, the obstacles Chiyoko and Yasuo introduce to foil the wished-for union ultimately confirm its strength and good health.

The book's ending makes one wonder how clearly Mishima has perceived and thus controlled his materials. *Sound* is a work of fluency and finesse that lacks a heartbeat because Mishima modeled it on literary formulas rather than his own creative instincts. But he could not sink his impulses entirely. Those that flare out of the book's last paragraph imply that he cannot end a story in which the boy *does* get the girl. Perhaps it also implies on his part a disbelief that boy-girl love *can* end happily. Let me set the scene for the book's slack, diffuse finale. Hatsue and Shinji have just toured the lighthouse. They have seen the electric generator that supplies the island's power. Their having witnessed this first cause, the very source of their community's energy, counts as an affirmation. The trim, shipshape lighthouse exists to protect life and property, and its up-to-date scientific apparatus helps it do this essential work more effectively. The lighthouse containing the generator eases snugly alongside Hatsue and Shinji in a mirroring universe where everything works to promote harmony, happiness, and virtue.

Then Shinji looks at the picture of Hatsue she had given him before he shipped out on her father's steamer. Like a medieval knight carrying his lady's token, he had this picture with him during the Okinawa typhoon. He shows it to Hatsue. But rather than telling her that it protected him during his ordeal, which she wants to hear, he directs his thoughts to himself:

Hatsue touched the picture. . . . Her eyes were full of pride. She was thinking it was her picture that had protected Shinji.
But at this moment Shinji lifted his eyebrows. He knew it had been his own strength that had tided him through that perilous night.

This surprising assertion of male supremacy comes as a shock. Besides breaking the mood of wholeness and joy that has been building, it goes against everything attributed to Shinji up to now—humility, devotion, strength, and generosity. What kind of husband will he be to Hatsue? Did the heroism that won her as a bride also fill him with the egotism that will rule out a happy future with her? Finally, does the spurt of masculine pride thrilling his blood mark the onset of homosexuality? None of these questions were invoked by the action preceding the book's last paragraph. None makes sense in the light of this action. By calling forth all of them without warning, Mishima both cheapens his earlier affirmations and smears the luster of what had been, up to now, his most lyrical novel.

2

Based on a true story, the firing of a national treasure by a despondent young monk in 1950, *The Temple of the Golden Pavilion* won great popularity in Japan. Nancy Wilson Ross tells how it sold 300,000 copies in Japan within three years of its publication and also succeeded as a stage play. This renown has persisted. A third paperback impression of the book remains in print in the United States, and, as recently as March 1987, Yoshio Iwamoto, writing for

Insight, called it "Mishima's best work."[2] Part of the book's appeal stems from its subject. Its Japanese title, *Kinkakuji,* reminded native readers both of the mad event that gave rise to it and the pleasing outcome of this madness. Enough of Kinkakuji survived its firing to allow it to be rebuilt quickly; some visitors, Ross explains, find the rebuilt version of Kyoto's storied Golden Pavilion even more wondrous than the original.[3]

The manner in which *Temple* is told attracted Japanese readers as much as the book's matter. Mishima's 1956 novel returns to that most popular of literary genres in Japan, the "I-novel." Like Kochan the Mask, Mizoguchi, the main figure and narrator of *Temple,* wants both to discover and locate himself in reality. *Temple* is a still life in motion, a record of the process of self-creation; it describes both the activity inside the seminary adjoining the golden pavilion and the consciousness looking at it. This consciousness is both warped and hostile. Mizoguchi's neurosis not only restores the baroque darkness pervading *Colors;* it also gives Mishima a frame of reference more congenial to his morbid sensibility than that of the cheerful, upbeat *Sound.*

A loving, trusting heart does not actuate Mizoguchi, as Keene explains in *Landscapes and Portraits:*

Mizoguchi emerges as a character worthy of Dostoevsky. As a boy Mizoguchi was told by his father of the incomparable beauty of the temple, and when he comes to live nearby as an acolyte its beauty so dominates him that he is even incapable of making love to a woman of less absolute beauty. In the end he realizes that he must destroy the temple if he himself is to live.[4]

Keene's summary of Mizoguchi and his problems needs fleshing out. Mizoguchi grew up frail and weak on remote, lonely Cape Nariu in northeastern Japan, the only child of a Zen priest. This alienation is aggravated by a congenital stammer. The book's swift, capable first scene recounts an event describing the pain caused by this stammer when an older boy embarrasses Mizoguchi in front of his classmates. A strong father might have helped him shrug off his early setbacks. But Mizoguchi's—so nugatory that he is not even named—coughs and stumbles through the early chapters of the book before dying. It is as if achieving his lifelong aims of showing Mizoguchi the temple and of introducing him to his ex-classmate, the temple's superior, had sapped all his strength. Perhaps he knew that Mizoguchi already despised him for condoning his wife's adultery and wanted to pass the boy on to a worthier father figure. The book's first chapter rises to a double climax; Mizoguchi sees the fabulous pavilion for the first time, and his father dies.

Denoting Mizoguchi's contempt for his father, neither event means much to him. He does obey his father's deathbed wish by returning to the temple as an acolyte. But the sick, dying cuckold who was both a natural and a church father has smirched authority in his son's impressionable mind. Nor is authority's poor image improved by the Japan that loses the Pacific War, the Father Superior Mizoguchi misreads and misprizes, or the mother whose adultery he wants to punish (even a relative of hers fails in business). This punishment he exacts by cutting himself off from her, an easy task for him because of her powerlessness. Like the mothers of the main figures of *Colors* and *Sound,* she is both widowed and financially squeezed. He calls her "poor and shabby," and, when she visits him soon after he enters the seminary, he feels so ashamed of her faded, baggy clothes that he tells her not to come back. She obeys his wishes for three years, at which time she returns because he has gotten into trouble and she wants to help. But when she appears at the temple gate, he sees her as run-down and disheveled, "like a dead person" rather than as the loving, protective mother who came straightaway to Kyoto on his behalf.

Had she known of his long-standing contempt, she would not have mocked his stuttering in chapter 3. His stutter is his greatest emotional burden, and he can never forget it. A young lady he has a date with in chapter 5 throws it up to him, as does the fellow acolyte who introduced him to her, the clubfooted Kashiwagi. Kashiwagi, in fact, mentions it practically every time he is with Mizoguchi. And Mizoguchi never tells him to stop. That he never stammers while speaking English and while managing to bed a Kyoto prostitute against all expectations shows that he views his speech defect as fixed and necessary; only when he slips out of character will his defect leave him. Perhaps he should have thought better of himself.

His stammer never discouraged the superior from designating him as the next Master of the seminary; the superior only disclaims Mizoguchi as his successor after he transgresses many times.

Mizoguchi's defiance of authority has split his psyche. Like Shunsuke of *Colors* and Isao Iinuma of *Runaway Horses* (1969, 1973), he is searching for an absolute system that will explain everything. Yet his antiauthoritarianism makes him more intriguing than these other searchers; he is looking for authority because he wants to deny or even crush it. Authority blocks his drive to being. This attempt to live more fully occurs often in Mishima. Unfortunately, it usually ends in defeat. And no cruel, mocking, or indifferent world can be blamed. The defeat comes from within; a product of self-knowledge and, in Mizoguchi's case, self-loathing. But, paradoxically, it also stems from a drive to self-authentication. Mizoguchi rebels against the conformism that Ruth Benedict found so damaging to the Japanese in *The Chrysanthemum and the Sword*. Curiously, his rebellion looks more Western than Eastern. Christian ethics has made individual salvation the fulcrum of moral activity and thought in the West. Miyoshi's linking Mizoguchi to the archetype of the artist[5] broadens the argument. The poets Byron, Shelley, and Whitman knew that the quest for self-definition could end as easily in destruction as in creation. Running the same risk as these Romantics, moderns like Joyce, Mann, and Eliot saw themselves surrounded by chaos. Their quest for order turned their attention inward; convinced that external reality was lawless, they sought permanence and truth within themselves. In the same vein, Mizoguchi looks for authority figures—but in order to hurt them and cast them off. He mentions *Hamlet* and Polonius in conversation, and in chapter 7, eager to direct his fate, he defies the warning of a fortune-teller:

> "Travel—unlucky. Especially avoid traveling in a northwestern direction."
> On reading this, I decided to make my journey to the northwest.

This defiance includes motives of masochism; perhaps he deserves the battering he has absorbed all his life. He encourages the superior to reject him, and at times he feels such self-disgust that he wants to flee his own skin. Yet he also wants to lash out at the world that has poisoned his self-image. Mishima places that self-image inside the context of Mizoguchi's growing belief that destroying the golden pavilion would entail a truer, more potent rebellion than bringing down any person, regardless of his/her power. This focusing reflects surprising judgment and skill, even for a writer as sharp as Mishima. Mizoguchi's first impulse is to reject the temple as he has rejected its great spokesman and booster, his puny father; denial of the temple *means* denial of the father. He reaches this double goal with great ease. His first glimpse of the glorious temple lets him down; in fact, what he sees as its smallness, darkness, and age makes him feel swindled. He much prefers both a table-size model and the reflection made by the temple in a nearby pond to the temple itself. But Mishima knows that masterpieces can play tricks by pretending to look like failures. Equally important is his knowledge that, whereas fashion will dazzle the beholder at first glance, art, which releases its beauty more subtly, can repel; the great artist forays into realms heretofore unknown and unchartered. Thus the letdown, puzzlement, and resistance created in Mizoguchi by the temple must subside before any aesthetic appreciation can take hold.

This appreciation both takes hold and overwhelms. Mishima's chief interest, through it all, remains Mizoguchi's complex response to the temple rather than the temple itself. To show how deeply the temple's beauty jars Mizoguchi, Mishima calls upon his best rhetorical skills. Mizoguchi feels dwarfed by the temple's radiance and harmony. Twice, the stupendous beauty of the temple causes him sexual disfunction; how can he embrace a woman whose beauty falls so short of the temple's? Then his rebellious streak imposes itself. He resents feeling nullified. To protect himself, he comes to see the temple's beauty as lifeless and inhuman. Like any other work of art, it is an empty play of forms severed from reality. He disparages the temple in order to protect himself. All along, the temple has been calling attention to his faults by embodying an excellence he can never attain. But this reproach also rests upon an irrelevancy. Though disorderly and shapeless, life nonetheless has a vibrancy, freshness, and warmth not found in any artifact. And perhaps it is just as fragile as the greatest art; a flood or fire can rip through an apartment building as quickly as through a museum. What Mizoguchi does with this insight forms the central drama of *Temple*.

At first he is angry because the pavilion preexisted his perception of it. By disregarding him, this architectural wonder has deepened his inferiority complex. Perhaps all beauty requires his ugliness as a counterpole. So low is his self-esteem that he even believes that his perception of the temple has dimmed its sheen. His feelings take a major turn at the end of chapter 5 of this ten-chapter book. The report of a typhoon in the area prompts him to volunteer to stand watch in the temple until the threat passes. Having just failed at sex with a willing woman, this virgin of eighteen enters the temple as he would a woman. But his penetration of the temple's dark, perfumed luxuriance also becomes a mystical communion: "Did I possess the temple, or was I possessed by it?" he asks in an atmosphere of danger and darkness. The mystical merging that has occurred in his mind's eye dissolves the subject-object dualism together with other known categories of judgment. In his transport, he both shares and enhances the temple's miraculous beauty. The book's fifth chapter and halfway point ends with the sexton's report that the typhoon menacing Kyoto has left the area. But the temple is not as safe as the sexton believes. The novel's second half will show that storms and American bombs, spectacularly violent as they are, threaten it less than the stammering neurotic Mizoguchi.

What gives this threat power is Mishima's unfolding of it. Though *Temple* develops within the crabbed, ratlike confines of Mizoguchi's psyche, it dramatizes a universal point—that life without self-respect will degenerate into a moral wilderness. A shrewd psychologist, Mishima appreciates the tricky interplay of beauty and ugliness within the human spirit. His Mizoguchi shows that people who downgrade themselves will reject the good and the beautiful. Their low self-esteem will also lead them to monsters like Mizoguchi's fellow acolyte Kashiwagi, who perverts goodness and beauty systematically. Mizoguchi's very attraction to Kashiwagi shows that he underrates himself. Unless he possessed the sublime, he wouldn't have perceived, let alone appreciated, it in architecture or women. But sublimity in any form both intimidates and paralyzes him. While fantasizing about a local beauty during masturbation, he turns into "an incomparably small, ugly insect"; his subconscious has punished him for craving intimacy with a woman beyond his station. His self-derision persists. Two chapters later, he labels himself "the one person who could have no . . . good points whatsoever." This familiar of ugliness can only debase beauty—i.e., re-create it in his own vile self-image. And re-creation to the person suffering from a pawn complex means destruction. "Other people must be destroyed," mutters Mizoguchi to himself in chapter 1; "In order that I might truly face the sun, the world itself must be destroyed." He feels like such a nobody that he cannot imagine himself achieving full growth in the world as it now exists. Annihilation of the status quo is his only escape from shame and ridicule.

But the sundering of galaxies could not help him. His statement in chapter 2, "Derision and insults pleased me far more than sympathy," confirms his nobodiness as an internal hurt. Even his stammer he views as attributive. Were this defining mark to go away, he would not know himself. The contempt he feels for his parents has recoiled on him, as it must. But his lowliness still has not erased a similarity he shares with the temple. As magnificent as it is, this great treasure is destructible. Its vulnerability to American bombs lends it a tragic grandeur in Mizoguchi's eyes. But to someone as unstable and self-loathing as he, its destructibility also argues weakness and defenselessness; it becomes fair game for burning. Mizoguchi is elated. The knowledge that he can burn the temple allows him to have sex. This acolyte whose rusty knife defiled the beautiful sword of a persecutor knows how to get even. In chapter 2, his daydream about the temple is broken by a classmate's remark, "I hear that your father died." The classmate adds that the temple reminds Mizoguchi of his dead father. A shrewd insight, but one that needs development; had the classmate known Mizoguchi better, he would have predicted how his friend would try to insult both his father and the temple his father loved in one mad act.

Burning the temple that has stood since 1400 and was declared a national treasure in 1897 thus emerges as the perfect rebellion—more potent and dazzling than any he has ever imagined. To raze the golden pavilion is to raze beauty itself, reasons this underdog who has seen his chance to win people's attention for the first time. The firing of the pavilion will disjoint the aesthetic standards, categories of reason, and moral certainties that have ruled Japan for centuries. The world that once discounted him will now wonder at his might. His mad scheme boosts his self-image in other ways. While planning his act of arson, he sees his sexuality spring to life. He loses his virginity to a Kyoto prostitute at the point when he has yoked his very survival to the burning of the temple. But the actual burning fails to bring any climactic revelation. *Temple* ends with a mad person setting a great building ablaze, as did Charlotte Brontë's *Jane Eyre* (1847) and Jean Rhys's *Wide Sargasso Sea* (1966). And madness begets only madness; another Mishima hero has aimed for self-transcendence and found himself looking into a fogged mirror. The book's ending leaves as many questions unanswered as those of *Colors* and *Sound*. Here is that inconclusive ending. It shows Mizoguchi watching the smoke rising from the National Treasure he had set fire to less than an hour before:

I noticed the pack of cigarettes in my . . . pocket. I took one out and started smoking. I felt like a man who settles down for a smoke after finishing a job of work. I wanted to live.

The importance of the idea evoked by this finale needs fuller treatment. Mishima has just shown Mizoguchi nearly choking to death inside the smoking temple, managing to escape, and then racing wildly across the nearby terrain. Mizoguchi's licking his wounds "like an animal" as soon as he stops running implies a new start. But it also falls short of the revelation he has sought. The novel's conclusion brings to light but fails to draw enough attention to the drabness and triviality of his rebellion. Even if the destruction of the temple had allowed him to live normally, the world would have gained no bargain. Mizoguchi's normality would have merely meant trading neurosis for common discontent, and a great art treasure would have vanished forever. In real life, the episode ended differently—and more agreeably. Kinkakuji was rebuilt within years of its partial destruction, and the stammering arsonist who set it ablaze turned himself over to the police. Within hours, the police saw that he belonged in a hospital rather than a jail.

Then why did Mishima build a novel around him and his woes?

3

An answer to this question lies in what is new and what is familiar in *Temple*. The novel restores the alienated hero; Mizoguchi's stammer, his frailty, his burdensome parentage, and the rural obscurity he grew up in all make him more of a misfit, in fact, than Kochan or Yuichi. His many false starts create the same bitter tone found in Mishima's earlier work; perhaps the bitterness will vex readers more deeply because of the religious context from which it springs. Finally, the observation made by Miyoshi, "Beauty . . . [exists] only where life is threatened with annihilation,"[6] recalls the devastation overhanging Mishima's fictional world. The tension created by the ancient wisdom informing this beauty and the neurotic perspective from which it's observed resonates throughout the book.

Imparting that resonance is the setting in which most of the action unfolds. Mishima moves as confidently and insightfully within the seminary where Mizoguchi lives as he did in the postwar Tokyo or offshore island village of his earlier work. Unhampered by having to rely on real-life sources, he describes the daily routine of the seminarians with extraordinary skill, showing the young men eating, praying, attending class, performing chores, and pondering the *koans,* or Zen riddles, put to them by their masters. The gift for subtle, convoluted thought shown in these deliberations carries into Mizoguchi's ongoing attempt to define the subject-object relationship. "The corpse was being looked at, I was just looking," observes Mizoguchi early in chapter 2. The observation implies the activity and thus the dynamism of the perceiver, or subject. Later in the chapter, this power builds when he claims that the glorious temple only confirms its reality to him when he is looking at it. His perception, he has inferred, validates not merely the beauty but rather the very existence of the temple. Instead of simply diminishing him, as he has believed, his obscurity has even helped him. He can perceive without being perceived himself.

But the uplift caused by his ability to move about unnoticed vanishes quickly. To be unnoticed is next to not existing. What is the use of seeing clearly if your perceptions go ignored? The free looking that creates the illusion of power really deepens his negation.

Mizoguchi must return to the mirror, which defines him as a trapped victim. In the last chapter, his helplessness confronts him anew. The golden pavilion takes on a new beauty and splendor on the eve of its destruction. Should he follow through on his plan to burn it? His arson occurs under the blank gaze of a famous statue housed inside the treasure. The statue offers no guidance. Art is mute, as in Henry James; it neither approves nor condemns Mizoguchi's crime. Lacking both the imagination and the artistic sensibility to rise to its example, Mizoguchi proceeds to burn the temple. He does not finish the job. Owing to his ineptitude, he scamps his work and nearly dies anyway. His failure withal, he has acted decisively. Courage he has. Pollack has missed Mishima's irony in naming him. Like Graham Greene's Quiet American, he substitutes action for talk; he also follows Greene's Alden Pyle in acting alone. His failure is not that of the coward or the nonstarter, as Pollack claims. He fails because his heart is desolate, and he cannot overcome his neurotic compulsion to reduce life to his barren, wretched level:

The name Mizoguchi . . . means literally "estrangement-mouth" or "rift-mouth". . . . It is his stuttering mouth . . . that creates an alienating and unbridgeable "gulf" between him and the world. He quite literally "cannot say," and, since language fails him at every turn, cannot act at the decisive moment.[7]

Just as Mishima captures in Mizoguchi the psychology of the loser, so does he infuse descriptive power and flair into his re-fashioning of the golden temple. He sees in the temple a magical blend of meaning and form, sensuality and design. Describing the interplay of contrast and symmetry, he shows the temple's exterior both permeating and mingling with its interior. He communicates this rhythm, moreover, as something that can be felt and heard as well as seen. One is convinced that the glittering, chiming temple is both firmly anchored in its piles and constantly aflutter.

The same high-level artistry that brings the temple to splendid life also radiates the novel's character portraits. *Temple* displays for the first time in one of Mishima's English-translated works the power of multiple identification. Several characters in the novel stand forth in depth, rather than just the one or two through whom Mishima is trying to work out his private salvation. First, there's Uiko, a beauty from Mizoguchi's native village, whom Mizoguchi wanted to have sex with. One night he stops her on a dark road. But after leaping in her path, he finds himself immobilized; the effort of accosting her has drained all his strength. She later explains his bizarre action to his uncle, who rebukes him harshly. The scolding he receives makes him wish her dead. And he gets his wish more explosively than he would have imagined. Uiko betrays to the military police a navy deserter by whom she has become pregnant. The deserter then shoots her in the back while she is presumably bringing food to his hiding place, a local temple; the action shocks Mizoguchi. It yokes female beauty and sexuality to betrayal, death, and religion. By extension, it includes his priest-father and his mother, since the pregnant Uiko dies while perverting the maternal or wifely office of bringing food to the man she was protecting.

Even more than his faithless mother, Uiko personifies woman-hood to Mizoguchi. He automatically judges all the women who move him sexually by her standard of beauty and treachery. It is even hinted that this judgment carries the force of punishment. A woman he later sees in a different temple loses both her child and the officer with whom she conceived it. The motifs of religion, death, and betrayal will fuse again in a military context when an American soldier brings a heavily pregnant Japanese prostitute to the golden pavilion and persuades Mizoguchi to trample her stomach. The prostitute miscarries. Mizoguchi's walking on her constitutes an attack on woman's very power to create life. Later, when he goes to a Kyoto brothel, he imagines that he will find Uiko working there. Even though five years have passed since her death, he is driven to wrong her. Her having been shot to death by the lover who impregnated her obviously does not satisfy Mizoguchi's urge to get even with her for having shamed him. He must soil and damage her anew. He has missed the irony that, in looking to have sex with a corpse, he has been hurting himself more than she could have ever done.

He confuses dead and living values again by underrating his cheerful, gentle fellow acolyte Tsurukawa and by then overrating and letting himself be swayed by Kashiwagi, whom Miyoshi rightly calls "the clubfooted evangelist of evil."[8] Perhaps a stiffer challenge to Mizoguchi's moral imagination comes from the seminary's superior, Father Tayama Dosen. The superior's very looks baffle Mizoguchi. Plump and pampered looking, "like a pink cake," Father Dosen also has a long nose and shaven head that impart disturbing animal gleams. Mizoguchi cannot fathom this apparent contradiction. His impatience soon outpaces his intellect. As both a figure of power and an ex–school chum of Mizoguchi's father, Dosen provides a perfect target for the young acolyte's anti-authoritarianism. How much does the superior know? Mizoguchi wonders. How much is he willing to ignore? These questions are important. Right after hearing about the incident of the pregnant prostitute, Dosen tells Mizoguchi to his surprise that he is sending him to a nearby university. He then pays the prostitute not to incriminate either the seminary or Mizoguchi. He tells Mizoguchi that he will be the master of the seminary. Mizoguchi abuses this outstanding kindness. He neglects his books, he skips lectures, and his grades drop. When he graduates, he finishes last in his class. But instead of dismissing him from the seminary, Dosen both pays his debt to Kashiwagi and, rather than mailing his tuition money to the university, hands it to Mizoguchi along with his living allowance. This vote of confidence is lost on Mizoguchi because, lacking the virtues of trust and love, he cannot prize them in others.

He is often baffled and thrown off stride. The news of sweet Tsurukawa's death makes him cry, which he did *not* do after his family died. Then he worries that he betrayed his dead friend by ignoring his advice to stay away from Kashiwagi. Yet three years after Tsurukawa's accidental death, Kashiwagi displays a bundle of letters Tsurukawa had sent him. Mizoguchi deserves to feel puzzled—and hurt. Besides warning him to avoid Kashiwagi, Tsurukawa has not written him once after leaving the seminary. Did Kashiwagi have some secret hold on him? Ugly, cynical Kashiwagi, the recipient of his letters, takes on a new mystery, which is enhanced by his skill at both floral design and flute playing. Yet Mizoguchi dwells too much on this mystery. Whenever he forgets Kashiwagi's malice and approaches him with a friendly heart, he is insulted and betrayed.

His common practice of rejecting the good and the true in favor of the degraded shows him insulting and betraying himself. It also makes *Temple* a downbeat, negative book. *Temple* forecloses on, rather than celebrates, possibilities. The choices offered by Mizoguchi's insights are joyless and life denying. Love remains forever out of his reach. Kashiwagi's suspicion that his clubfoot has made him unlovable drives him to divide sex from love. After failing at sex several times with young women, he finally wastes his virginity on a dimwit of sixty. Kashiwagi is also the person Mizoguchi chooses to emulate. He would not have gone to the Kyoto brothel had he known how love operates, nor would he have defied Father Dosen had he understood the challenge imposed by faith, which outstrips that of belief. His failures make grim reading. But their consistency and pathos both seize us. And they also reflect the outlook of Mishima, a writer who engrosses us but rarely warms or brightens our hearts.

6

Breaking the Rules
After the Banquet
The Sailor Who Fell from Grace with the Sea

Full of people, parties, and clashes, *After the Banquet* (1960) explores the lines joining marriage, business, and politics in a busy, novelish way. Both its immersion in sensual reality and its brawling vigor make it Mishima's most Dickensian novel. It contains crowd scenes, political cabals, and, thanks to its use of an elegant Tokyo restaurant as a major setting, some lavish displays of food. Here are just the hors d'oeuvres from a wedding dinner served in chapter 8; four large courses will follow: *"Horsetail and sesame salad Smoked carp Butterball-flower rolls Conger eel boiled in salt water Perch on rice wrapped in bamboo leaves."* This abundance disguises neither the seriousness nor the pessimism the reader has learned to look for in Mishima. *Banquet* takes a typically dark look at both the modern quest for fame and the cult of personality that Mishima deplored but also found so fascinating. The action he depicts shows him frightened by both the lack of meaning and the black emptiness underlying most of man's efforts. He also uses as his main characters a woman of fifty-five and a man of seventy not so much to extend his artistic range but, rather, to argue that too much freedom may be worse than too little.

He had already shown, in *Thirst* and *Temple*, freedom running to waste without the necessary constraints provided by checks and

116

balances. The Buddhism permeating *Temple* and the secularism of *Banquet* join the absence of these constraints to crises in both the Japanese urban state and private conscience. The main figures in the later novel are too intelligent and mature either to misconstrue or excuse their wrongdoing. They marry because they want to arrange each others' lives while also brightening and defining their own. Their joint goal makes them both ask, Who is using whom? Each responds to this question by maintaining his/her earlier life-style, by undertaking major decisions alone, and by frustrating communication. What looks at marriage's outset like a brave last chance for mutual self-renewal soon hardens into a dual act of self-retrenchment. But perhaps not self-justification; the marriage of Yuken Noguchi and Kazu Fukuzawa does not depict the loss of bravery. Instead, it shows bravery steering both parties into a sea of dangers, perhaps as self-punishment for unexorcised guilt. The Mishima character who concocts his own downfall is already familiar to us. Fresh to the canon is the slow parabola traced by the downfall.

Both Kazu and Noguchi juggle motives of trust and deceit, of self-enhancement and self-destruction. Mishima directs most of this juggling to their marriage. Lest the reader forget, in the buzz of activity the novel depicts, that the narrative focus is the Noguchi marriage, Mishima entitles chapter 13 of *Banquet* "An Obstacle in the Path of Love." The love of Kazu and Noguchi had already seized us—mostly with its promise of happiness. Hewing to the optimism of Carl Jung's ideal love dynamic, both parties have reached out for their opposites. Rather than double their losses by choosing mirror images, Noguchi and Kazu each opt for someone of a different age group, social background, personality, and value system. Their mutual quest for self-enrichment even includes looking for a spouse with a different body build. Thus the marriage of dry, scrawny Noguchi and plump, effervescent Kazu rests on a tacit recognition of the parties' own faults, a willingness to take risks, and a suspicion that each represents for the other a last shot at self-renewal and emotional growth.

But this novel that gainsays theory and principle not only describes the defeat of the couple's hopes; it also shows the couple as too selfish and stubborn to break the loveless habits crushing those hopes. Kazu learns that the energies that helped her claw her way from rural obscurity to power and riches in Tokyo also hamper her as a wife; she must temper her will. She also learns that she is too committed to the discharge of energy to become the wife she wants to be. A woman of intelligence and kindness, Kazu acts like a displaced feminist heroine. Miyoshi speaks of her "tenacious optimism and will to live." Referring more pointedly to her refusal to depend either financially or emotionally upon men, Petersen calls her "a woman with a man's resolution and a woman's reckless enthusiasm, preferring to love rather than be loved."[1]

These assessments speak home. Earthy and frank, impulsive and vital, "beautiful vivacious" Kazu, as Petersen implies, craves control. Instrumental in winning her the power to take charge is her impoverished rustic background. The hardships she suffered in her youth have honed her sights on material and social success; never again will she endure the squalor of poverty if she can help it. The title of the novel's first chapter, "The Setsugoan," refers to the elegant, expensive restaurant she owns and runs, mostly for the pleasure of the rich and powerful. Her have-not country past has also made her an expert in producing this high-toned pleasure. Like a Dr. Johnson or a Scott Fitzgerald, she succeeds in the great city because, as an outsider, she is not gulled by the glitter surrounding her. Her skepticism hinders her while helping her. Even though she is lonely, she cannot stop running things and people. The reader can see why. Taking charge has helped her both protect and improve herself; the country girl who comes to the megalopolis with nothing needs more than looks, charm, and a kind heart if she hopes to survive. She needs cunning. The rank breath and the cruel, grinding teeth of the archetypal male who threatened to chew her up as a girl still haunt her. Her guard must stay up. Her earlier career as a prostitute has made her doubt the freedom, openness, and tenderness of the sexual tie. And why should she not be skeptical? Sex to the prostitute is a business deal, anyway. Kazu has remained a businesswoman, regardless of the psychological cost. Even though the exercise of power has isolated her, it has also brought her material security and she cannot discard it.

Any kind of reciprocity threatens her. An important politician who has known her for years says of her, "When the day comes that a man coaxes some honest-to-goodness love out of her, she'll really explode." He is wrong. Rather than changing her, marrying Noguchi heightens what she already was, exaggerating the traits, foibles, and values she brought to the marriage. This creature of routine has avoided love her whole life precisely because it is so disruptive. Her attraction to Noguchi lacks the outgoings that usually accompany love. A widower for over a decade, Noguchi wears shabby, if high-quality, clothes. By looking forward to smartening his wardrobe, Kazu is merely indulging her penchant to control and supervise. She refers, in a thank-you note written after a lunch date, to "the joy that someone who normally entertains others experiences when she herself for a change is entertained." But her euphoria soon fades; the novelty of being catered to only charms her briefly. Noguchi has arrived too late in the day to undo the influence of the past. This influence opposes the mutuality that Kazu as an ex-prostitute distrusts to begin with. The resolve that helped her in the kitchen and the dining room of the Setsugoan has inhibited her around the marriage hearth. She knows how to prepare, arrange, and serve food. An accomplished hostess, she can charm her clientele. Yet her impressive skills cannot stop this clientele from dwindling after her husband becomes the Radical Party candidate for the governorship of Tokyo prefecture. Nor is she surprised. The Conservative high-rankers who patronize her restaurant will naturally stop feeding the Radical exchequer. Why is she damaging her business after working so hard to build it up? Could she be choking off her money supply in order to focus her attention on a marriage she suspects she is unsuited for?

How she reacts to the imposition of restraints, both at work and home, reveals more deep-seated fears. Fear, in fact, steered her to the altar with Noguchi. So nagging have been her battles with loneliness that she sees them extending to the afterlife. Less devout than superstitious, she harbors the great fear of dying unmourned. One big advantage to be gained from marrying Noguchi consists of the assurance that his descendants will include her in their prayers when they visit the family's burial plot. These prayers, she believes, will redeem a past made up of "obscene parties . . . back alleys . . . [and] bought caresses." She needs them because she doubts her ability to redeem her guilty past on her own. Because of her maimed self-worth, she uses money to gain power, to vent anger, and to exact revenge. Her recurrent practice of donating big sums to memorials, shrines, or political campaigns also shows her trying to buy other people's favor. Donations will not buy her own favor, though. In chapter 7, she rates the prizes she has won throughout her spectacular career much lower than the wreckage she has strewn on the way:

Men had killed themselves for Kazu when she was young. Some had lost their wealth and position, and others had sunk to the lowest depths of society, all because of her. Strangely enough, Kazu had never known love for her to ennoble a man or help him to success. Through no evil design on Kazu's part, men generally went down in the world once they met her.

Noguchi represents for her a last chance to help, rather than ruin, a male intimate. Feverishly looking to make amends, she will go to any length, even if it means breaking the law. In chapter 11, she resolves to do all she can to get her husband elected governor: "I will do anything for that," she remarks inwardly; "It does not bother me what people will think or what the law has to say." The fanaticism with which she follows through on her resolve implies that she is acting more on her own behalf than on Noguchi's. She is forever hatching new schemes to promote herself. These schemes take predictable forms. For the purpose of improving Noguchi's chances at the polls, she pours money and energy into the campaign. She meets secretly with his chief adviser to plan strategy because she knows that Noguchi would condemn her tactics and halt their implementation.

Her zeal as a campaigner calls other motives into question. One wonders if her deepest heart has not led her to fulfill a prophecy dictated by the belief that she is tainted beyond redemption. Her dynamism wrecks both her husband's candidacy and her marriage, despite her professed hopes. Her worst enemy could not have sabotaged the central realities of her life more effectively than she does. Besides going behind Noguchi's back to formulate election strategy, this reckless, headstrong woman will also act on her own. The tone of the following passage, from chapter 11, implies that, rather than helping Noguchi, Kazu is conspiring against him: "Noguchi suspected nothing. . . . His lordly indifference . . . permitted Kazu to dispense with elaborate precautions to keep her activities secret from him." Most of these activities consist of secret meetings with party workers.

As often happens when deception cuts across love, the husband is the last to know. Suitably, Noguchi divorces Kazu on the grounds of betrayal. Betray him she did. After meeting in secret with Radical leaders, she conspires with the Conservatives. Conspiracy comes naturally to the person ashamed of acting in the open. Kazu has not fooled Noguchi. By asking her former patrons, the Conservatives, for money to reopen the Setsugoan, which she mortgaged to help finance his campaign, she has, in his view, committed adultery. Soliciting funds clandestinely from his old political foes is an activity he equates with sleeping with them. Does Kazu agree? She had to know that his old-fashioned sense of honor would disclaim any deception, no matter how slight. And she knows, too, that her deviousness always recoils on her. But she cannot rise above it. Perhaps she is using it to get out of her marriage. The book's next-to-last chapter shows her speaking with rare honesty when she admits (though not to her husband), "The trouble all started from my insistence on having my own way."

Her own way is that of the self-doubter, even the self-hater. She goes behind the backs of her intimates because she knows she would never win their approval or cooperation. Thus she misbehaves in spite of her better judgment. The disdain she feels for her actionism sometimes declares itself subtly. For instance, her living in "a cramped little room" on the vastness of the Setsugoan property reflects a belief that she does not deserve the luxury she lavishes on others. A would-be thief who invaded the property but fled without taking anything in chapter 10 sheds further light on her anxiety. This chapter, the book's midmost, describes a key event—Noguchi's being invited by his party chiefs to run for governor. But to Kazu, the chapter's title, "Important Visitors," would also include the young thief who fled rather than face capture and arrest. Like the thief, she is a gate-crasher. She knows of his troubles. She also wants to reward him for stirring up her life. Thus she buries the wads of discarded chewing gum that could have been used as evidence against him. Her reference to the "young . . . strong, rough rows of teeth that had chewed the gum" she hides from the police gives her little rebellion a sexual coloring consistent with her inner malaise.

Kazu is as deeply divided as Ibsen's Hedda Gabler or Strindberg's

Miss Julia. But unlike these bored upper-class beauties, she has used wit, guile, and craft to achieve success in a country whose traditions and social norms frustrate womanly initiative. Her success has had surprising by-products. She still feels the force of the controls she flouted to win wealth and prominence. Unfortunately for her, this force, though persistent, is slight. Rather than curbing misconduct, it only steps in after misconduct has occurred in order to frown and to scold. It cannot compete with her will. Thus the dynamism that Kazu disapproves of but cannot control spurns the everlasting bliss of Noguchi's burial plot in favor of the hurly-burly of business: "She had found her tomb," Mishima notes of her in chapter 10, adding wryly, "But people cannot go on living inside a tomb." The prayers offered by Noguchi's descendants have paled before the vital and the tangible. Though stretching to infinity, the prospect of salvation stirs her less than the vigor and the throb of restaurant management. She gladly trades Noguchi and his promise of eternal bliss for the vibrancy of the Setsugoan. Her choosing vitality over resignation, passivity, and obedience costs her dearly. It probably also voices Mishima's disbelief in change and progress. Her actionism has aggravated her nagging isolation. In fact, it carries that isolation all the way to the "lonely, tumbledown, unattended grave" she has doomed herself to by divorcing Noguchi. Her outlook in the every-day world is not much brighter. She sees herself hopelessly com-mitted to habits of mind that preclude continuity and connection, let alone intimacy.

What remains to console her is money. It is a dubious consolation. In postwar industrial Japan, it buys freedom and power. It also buys the real estate and the wardrobe that can hide frailty. But it cannot hide a secret hurt or soothe nerve endings raw with long-standing guilt. During a campaign speech in chapter 14, Kazu sees a face that terrifies her. Though hardly terrifying in appearance, the face, now "gone to seed" and further degraded by nicotine-stained teeth, belongs to a smirking ex-lover. She could have easily walked away from this figure from her guilty past. But Totsuka's foreknowledge of her compliance justifies his smirk. Not content to blackmail her, he insults her as well. Her conduct with him shows her disregarding expediency and self-preservation, just as he had expected. It is as if Totsuka were a figure of both destiny and retribution. First of all, she approaches him, rather than waiting for him to address her, and she detaches herself from her friends in order to talk privately to him.

The guilt welling up from her past has been aggravated by the knowledge that she has been deceiving her husband. That her conversation with Totsuka takes place under a calendar shows how time has both caught up with and is running out on her. In another trick of time, the appearance of a lover from the past gives her deception a sexual aura. She feels mean and tainted. So disarmed is she that blackmailing her is child's play for Totsuka, and he knows it. To solidify his advantage, he prolongs the encounter with Kazu rather than going for the quick kill. He peers inside his shabby brief case "for an interminable length of time," letting her anxiety mount every second, before removing a copy of a pamphlet he allegedly wrote, "The Life of Mrs. Yuken Noguchi." The pamphlet describes her as a ruthless opportunist and nymphomaniac. The haste with which she meets Totsuka's demands shows her assent to this verdict. Without receiving any assurances that no copies of the pamphlet will circulate, she gives Totsuka his asking price of a million yen. Naturally, he takes her money and distributes the pamphlet, anyway, "to well-known persons throughout the prefecture." Her guilty conscience has connived at this defeat. Most notably, it has duped her into acting alone with Totsuka. Rather than report the blackmail threat to her husband's campaign manager, Soichi Yamazaki, she breaks confidence with her confidant (who would have wisely told her to keep her money).

Both her judgment and her timing have failed her. The blackmail threat came at a time when the Radical Party's funds had already ebbed; also, its success encourages the Conservatives to step up their dirty tricks, like tearing down posters, planting hecklers at rallies, and buying votes. Though not a normal campaign maneuver, the pamphlet neither surprises nor offends the cool party pro, Yamazaki. He does learn from it, though, that the more desperately Kazu acts to fend off trouble, the worse that trouble will become.

1

The character of Yuken Noguchi, agree Nathan and Scott-Stokes, derives from a foreign minister of liberal bent who fell in love with a

Tokyo restaurant owner. In February 1961, the ex-minister sued
Mishima for invasion of privacy.[2] *Banquet* has outlasted the stir
caused by the suit. Part of this favor stems from the skill with which
the Kazu-Noguchi tie is handled. The two characters meet in chapter 2 at a dinner party held at the Setsugoan. Noguchi impresses
Kazu by being the only nonretiree and the only former diplomat at
the gathering who talks about the future. But his outlook soon
darkens. Dramatizing Mishima's belief that character decides everything, Noguchi blights his own hopes by being too harsh and rigid.
In both his marriage and his election campaign, he sets too much
store by principle and too little by experience. This cold, distant ex-
ambassador despises compromise, a little of which would not have
hurt him. A childless widower who has lived alone for more than a
decade when he enters the novel, he impresses Kazu with his background of travel, his knowledge of foreign languages, and his indifference to society's prizes. On the other hand, she winces when she
hears of his small pension, and she feels indignant over the news
that, as a defeated ex-candidate for Japan's diet, or parliament,
he travels to Radical Party meetings by streetcar rather than by
limousine.

She also sees quickly that losing political prestige has not dimmed
his self-esteem. He is content to listen quietly at his club's dinner
party in chapter 2 while a cocksure ex-minister to Germany brags
about meeting Hermann Goering and Marlene Dietrich. Though
smaller and less flamboyant than Hisatomo Tamaki, Noguchi
proves his superiority over his Party colleague—by outliving him.
Overstuffed with food, talk, and self-importance, Tamaki collapses
in the men's room of the Setsugoan and dies soon afterwards.
Noguchi earns Kazu's favor again when he scolds her for her handling of Tamaki's wife during the crisis. And if this rich, accomplished hostess is rarely scolded, she is never rebuffed physically.
When Noguchi releases his hand from hers the next day, after hers
had sought his in an intersection, he thrills her. She will fall in love
with him in a week.

But the moral assurance that lets him rebuff and reproach her
stems from his sense of superiority. He does not need much provoca-
tion to hide behind his stubbornness and aloofness. His wearing an
overcoat and carrying a pocket comb that are both thirty years old

may pass as endearing eccentricities in an aristocratic elder. Seen in tandem with other traits of his, these practices confirm his dryness, arrogance, and resistance to change. He does not know when to stop any more than Kazu does. "His ingrained authority" has blinded him to the feelings of others. Nor will he waste social niceties on these others. The gaffe, unintentional but stinging, is more in his line. When he invites Kazu to lunch with him after leaving Ambassador Tamaki's hospital room, he implies that, were they busy people, they would be spending their time more profitably than by dining together. Over lunch he dogmatizes, "Diplomacy boils down to knowing how to size up people. That's one art I've acquired." He is absolutely wrong. He looks down from such a moral height on people that he despises them all. Though he calls his deceased wife "a splendid woman," there is little indication that he made her happy or even cared about her happiness. Her splendor faded quickly if it ever existed. Her dying presumably in her forties without having had children invokes the joyless marriages of Shunsuke in *Colors* and Honda in *The Sea of Fertility* cycle. A good marriage needs more humanity than he can dole out. The temporary loss of a cigarette lighter he has carried for twenty years rattles him so much that he is accused, by a virtual stranger, of rating things over people.

The accusation rings true. The tenacity with which he clings to old possessions and ideas hurts both his marital and his political hopes. In his steely self-righteousness, he rejects the honeyed rhetoric that Shakespeare's Coriolanus scorned as fooling the people. He will not play the game of vote catching any more than he will permit Kazu to brighten his faded wardrobe. The deadpan, colorless delivery of his first campaign speech embarrasses his young backers. Ironically, his chances for winning the election gain a big boost from Kazu's public appearances, which include songs, dances, and costumes that he would ban if he knew of their existence.

And would his ban have stopped the theatrics, anyway? Probably nothing short of his threatening to withdraw from the election could curb Kazu's passion for ballyhoo. This doggedness invokes more important truths. Neither the election nor the marriage of plump, rosy Kazu and stringy, humorless Noguchi changes either person. Rather, these two events accentuate crotchets and quirks the persons already possess. Each views the marriage less as an adventure in development than as a threat to cherished patterns of behavior. From the outset, this commitment to patterns firmly in place had confirmed itself: "Married life had . . . not brought with it any surge of happiness," says Mishima of Kazu in chapter 9, entitled "The So-called 'New Life,'" which takes place right after the wedding. But how could the marriage of Noguchi and Kazu bring a surge of anything at all? Those who give little, get little. By continuing to live as they did before the wedding and getting together only on weekends, Noguchi and Kazu change neither their routines nor lifestyles. She satisfies her passion for movement and change at the restaurant, and he—spied upon by the domestic servants she hired to tend to his needs—follows his dry academic schedule. This arrangement can bring no refreshment or renewal. The couple's weekend reunions yield predictable results. Preferring his surroundings simple and lean, the stoical Noguchi snubs the "immense stack of presents" Kazu, replacing effort with extravagance, brings him each Saturday. Perhaps the presents deserve to be snubbed. Had she loved him, she would have spent more time with him. She would have also trusted him enough to let him run his own election campaign.

Neither ideology nor love explains why she surges ahead full throttle in the campaign, riding roughshod over precedent and analogy. She is too caught up in campaigning to seek explanations, anyway. For some weeks, until the "scurrilous pamphlet" stops her breakneck momentum, she enjoys great success with the electorate. Just as Noguchi improves the minds of the voters, so does she, with her dramatic flair, gladden the voters' hearts. This balance addresses larger issues. In describing the breakup of her marriage, Mishima neither takes sides nor casts blame. If she ignores civilized restraints and controls, she nevertheless embodies a rude driving vigor that Noguchi could have heeded more, just as she could have taken more seriously the ethical purity in him that attracted her to begin with. Kazu blunders seriously at least twice—when she helps Totsuka cheat her out of a million yen and when she takes out a second mortgage on the Setsugoan at a time when the restaurant's earning power has all but vanished.

But any condemnation of her actions must also take into account Noguchi's harshness, stubbornness, and stiff-necked resistance to change or compromise. With sniffing indignation, he assumes an all-or-nothing stance when the Conservatives offer to withdraw their candidate in exchange for his promise to pick a Conservative as his lieutenant governor. Their offer is reasonable, even generous. Noguchi can become governor of the Tokyo prefecture without going through the toil of campaigning during an unusually hot summer. But he rejects the chance. By asking for everything, he gets nothing, an outcome he deserves. His rigidness hurts him elsewhere. He is as cold, commanding, and abrupt with Kazu as he is with his Party colleagues. Never saying please or thank you, he orders her to do his bidding. He certainly wastes no graces on her the night he is expecting his Party chiefs to offer him the Radical nomination for governor. When she asks him why she must drop everything immediately, he snaps back, "You're to have dinner ready and return home by five o'clock. I won't take no for an answer." Then he hangs up.

Rudeness like this makes one wonder whether Noguchi or Kazu does more to wreck their marriage. He communicates as badly as she. This is going some, since she takes offense when she hears that her adviser, Yamazaki, whom she deceives regularly, has taken important action pertaining to the campaign without first telling her. In chapter 11, she learns that Noguchi is running for governor—but from a Conservative leader and not from Noguchi himself. In fact, the news of his candidacy appears in the local press before he mentions it to her. Politics cuts across love and merges with Mishima's death wish less boldly in *Banquet* than in the famous story, also from 1960, "Patriotism." But this restraint is not a fault. Part of the novelistic amplitude and many-sidedness of *Banquet* impinges on Mishima's treatment of the election. With a Tolstoyan disdain for single causes, the book shows that the election, as dramatic as it is, merely speeds an event that would have occurred sooner or later anyway. The letter from Yamazaki that ends the book claims that the election, no real calamity, caused the Noguchis to display "their naked selves." "Everything has found its place," Yamazaki adds; "the birds have all returned to their nests."

2

Like *Banquet* before it, *The Sailor Who Fell from Grace with the Sea* first looks like a love story with an unusual twist. Again, a widowed person marries a stranger to matrimony. But their marriage ends even more quickly than that of Kazu and Noguchi. What ends it is death, not divorce. Published in 1963, *Sailor* features, much more than *Banquet,* the fascination with death that was to overtake Mishima as the decade advanced.

Had death not intervened, the marriage of naval officer Ryuji Tsukazaki and Fusako Kuroda might have succeeded. Both parties need love and nurture. At thirty-three, shapely, beautiful Fusako lost her husband five years before the time of the novel. She has not spent her widowhood languishing. She owns a chic Yokohama haberdashery, called simply Rex, Ltd., which stocks items like English spats that cannot be bought on Tokyo's fashionable Ginza, about an hour's car drive away. Rex, Ltd., imports most of its luxury wares from Europe and the United States and sells them to celebrities; one of Fusako's best customers is a well-known film star. Mishima's knowledge of merchandising makes this success credible. His insight into her personality makes it a function of her skill, her values, and her temperament. Fusako lunches in expensive French restaurants, belongs to a tennis club, owns a mink coat, and has both a housekeeper and a chauffeur. Yet she does not hide behind this privilege, neither her fine trappings nor aristocratic tastes masking her loneliness. Her life changes when she and her thirteen-year-old son Noboru tour a freighter docked in a nearby harbor. To thank the *Rakuyo*'s second mate, Ryuji, for showing her and Noboru the ship, she invites him to dinner. But the couple do not part company right after dining. Instead, they walk through a local park, continue their conversation in Fusako's house, and wind up sleeping together.

If Fusako has not had sex with a man for the last five years, Ryuji has also known loneliness. They go to bed so quickly because of a mutual need to share and to be close. Nor have their instincts betrayed them in choosing a lover. Repeating the Jungian sexual dynamic that brought Kazu and Noguchi together in *Banquet,* Mishima shows a worldly sophisticate (who, ironically, has traveled little) and a world-traveled but socially awkward sailor reaching out for one another. Ryuji's rough-hewn ways even embarrass Noboru. To cool off one summer afternoon, Ryuji sprays himself with water from a public fountain. And when he returns to Yokohama after an absence of four months, he brings Noboru a stuffed crocodile and Fusako an armadillo pocketbook.

These reptilian gifts convey more than Ryuji's tastelessness. They also conjure up the pervasiveness of primitive emotions amid the urban chic of postwar Japan. All of the important characters in the book are lonely; all have something to hide; all harbor secret longings. While sporting English tweeds and studying techniques of merchandising, Ryuji covets the clean male athleticism of the sea. To this rugged, decent man of goodwill, the surge and swell of the ocean calls up visions of a glorious death. This romantic destiny moves him deeply. Yet he also knows that he has never come close to achieving it, even during his nightly watches from midnight to 4:00 A.M. with only the stars and sea as company on the ship's bridge. He cannot decide whether his 10,000-ton freighter offers freedom or entrapment. It both joins him to and separates him from the immensity rolling and heaving underneath. Yet the same immensity that rouses visions of splendor also kills. Is his surmise that he has been ordained for glory and grandeur a mad fantasy? Making love to Fusako makes him wonder if he should renounce the sea for the wholeness and warmth of a family. He continues to wonder. Though he refers to "the squalor and the boredom of a sailor's life," he cannot say whether giving up the sea represents a mature decision or a concession to banality. And neither can Mishima. What his heart accepts as male strength, fearlessness, and dominance, his mind scorns as bogus and stereotypical. Ryuji does not help him break the deadlock. The sailor has saved almost two million yen, "an extraordinary sum for a Second Mate," and he is searching for both a cause and a person to invest in. Meeting Fusako sensitizes him to the anchoring warmth of a family. Yet the same shore life that brings coziness and intimacy also unleashes complexities.

The greatest of these comes from Noboru. Now that Ryuji has forsworn the sea, he can do no right in Noboru's eyes. His having opted for the regularity and respectability of the landlubber means that he must die. In a motif that will recur in *The Decay of The Angel,* the hero's brilliance fades and tarnishes once he descends to earth. Like the decaying angel, the proud adventurer now has pits and blemishes on his hard exterior. Noboru wants to drive a knife into these soft places. And what does Mishima want? It is hard to know if he is celebrating Noboru, presenting him as a fact of life, or describing his cruelty as a logical outcome of postwar Japan's cultural upheavals. One suspects that Noboru is being admired for qualities most would find abhorrent. Still, much of the book's force comes from Mishima's sensitivity to how Noboru guards his privacy and autonomy. Noboru is secretly glad that his father's death has removed an authority figure much harder to deceive than his mother. Yet he also craves male authority, which he defines in a loveless way. Incapable of reciprocity or love, he scorns the kindly and the gentle in Ryuji, his father's successor. The naval officer must scowl and threaten, not smile and commiserate. Noboru likes him much better when he barks "brisk instructions" during an annual New Year's Eve cleaning ritual than when he extends friendship. Noboru's carrying out these instructions "with delight" also discloses a preference for a society that is simple, mannish, and rigidly hierarchical.

He is not alone in this juvenile preference. The end of the novel sees Ryuji recounting his naval experiences to Noboru and some of his friends. As he dives deeper into his memory, though, he finds himself talking for his own sake. Dredging up his seafaring past excites him. It restores the poetry of the tides, of the surf breaking on tropical shores, and of lost, doomed love. He longs for the grandeur of the open sea, always a symbol of death in Mishima because of its vastness and mystery. Has he betrayed himself? Ryuji wonders. In one of the most brilliant finales in the Mishima canon, the closing pages of *Sailor* show him being lured to a remote place where he is to be killed for smirching the heroic ideal of seamanship. The death plot concocted by Noboru and his friends has roused Ryuji to new imaginative heights. This broadening and deepening of his psyche ("the things he had rejected were now rejecting him") prompts an intimation of his coming death. But he not only intuits his end; he also consents to and even welcomes it. By serving him poisoned tea, the boys effect the deathly consummation he had been viewing as majestic and grand but, wrongly, as "eternally beyond his reach." The novel's beautifully understated last paragraph—whose haunting magic is caught by translator John Nathan—fuses his secret longings with the punishment the boys are inflicting upon him: "Still immersed in his dream, he drank down the tepid tea. It tasted bitter. Glory, as anyone knows, is bitter stuff."

This passage proves that *Sailor* betrays no laxity or decline from the high artistic standards of *Banquet*. But the cruelty the brilliant finale foreshadows serves a diminished, defeatist view of life; Ryuji will be stabbed, carved, and eviscerated as soon as he passes from consciousness. A work of warped genius, *Sailor* opens exciting realms of response, but only to slam them shut. The book's artistry serves dead values. This deathliness overrides logic. Insight into the muddle that inspired this strange, bruising novel comes from Edmund White's review of another Mishima novel, *Runaway Horses,* which was published six years after *Sailor* but rests upon the same premises: "Purity is the special property of youth. . . . It is preserved through constant contemplation of death. And purity hungers for bloodshed."[3] The purity-bloodshed circuit White refers to is strong enough on its own to ignore the drum rolls of emperor worship. It is also strong enough to bypass the benefits of interchange. The book contains little fugue or counterpoint. Ryuji's purity craving merely differs from Noboru's in degree. As beautifully orchestrated as it is, the one-note finale of *Sailor* is predictable. By the time Ryuji sips his poisoned tea, the book's adolescent theme has already swamped its domestic one. A pity because, perhaps more than any earlier work of Mishima's, *Sailor* conveys his insight into people and their feelings. The twice-widowed Fusako, who faces the desolation of living with her husband's killer, stands forth as more than brave, resilient, and resourceful. She is also a shrewd, stylish businesswoman and conscientious mother to whom the love of a good man outweighs considerations of social rank and money. The setback and drudgery of the last five years have not jaded her on love. Through her, Mishima shows his understanding of female charm—what it is and how it is exerted. She uses flawless timing to tantalize both Ryuji and the reader with glimpses, scents, and hints of delight that combine elegance and carnality.

Before going to waste, this tantalizing blend emits rays of promise. Her heat-and-light display impresses all the more for occurring so quickly against heavy odds. The book's first page finds Noboru angry and humiliated as he hears the lock turning in his bedroom door. He perceives Fusako, who tells him to sleep well in the book's opening sentence, as more of a jailer than a protector. She locks him in every night to prevent a recurrence of a recent misdemeanor—his having sneaked out of the house after bedtime to meet a friend. This reversal-rich novel starts with Noburu converting his resentment into uplift and exhilaration, but in a way that prefigures a still-deeper resentment. The voyeurism that surfaced in *Colors* and will prove itself so damning in *Decay of the Angel* flares out immediately in *Sailor*. Noboru discovers that he can remove a drawer from the clothes chest built into the wall adjoining his and his mother's rooms. By fitting himself into the empty space created by the removal of the drawer, he also discovers a peephole he can look through. And look he does after hearing Fusako climb the stairs and enter her room with Ryuji. What he sees—his mother and Ryuji having sex—excites him more than he has ever believed possible. What gives him his first orgasm, specifically, is the spectacle, "ripping up through the thick hair below the belly, [of Ryuji's] lustrous temple tower . . . [soaring] triumphantly erect." Again in Mishima, as so often in D. H. Lawrence, male sexuality evokes religious associations. Noboru feels as if he has just participated in a miracle; so jolting is his response to Ryuji's nakedness that it crushes any unstated Oedipal impulse of father destruction he may feel. But other feelings assail him, as well. He takes offense that the possessor of Ryuji's heroic, muscular body should fall prey to the middle-class domesticity Fusako represents.

He takes his objections to the gang, a group of would-be Raskolnikovs or proto-Nietzscheans who commit acts of violence to prove their superiority. As has been seen, the gang will kill Ryuji for rejecting the rough masculine adventure of the high seas. A man should be stern and rigid, brave and athletic, they insist. Ryuji embodies enough of this ideal to be labeled a traitor who deserves to die. Noboru, who delivers him to his murder site, acts on mixed motives. Now the vision of brave sturdy Ryuji commuting to the shop every day, budgeting money, and learning English offends Noboru. But the lad also feels that his status in the gang needs boosting. Insecurity goads him into launching an attack lest he be attacked himself. The following passage shows him gifted with a vivid, pictorial imagination that should have been immune to peer pressure:

Noboru still believed in the adventures lurking in some tropical backland. And he believed in the many-colored market at the hub of clamor and confusion in some distant seaport, in the bananas and parrots sold from the glistening arms of black natives.

Yet peer pressure makes him forfeit this rich plenty; he gives into the abstractions and the imperatives of the gang. His mistake carries forward an important insight from *Banquet*, i.e., that those who betray the people closest to them also betray themselves.

Noboru's having joined the gang of thirteen-year-old nihilists constitutes a betrayal in itself. The gang's agenda consists of destroying whatever they condemn as false. And since falseness has seeped into everything, the gang wants to destroy the world itself. They even have a plan. In order to dismantle the status quo and restore the primeval chaos where they can be free, they look to overthrow vested authority in the forms of school, society, and fatherhood. And the overthrow will be sharp, swift, and violent; death confers meaning upon life. Mishima shows his disdain for this butchery by withholding the names of its spokesmen, the gang members. Except for Noboru, whom the reader already knew before the gang first meets within view, and the gang's leader, the chief (whose designation is denied a capital letter), Mishima refers to the boys only by numbers, a device that symbolizes the bleakness and sterility they stand for.

But Mishima's intellectual scorn for this negation runs afoul of his night side. Though the chief condemns fathers as "the worst things on the face of the earth," he also wants to be led. Like the later Mishima, he leads by default. His arrogant will to power takes root in despair. What he wants most is a father he can love and trust, a stronger, older male he can submit to. Mishima would find the images of desire and worship conforming to male supremacy in the emperor, in the warrior, or Bushido, code, and in the ideal penis. Much of this highly charged symbolism informs his portrayal of the gang. No Freudian rebels, Noboru and the chief would have Ryuji harsh, brutal, and punishing—a masochistic gay's dream of male authority that includes the cruel, rigid nightsticks of angry policemen. How much of this masochism Mishima understood cannot be known. Yet the artistry he infuses into his portrayal of the chief, the gang's intellectual leader and scold, reveals an insight and judgment he never successfully applied to himself.

The chief resembles and could descend from those frail, puny, and sometimes diseased artists in Thomas Mann who crave forbidden knowledge. An excellent student, this precocious son of rich parents who ignore him has a piping voice, dimpled cheeks, and dainty white hands that he protects with surgical gloves whenever he slices into organic tissue. His statement, "that . . . genitals were for copulating with stars in the Milky Way," reflects a failure to cope that his rubber gloves are meant to hide. His instigating the death of a kitten in part 1, chapter 5, whose sex is carefully unspecified, shows him fighting life itself. Advisedly, though he will disembowel the cat after it is dead, he insists that others kill it. Analogously, he instigates the death of Ryuji without raising a finger to kill the sailor himself; only after the poisoned tea does its fatal work will he slice into Ryuji with his gleaming knives and scissors. Instigation is his specialty. After accusing his friends of talking too much, this loudmouth reads them a passage of the local penal code that excuses all crimes performed by juveniles under fourteen years of age. He is tempting them with their last chance to literally commit murder and get away with it. Delighting in the paradox that the gang's enemy is also its protector, he represents an extreme of evil that entices Mishima as much as it horrifies him. By having made the undersized chief the gang's leader to begin with, he conveys his awareness of the attraction generated by the sinister. Most of the other boys in the group could probably crush the chief in a fight. They probably also see behind his sonorous cadences the pain he feels over being small and neglected. Yet instead of laughing at him, they follow him, perhaps because of his morbid streak rather than in spite of it. *Sailor* does not reinforce constricting values so much as light the dark currents that flow within us all. The echoes accompanying the screams tearing from the book rescue it from the charges of perversity and sensationalism. Stifling our protests, these echoes extend our humanity.

7

Tragedy at the Crossroads
Spring Snow

Set in Imperial Japan in 1912–13, *Spring Snow* is both a tragic love story and the first installment in *The Sea of Fertility,* the tetralogy Mishima completed the day of his death. Western readers will find much of the novel's turf pleasingly familiar. Both the society and the characters Mishima writes about feel the influence of the West. The telephone, the department store, European films and phonograph records, and Western styles in both building and dress have already permeated Japanese life. One rich family keeps warm in the winter with a steam-heating system imported from Chicago, and another owns a Rolls-Royce, "the second ever purchased in Japan." A notable attorney who studied law in Germany enjoys his Western food served on English china. Though Mishima shares this fascination with the West, his roots and ties, like those of his people, lie in Japan. In fact, the influx of Western artifacts and values characterized the Meiji era (1868–1912). To omit this trend would have created a false picture. Its inclusion lends credibility to the novel, mostly because of Mishima's tact. Numerous court rites and observances exhale an oriental perfume that no Western force can dispel. These flower festivals, banquets, and coronations also set the novel in the Japanese aristocracy. One of the book's main figures showed the Imperial Prince around Paris during the 1900 Olympics.

The action turns on this rhythm of stability and change. This change can be violent. The book's first sentence refers to the Russo-Japanese War, which ended only seven years before the present-tense action, and the next paragraph begins by referring to two battlefield casualties from the war. The book's second paragraph also discloses a photograph that will haunt the whole tetralogy. Exuding an atmosphere of "infinite poignance," the sepia-tinted photo shows thousands of Japanese soldiers grouped around a cenotaph and an altar to honor their comrades in arms who died in battle. Like the photo, *Spring Snow* will also honor the dead, lament their lost hopes, and commend their energies and purposes.

This tribute covers a wide sweep. The novel divides its characters between those who do and do not remember the war. Members of the latter group will fight wars of emotion rather than the glorious battles of gunpowder and flashing steel that ended with the Meiji era. But these wars of the heart will also produce casualties. The endangered lovers in *Spring Snow* (1968) are Kiyoaki Matsugae and Satoko Ayakura, the beautiful, sensitive daughter of a court nobleman. Of the two, Kiyoaki gets more of Mishima's attention. Poor student, false friend, and indifferent son, Kiyo is a first-rate brat. Yet, like the epicene Yuichi in *Forbidden Colors,* he charms people. His schoolmates and family cannot resist him. Even though he snubs them, he wins their fanatical devotion.

His gusty romance with Satoko, like his other ties, reflects an uncanny authorial insight into motives. Mishima knows how the reader's feelings work. Like the Shakespeare of *The Taming of the Shrew,* the Noël Coward of *Private Lives* (1930), and the Raymond Chandler of *The Long Goodbye* (1953), he describes sexual love as combat. Cruelty as well as death overhangs the battlefield of erotic passion in *Spring Snow.* Kiyo cannot simply accept or reject Satoko; he either pulls her wildly to him or drives her angrily away. When circumstances put her off-limits, he positively craves her. His craving surges forth when a prince of the court receives royal permission to marry Satoko. This sanction makes the marriage more of a state than a private matter, since it welcomes Satoko into the emperor's family. Thus Kiyo's romance with her challenges both the dynastic succession and an imperial loyalty that informs all aspects of Japanese life.

The affaire also carries the two young lovers to a flame-tip of emotion that refines as it consumes. By defying an imperial decree, they must maintain maddening security precautions to avoid detection. The dazzling heights they scale together during their trysts entail terrible risks and awful retribution. This retribution will be exacted ironically. The passion that gives Satoko the dignity of a princess also stops her from becoming one; the love that ripens Kiyo into manhood also snuffs out his manhood. A savage power permeates the scenes describing this process. The taboos restraining the lovers transform common experience into pure poetry. Mishima's symbol for this fleeting agony of delight is the fragile, finely articulated snowflake, which either melts or breaks at first earthly contact.

But snow refers more directly to Kiyo. He and Satoko spend their first time alone together in the novel taking a rickshaw ride through the snow. They also kiss here for the first time. Satoko, who falls in love with him during the snow ride, writes him a letter soon afterward in which she says, "I think of Kiyo as the spirit of snow." The traditional equation of snow and death aligns death with rebirth in the novel's title—but in a way that criticizes and even mocks Kiyo. The title only appears very late in the action, namely, in chapter 52 of this fifty-five-chapter work. Its appearance serves the purpose of foreshadowing; Kiyo's death will coincide with the enactment of his resolve to close with Satoko. No easy task, this; she has just had an abortion and then, surprising everyone, stayed on as a novice in the convent she visited afterward. Kiyo shows admirable courage and resolve by returning to the convent day after day despite physical pain and loss of health in order to see the cloistered Satoko. As his life shrinks and dims, it takes on a new intensity. But this process also describes his unfitness. As soon as he leaves home for the first time, he shrivels, suffers, and dies. He cannot survive on his own, even when he is coddled. And coddled he is, by both a Tokyo friend who visits him and the proprietor of the Nara inn where he stays during his pilgrimage.

Kiyo descends from a prominent samurai family. His grandfather, a general, was a great national hero, and his rich, powerful father owns a sumptuous hundred-acre estate in suburban Tokyo. The Emperor Meiji himself once visited the estate, and members of the imperial family still dine there. The Matsugaes entertain other royalty, too. In chapter 17, two Siamese princes, one of whom is heir apparent to his country's throne, attend one of their dinner parties. But because the Matsugaes' wealth and social power are both relatively new, the marquis and marquise sent Kiyo as a small child to learn elegance and grace from old court nobility. The family they

picked to raise Kiyo, one that has been enjoying the imperial favor
for twenty-seven generations, is the Ayakuras. Despite their charm
and culture, though, Satoko's aristocratic parents have financial
worries. Their money supply has fallen far short of both their
cultural attainments and social obligations, and Satoko's indolent,
ineffectual father, the count, can't brighten their outlook, as if
expediency would violate the good taste centuries have bred into
him. Fortunately for him, the Marquis Marsugae will pay his family's bills in gratitude for their having taught Kiyo courtly elegance.
The size of these bills is no deterrent; Matsugae agrees immediately
to underwrite the "incredible expenses" that will face the Ayakuras
as intimates of the crown. The prestige once enjoyed by this family of
spotless lineage has again come within reach, despite the resentment
the count must feel toward his rich benefactor. No aberration, Kiyo's
intrusion into the Ayakuras' royal hopes shows how the deep-run-
ning connections between the two houses have been branching off,
twisting, and recoiling on themselves.

1

Kiyo makes one wonder at different times whether he has ignored
the refinements the Ayakuras have taught him or whether he has
learned them all too well. This pampered, lounging eighteen-year-
old of "exceptional beauty" hates the rude vigor displayed by his
extroverted, sports-minded classmates at Peers School. Like one of
Evelyn Waugh's stylishly weary Cambridge undergraduates, he cultivates aloofness and elegance. His keeping of a dream diary suits his
well-bred indolence. More pointedly, it conveys a failure to cope.
Saddled with low self-esteem, he automatically rejects people who
like him. He also keeps people at bay because, lacking inner security,
he finds himself easily upset by them. Though he knows that they
can cheer him, he fears the emotional risks. He prefers to take
refuge in his charm and good looks. These assets, he tries to believe,
have conferred unique privileges on him. In chapter 4, he says that
he is searching for "something absolutely definitive"; he also calls
Satoko "the barrier that prevented him from taking a single step
toward it." His callowness has stopped him from seeing that, rather
than thwarting his drive to fulfillment, Satoko constitutes it. Like

Jane Austen's Emma, he has failed to see that his best chance lies close by.

This failure stems from a pseudoromantic preference for the remote and unattainable; to him, the attainment of desire kills desire. He wishes it were otherwise. The contempt he feels for his contrariness fills this dreamy young man with anxiety. Only the unrealistic forgo the here and now for the thunderclap moment that reveals all, he knows; as Shunsuke proved in *Colors,* the only terminal answer and ironclad assurance is death. A searcher for absolutes himself, Mishima understood the destructiveness of Kiyo's search. And he used it to work through his own anxieties. Did he judge wisely? Languid, pale-cheeked Kiyo is more dangerous than he appears. Frightened as a small child by the snapping turtles in his family's pond, he drinks turtle blood at age nineteen. The potential victim has become the unsuspecting victimizer.

Yet, because of his beauty, Mishima can side with him emotionally while condemning him morally. A homosexual bias colors Mishima's portrayal of him throughout. By surrendering to his beauty, Mishima not only puts his mind and heart at odds. He also bases Satoko's love for him in his looks, a response more homosexual than hetero-. But this inconsistency hurts the novel less than might be expected. Although Mishima does not validate Satoko's love for Kiyo psychologically, his own struggles both to perceive and judge Kiyo create terrific narrative pressure, some of which can be imagined stemming from her. Mishima will fault Kiyo; he will accuse him of vanity and stubbornness; he will show him acting destructively. But these objections will dissolve into admiration for Kiyo's "delicate skin," "the graceful lines of his body," and "the incomparable smooth white of his back." As these effusions show, he enjoys posing and rhapsodizing over Kiyo. But, as an accomplished novelist, he also knows that a work of fiction is not a still life; static characters do not a novel make. This knowledge causes him to be nervous and resentful. At the end of chapter 35, death divides a young couple. Kiyo's Siamese classmates must return home because the fiancée of one of them (and the sister of the other) has just died. Kiyo intuits in their wild grief the heartache that awaits him. And his premonition proves true. But Mishima, by denying him room in which to grow, *makes* it true. To Mishima, Kiyo is already complete; a beautiful youth with long lashes, pale cheeks, and a delicate red mouth needs no inner resources. Activity cannot enhance these gifts. In fact, it can undermine them. Mishima relishes Kiyo's silky indolence and indifference so much that he punishes him for charging headlong into his romance with Satoko. Kiyo dies because his author could not imagine him functioning as a vital young adult. Unlike Yuichi, who drifts aimlessly into the wings at the end of *Colors,* beautiful young men in Mishima's later work suffer and die.

Mishima's homosexuality also smudges his portrayals of women. But because he responds more vitally to youths than to damsels, the smudging is subtler. It may also be crueller. In chapter 34, Satoko tells Kiyo, "We women have no real friends at all." Her assessment includes Mishima. A figure of strength and courage, she inspires friendship. Guided by sound instincts, she accepts both her loss and her punishment; she may even convert these setbacks to gain. What is so winning about her is how much she is in command, despite her youth. *Spring Snow* does not merely recount *any* woman's unfaithfulness. Satoko's misconduct touches the royal family. But it does not become a metaphor for what is happening in the state because Mishima's approval of her runs afoul of his dark side. And of his artistic shortcomings, too? No author should be criticized for the book he did *not* write. Perhaps Satoko deserved better from Mishima than being stowed by him in a cloister. Her brief appearance at the end of *Decay of the Angel,* the last work in the tetralogy, reveals her as smooth, accomplished, and profound. But, just as Mishima omits the interview with the abbess of Gesshu Temple that wins Satoko permission to enter the order, neither does he dramatize the steps by which she acquires her vast social and spiritual gifts.

Nearly sixty years pass between the reader's last glimpse at a newly tonsured Satoko in *Snow* and the paragon she reveals herself to be in *Decay.* It is never known whether her life in the convent was one of denial or fulfillment, a form of suicide or a soaring adventure of the soul. Mishima invites the ambiguity. Even though Kiyo dies for love, she loses more than he does. Her body is violated by an abortionist; her reputation is ruined by the rumor that she is mad; by cloistering herself, she forfeits the rich variety of the world, including the love of her parents. Did she choose wisely by entering the convent? Because her heart is more sensitive and mature than Kiyo's, her understanding of what she has lost drives deeper than his. Thus her need is greater. But where this need takes her is a question Mishima sidesteps. By fixing his attention on Kiyo, he slights Satoko, a figure of greater charm, vivacity, and self-control. His preference for Kiyo causes regret because the reader never knows if it is based on a preference for death over life or on one for a quick death over a slow one.

To be fair to him, these regrets only surface because of the sustained brilliance of his portrayal of Satoko, perhaps the outstanding woman in the canon. Ironically, the robust clarity and superfine detailing with which Mishima presents her whet our appetites for more time with her. She makes the blood sing. One can easily understand why she inspires the following conceit, bold as it is, in chapter 19:

He looked down at her ear, half-hidden by her hair. With its tinge of pink and its fine curve, the wonder of it made him think of a delicate coral recess that might appear in a dream, containing a tiny, beautifully carved Buddha. There was something mysterious about the hollow of her ear, now fading in the darkness. Was it there that her heart was hidden, he wondered.

This enchantress first appears in the company of her great-aunt, advisedly the abbess of the convent she will later join (and whose exalted post she will later assume). Despite her beauty, she has saddened Kiyo, whose parents' estate she and her great-aunt are visiting to view the autumnal blaze put out yearly by the Matsugaes' maple trees. A sentimentalist, Kiyo is not looking for a familiar face but for a beautiful stranger who will excite and ennoble him. This juvenile hope has blinded him to both Satoko's charms and the depth of her heart. On the basis of his conduct with her later, in chapter 10, it has also deafened him to the lyricism of her speech. Her fresh, loving outburst, "Oh, Kiyo, when I'm happy, my words come tumbling out like the doves they release at a launching, flying up through a burst of confetti," angers rather than delights him.

This sourness typifies him. He lacks the self-trust to be happy. The psychic distance established during their first exchange between his defensiveness and her cheer declares itself dramatically. The spiritual associations she calls forth by entering the action alongside an abbess betokens a faith in life. In both this early foreshadowing and what follows, she will outclass and outperform the anxious, disdainful Kiyo. She is aware of her advantages. No angel, she will use her agile wit to tease him, to catch him off guard, and to make him feel slow-footed. But she controls her mischief. In chapter 3, where she is introduced, she sacrifices propriety to candor when she points out the corpse of a dog wedged into the stony lip of a waterfall. Kiyo also saw this horrible portent. But timidity silenced and ultimately shamed him. He will be cowed again. Without waiting for anybody's help, she picks some flowers for the impromptu burial service her great-aunt has offered to conduct for the dog. His avoiding Satoko's eye during the flower gathering sharpens Mishima's portrait of her as a younger, more radiant descendant of Kazu *(Banquet)* and Fusako *(Sailor),* impulsive energetic women of goodwill trapped in a system that both discounts and thwarts them.

Satoko again takes the initiative when, in chapter 12, she invites Kiyo to miss school in order to ride through the snow with her. Recalling a scene in Tolstoy's *War and Peace* in which a young couple ride joyfully through the snow, this outing brings Satoko and Kiyo much closer than ever before. But the aforementioned equation of snow and death joins with Kiyo's negativism to crush their joy. Mishima sets up this defeat carefully. The snow ride marks the second clandestine meeting of Satoko and Kiyo in two chapters; one meeting takes place indoors and after dark, and the other occurs outdoors during daylight. The ride also represents the first time the couple is seen alone together; the normally guarded Kiyo has flouted schoolboy duty in favor of his adult heart, forgetting classwork in order to give his shadowy, suppressed love for Satoko the confirmation of sunlight. She responds to this tribute with a love letter in which she praises his gentleness, his masculinity, and his beauty. But in the meantime, his disdain for anyone who accepts him has snapped back into place. Being close to her has scared him. He imagines wrongdoing on her part, and, lacking the reserves that come with self-confidence, he manufactures a crisis around having missed school, all to distance himself from her. Mishima's psychology is right on target. The sensitive, unstable personality will usually blame others for real or imagined wrongs, he/she fearing the responsibilities rising from guilt.

Satoko's beauty has always confused, upset, and annoyed him. But what infuriates him is her wisdom. Besides being quick and bright, she is also two years his senior. These advantages, he feels, give her insight into his every move; he feels that she has blocked all his lines of both approach and retreat. Both to shock her and to repay her for an imagined hurt, she sends her a "wildly insulting" letter in chapter 6. For once, his cowardice has served him well. For had he confronted her in person with his grievances, he would have had to engage in a one-on-one duel of wits, which he would have surely lost. More significantly, he would have also lost the chance to retract his charges. And he would have bilked the book of a great moment, too. Deciding within hours of writing the nasty letter that introducing Satoko to some new friends would boost his social reputation, he phones her late at night to ask that she destroy his letter unread. Not content to dazzle the reader with this inventiveness, Mishima weaves it into his plot. He also keeps his narrative embroidery free of snags. Though Satoko breaks her promise to Kiyo by reading the forbidden letter, she reacts creatively to it. So easily does she shrug off his insults that, within days of reading the letter, she proposes the snow ride. And she only discusses with the marquis his son's sexual boasting in order to understand—and love—him better. Nor does she report this secret meeting to the virginal Kiyo, particularly the exposure of his lies.

Naturally, these graces are wasted on him. His defensiveness causes Mishima some embarrassment. The consistency with which Kiyo either underrates or misreads Satoko keeps the reader's skepticism to the fore. What could she possibly see in him? But the same question has been asked many times about the intrepid Dorothea Brooke's attraction to her two trivial husbands in George Eliot's classic *Middlemarch*. Furthermore, the qualitative differences between Satoko and Kiyo, instead of discouraging reader involvement, sharpens it. While savoring the excitement generated by these differences, we wonder if Kiyo can become the man Satoko deserves. Most of the way, we doubt him. He misconstrues her loving actions as insults because anger comes more easily to him than love; anger he can trust. Narrative structure helps show that she has overrated him as badly as he has undersold her. For, just as she reads a letter of his against his will, so does he destroy unread many letters written to him by her. These letters concern the royal proposal of marriage she has received. Always open and up-front, she wants to know his feelings about the proposal. These feelings he will not share with her. In keeping with his inferiority complex, he gloats while she suffers alone, mindless of the way she has been defying very strict conventions for his sake.

He thus gives up his chance to block her engagement to Prince Toin. Driven to belittle both her and his bond with her, he enjoys parading his alleged immunity to her charms; he is relieved that she is out of his care, he claims. He even boasts about how quickly he has forgotten her. He has failed to learn from the wild grief of the two Siamese princes, following the death of a princess from their court, how to respond properly to the loss of love. Unlike those of the princes, his emotions are not honest. They continue to flow in muddy channels. The granting of the imperial sanction prods him to pursue Satoko. Now that she is out of reach, he decides that he loves her. Whereas she was his for the asking just days before, now he has to flout a royal edict to steal a little time with her. Her unattainability has made her so alluring that he is willing to insult the throne to become her lover.

He even overlooks the truth that the external pressures that are driving him and Satoko together must also drive them apart. Resorting to lies and threats, he persuades her to keep seeing him after the fixing of the wedding date, a step that gives the engagement national importance. Satoko perceives both the new dangers she faces as Kiyo's lover and the sleaziness of the tactics he is using to be with her. But she also loves him and wants to be with him as much as she can. Thus she carries forward with a quiet dignity, assurance, and resolve. "Kiyo and I have committed a terrible sin, but I still don't feel defiled in any way. In fact, I feel as if I'd been purified," says this self-acting young beauty. She regrets nothing. Her acceptance of the consequences of her treachery raises the question, central to Graham Greene's *The End of the Affair* (1951), of whether sin can serve as a foundation for grace.

This profundity never occurs to Kiyo; he has not seen things through with her clarity and depth. After making love to her in chapter 34, suitably in a derelict boat, he admits, "You know . . . if we had everyone's blessing, we would probably never dare to do what we've done." Analogously, the same immaturity that defies adult curbs also rejects the inevitable truth that the affaire must end. His refusal to accept limits causes great woe before it kills him. Not once does he consider leaving Japan with Satoko, even though a friend suggests it to him; his love for her belongs outside the law. The contrariness that feeds his love also stops its legitimization. Yet when she tells him in chapter 36 that the passage of time will help him forget her, he recoils sharply. He has failed to see that she has always been bolder, more honest, and more realistic than he. When he senses her slipping away, all he can do is feebly pray for an earthquake or a major war to delay her wedding and thus win him some more time. The youth who once destroyed her impassioned letters unopened and unread now lives for the merest sign from her. Had he bothered to know her, he would have saved himself a great deal of anxiety. The message he craves will never come, a truth conveyed by her cutting her hair within hours of visiting Gesshu Temple, allegedly to pay a social call on her great-aunt, the abbess.

The characters surrounding the lovers waver between condemning their conduct and reveling in it. A primitive streak in nearly all of them attracts them to the lovers' boldness when they are not recoiling from it in horror. Perhaps the most notable of them is Shigekuni Honda, a quiet, studious classmate of Kiyo's. Yourcenar's calling him "a good friend and a plodding student . . . the gray shadow of the adventurous Kiyoaki,"[1] touches on a key feature of the book's narrative strategy. Honda's diligence and discipline do make him a good foil for Kiyo, in both Kiyo's listless, limp-wristed phase and his later overcharged recklessness. Honda has inherited a legacy of fastidiousness from his lawyer-father ("Everything in the Honda household, down to the most trivial utensil," one reads in chapter 6, "had to meet exacting standards"). An aspiring attorney himself, he even attends a criminal trial, and, in *Runaway Horses,* the next work in the *Sea of Fertility* cycle, he will have attained a judgeship by age thirty-five. This honor is not surprising.

Neither is its cost. So full of purpose is he that he is baffled by Kiyo's relaxed charm in the opening pages. *Snow* begins with a

conversation between him and Kiyo because Mishima may have
already decided to build the tetralogy around him. Honda will not
only appear in all four volumes; he is also present in the first
sentence of the first installment and in the last sentence of *Decay*, the
final entry, which ends some sixty years later. But *Snow* does not
always make this prominence clear. Honda drops out for chapters at
a time, only to reappear in chapter 33, where he helps Kiyo gain
access to Satoko. The enjoyment he takes in promoting the lawless
romance adds an important humanizing touch. Up to this point, he
has mostly listened to Kiyo's stories about his romantic exploits and
voiced some philosophical ideas. After it, he will be more active and
take more risks. The closing chapters find him dropping his studies
just before exam time to nurse Kiyo; in *Runaway Horses,* he will
resign his judgeship to defend, free of charge, a young neosamurai
being tried for crimes against the state.

While Honda is poring over his legal texts, Mishima turns much
of his structural role over to Shikeyuki Iinuma, Kiyo's melancholy
tutor. Iinuma is more of an underdog than Honda. Besides viewing
Kiyo, to whom he is fanatically devoted, as "a constant, mocking reproach," he also suffers sexually. His pain takes on an added sting
from the impression Mishima gives that he will escape it. This false
hope stems from Mishima's including him in the classic pattern of
Western romantic comedy that emerges as a structural device a
quarter of the way through the text. Balancing the Kiyo-Satoko love
plot is the behind-stairs romance of Iinuma and the pretty house-
maid, Mine (there is even an elderly confidante, or keeper of the
secrets). But Mine has also been sleeping with Kiyo's father. More
nastiness follows. When the marquis tires of her, he marries her off
to Iinuma and sends both of them away. Iinuma's removal from the
action allows for the restoration of that other cold fish, Honda; to
feature them both at the same time would clog the action. Mishima
brings Iinuma back near the end as the author of a right-wing
broadside against the marquis, and for a good reason; Iinuma will
sire the young radical Honda defends in court in *Runaway Horses,*
and Mishima does not want him off the scene too long before
restoring him.

Much more colorful than either Honda or Iinuma is Satoko's
elderly maid, Tadeshina. Like Satoko and Madame de Sade, the title

figure of Mishima's 1965 play, Tadeshina confirms her author's belief that women are as complex and varied as men. This "self-possessed old woman" who has served the Ayakuras for forty years sends fresh breezes across the action. Called in chapter 41 "the equivalent of a master of arts in all sexual matters," she grows in importance as the plot builds. She feels "an agony of delight" over defying the imperial taboo to bring Satoko and Kiyo together. Much of this joy comes from her newfound zest for power. Though "hardly more than a dwarf," elderly, and a servant, she controls a matter of national import. But she never forgets her love for Satoko. Dreading the consequences of her young charge's pregnancy, she attempts suicide. But we have seen too much of her to dismiss her when her prospects darken. Our faith is rewarded. Propped up in her sickbed with heavy white makeup and lipstick embellishing her ancient face, she reveals that, despite being twenty years his senior, she once made love to Satoko's father, the Count Ayakura.

Mishima chose wisely to make the practical, also ethical-minded Honda Kiyo's interlocutor in this crucial scene. He implies Honda's centricity in what will follow by making him the recording consciousness of chapter 29, which opens the novel's second half. This chapter deepens Honda's participation in Kiyo's tie with Satoko. Another look at the dangers of erotic abandon, it describes the trial of a woman who killed her lover. Honda sees again in it that yielding to passion releases energies that are beautiful and exciting; the accused, a plump, drab mediocrity of thirty-one, takes on a distinction and a tragic grandeur during her trial. But she also sends out signals of foreboding. The book's second half has opened with a murder trial; love seems to be ending in crime and punishment. And though the parallel with Kiyo and Satoko is not exact, it is close enough to command the reader's attention. The ordeal of waitress Tomi Masuda also took root in a love triangle. Kiyo's later tendency, in fact, to view the continuance of his romance as more of a technical than a moral problem puts Satoko's fiancé increasingly in the picture as a victim.

The association of sexual love and danger acquires sinew from the early chapters of the novel's second half. Not only is a woman convicted of murder and an imperial decree violated. As if the illicit link between Satoko and Kiyo unleashed a curse, one of the Siamese princes believes that his missing emerald ring has been stolen. Then his sister dies, as has been seen, and he and his cousin, the dead woman's ex-fiancé, must return to their grief-torn families. Never mind that Honda is studying the law and that his father is already a prominent lawyer. The law cannot halt the contagion of suffering unmuzzled by the flouting of a royal edict. The convulsive process is symbolized by wild rains. Rain beats madly on the roof covering Satoko and Kiyo during their first rut in chapter 27; it pelts down again during Tomi Masuda's trial two chapters later; the following chapter shows the two Siamese princes combing the wet grounds of Peers School for the lost emerald during a shower while some of their fellow students, whose honor the princes impugned by saying that the ring was stolen, insult them.

Mishima does not include this rancor to indulge his pessimism. He has poised many of the book's key figures at a crossroads where a mishap or a misfire could possibly doom them. Satoko is poised between maidenhood and marriage, while Kiyo, Honda, and the two Siamese princes all straddle youth and manhood. In addition, an important scene takes place at a shoreline, or "border between land and sea." Here in chapter 32, Honda sees under Kiyo's left armpit the three small moles that will show up years later on characters in *Horses, The Temple of Dawn,* and *Decay.* Mishima underscores this piece of dramatic foreshadowing by having the Siamese princes discuss an idea germane to Honda's discovery, the transmigration of souls. One can nearly predict that the souls who descend from Kiyo will suffer; the border, or margin, where things become other things bristles with dangers. Shrewdly, Mishima describes the dangers threatening his characters-in-transit with different metaphors of noncommunication. Noncommunication covers a wide swathe in this novel of missed chances. At the very outset, the Russo-Japanese War divides those who remember it from those who do not; the Siamese princes, who never learn to speak Japanese properly, feel increasingly alienated from their fellow students; the permanence of Kiyo's separation from Satoko is spelled out by the convent walls that enclose her, the bricks of which both enjoy God's blessings and express the strength of His will. Also conveying the futility of Kiyo's pleas to see Satoko once more before he dies is his pleader. Too weak to keep visiting the convent himself, Kiyo sends

Honda. But Honda's failure goes beyond gaining no interview for his friend with Satoko; in the novel's final rift between hope and attainment, his mind also wanders during his audience with the abbess. It is in this climate of fragmentation that Kiyo dies.

Short-circuiting his hopes seven chapters earlier in a way consistent with the noncommunication motif was his learning from a newspaper that Satoko had enrolled as a novice in Gesshu Temple. He was not told of her decision to cloister herself even though he was surrounded by people who knew of it. This breakdown of confidence and continuity recalls Kazu's learning of her husband's candidacy for high office from a news bulletin in *Banquet*. More poignantly, it reminds us that Mishima's widow would first hear of his suicide on the radio. This reminder sends shock waves through *Snow*. It shows both how much of himself Mishima poured into the book and how keenly he felt the frustration gnawing his characters. His pain floods the action. It shows him sifting his feelings in an atmosphere of grief. At no time does he try to flatter or go soft on himself. Like the badgered Iinuma, he was a right-winger with a skin problem—and a hairy chest (a rarity among Japanese men). These likenesses invoke a key point about the novel; Mishima has made one of his major spokespersons in the book a stiff-necked prude and a sexual groundling. Using Iinuma to reflect his own disquiet argues unusual sophistication on his part about how the difficult and dangerous entity known as the truth can be approached. But his search does not stop here. Like Kiyo, he also had a domineering grandmother whose chief victim was her daughter-in-law, his mother. Both Kiyo and Honda followed him into Peers School; also like him, both boys lived at home rather than in the school's dormitory. And Honda's father probably attended law school in Germany because his author studied German law at Tokyo University in 1946. Finally, Mishima shared Kiyo's worst faults—a hankering for an all-embracing explanation of life's problems and a tendency to spurn anyone who showed him affection.

Unfortunately, as was seen in *Sailor,* his brave, honest practice of confronting personal problems through his art did not help him solve them. But it did enhance the richness and virtuosity of *Snow*. Challenging and educative, the novel increases our awareness of how we live. The illicit love affair at its quick stands as both "a tiny, brilliant crystal palace" and a rampaging brushfire whose flames destroy families, scorch the tables of the law, and blacken his imperial highness, the emperor. This wild blaze both drives the lovers together and divides them. In describing the paradox, Mishima does not try to be so clever that he forgets to be himself. "From the beginning you've been bewitched by *impossibility*," Kiyo hears in chapter 38. The assessment speaks home. His lyrical defiance of restraints damns him. At the same time, it lends his damnation both a beauty and an elevation that no army of Hondas could attain. He thrills us while enriching us. Yes, he dies pursuing the impossible. But so did Cervantes's Don Quixote and Conrad's Lord Jim. In his perversity flicker images of what we could become if we had the grit to follow him.

Snow is large scale and demanding, vital and sensual. Its colors are not drab or muddy. This novel is not to be read passively. You view it through a rotating crystal, catching in its multicolored planes an occasional glimpse of yourself. Kiyo and Satoko are humanity writ large; their emotions resemble ours along with their needs. But they also breathe a pure, highly charged air. In the process, they help make *Spring Snow* Mishima's best novel. Full of tension, the work is both intellectually exciting and emotionally challenging; something worth paying attention to is always going on in its lively, convoluted plot. It is courtly in that it focuses mainly on people of noble lineage. But its real eminence stems from its masterful conception and execution. Its dovetailing of materials rough and rare, savage and subtle, discloses a genius working at top form.

8

Echoes from a Waterfall
Runaway Horses
The Temple of Dawn
The Decay of the Angel

1

Runaway Horses opens in 1932. Kiyoaki Matsugae died eighteen years ago, and Shigekuni Honda is now a judge on the Osaka Court of Appeals. He studied criminal law because he liked it, not because he wanted to further his career. But if his ethics have remained spotless, they have not been seriously tested. This peripheral thirty-eight-year-old relates feebly to life. Dull and respectable, he does not go drinking with his colleagues after work, and his childless marriage is so sane and tidy that it barely exists. His centricity in the book's opening chapters augurs badly. In contrast to Kiyo, who died for love at the end of *Spring Snow,* Honda is tame and tedious. Reading a book about him would be like chewing dry straw. Although this fear will be allayed, Honda creates little bounce. He reads, observes, and reviews his youth (the memory of which has, naturally enough, sharpened with age). In line with his reactive personality, he hears a lecture, watches a kendo (dueling with bamboo staves) match, and attends a No play at different points in the action. His judge's faith in reason, control, and stability has shielded him from the wildness whose criminal offshoots he deals with every day in court.

His life changes when, always available, he stands in for a colleague at the last minute to represent the bench at a local kendo tournament. Looking to invest his emotions (he will adopt a son in *The Decay of an Angel*), he finds himself riveted by eighteen-year-old Isao Iinuma. The manly Isao not only scores five straight wins. He also reveals himself to be the son of Shikeyuki Iinuma, Kiyo's former tutor and now the head of the right-wing militarist Academy of Patriotism. A still-greater shock comes when Honda follows the kendoists to the waterfall where they have gone to purify themselves after fighting. After completing the grueling walk to the falls in Nara, where Kiyo collapsed trying to join Satoko, Honda recalls his friend's dying words: "Just now I had a dream. I'll see you again. I know it. Beneath the falls." A spasm rushes through the structure of reason he has spent the last twenty years building. While standing under the tumbling, clubbing waterfall, he sees that Isao has Kiyo's same three moles on the left side of his chest. The possibility that Kiyo has been reborn as Isao wrecks Honda's digestion and keeps him from sleeping. But not from persevering; even though he cannot know the meaning of Kiyo's rebirth, he rejoices in it. Here is a development worthy of his energies. Though totally different, Kiyo and Isao both ratify the splendor of youthful promise and striving.

Echoes from *Spring Snow* enforce the idea that Kiyo has returned to earth as Isao. Iinuma recalls the pain of being turned away from both Kiyo's wake and funeral service. Nor has he forgiven his wife Mine for having been the mistress of Kiyo's father, the marquis. Besides forcing her to have an abortion early in the marriage under the flimsy supposition that the child might belong to the marquis, he also battered her a decade later when he believed her too friendly with a student from the academy. Invoking Satoko as vividly as the abortion motif is the return to the tetralogy of her former fiancé, Prince Harunori Toin, now a beefy regimental commander of forty-five and a supporter of the band of young ultranationalists, led by Isao, who want to restore imperial rule. As in *Spring Snow*, the action of *Runaway Horses* (1969) casts shadows on the imperial family and thus encroaches upon the welfare of the Japanese nation. This encroachment deserves a close look, the prince's longest appearance in the book coinciding with rain, a condition that accompanied many of the calamities of *Spring Snow*.

Other echoes from *Spring Snow* invoke unrest while also summoning up Kiyo. But whereas Kiyo only dreamed of killing birds, Isao shoots one. His dismissing the pheasant's shooting death in chapter 23 as "a small shedding of blood and a small death" is nonsense. It shows how easily the thinking that turns kids into killers can spin out of control; the death certainly was not small to the pheasant because it ended the only life the pheasant had. As was seen in *Sailor,* the impulse to kill rarely stops at animals. The members of Isao's Showa League of the Divine Wind may be four to six years older than those of Noboru's gang, but they are just as sociopathic. Their deathliness validates Honda's visit to Kiyo's grave in chapter 25. But if time kills, it also resurrects. In what may be the book's most touching scene, the seventy-eight-year-old operator of a rooming house takes the witness stand during Isao's trial for sedition; the obsessiveness directed to sexual love in *Spring Snow* has taken patriotism as an object in *Runaway Horses.* When asked if Isao ever visited a certain infantry officer in the house, the old proprietor says that Isao brought a woman there twenty years before. This answer brings gales of laughter from the spectators at the trial, since Isao is only twenty years old himself. Only Honda sees the answer's merit. Having unconsciously rated the spiritual aspects of the trial over the factual ones, the proprietor, as if led by an unseen hand, has spoken more profoundly than anyone in the room besides Honda could suspect. Experience has repeated itself in such a bizarre way that the spectators can only laugh. They have been expecting something more prosaic. But what they dismiss as a senile blunder strengthens Honda's belief that Kiyo has come back as Isao.

This revelation occurs while Isao is being tried because he and a dozen or so friends were caught planning an insurrection. Their aim? To kill Japan's leading industrialists, to revive the nation's sagging economy, and, above all, to restore the absolute rule of the emperor. The trouble is that by burning the Bank of Japan and destroying all of Tokyo's electricity, they will only aggravate the pain, upheaval, and demoralization they see festering around them. The success of their proposed rising would convulse the imperial family as much as anybody. The emperor would be left with nothing to rule over and nothing upon which to rebuild Japan's economy, if that were, indeed, his aim; Isao and his friends have not bothered to find out. They have made other serious omissions, too. Lacking any concrete program to create jobs, heal the sick, or feed the hungry, they are only masquerading as freedom fighters. All they can create is disorder and bloodshed. Rather than restore national honor, they will damage Japan more than could generations of their professed enemies, communists—scheming capitalist officeholders, and Buddhists.

Then why do the Leaguers rush into action? Certainly, these young idealists do not want to worsen Japan's woes. They want to remove them by supplanting the greed and corruption they see infecting Japan with the ancient worship—the unification of government and religion, as personified by the emperor. Proper reverence for God and the emperor in these parlous times, they believe, must express itself as military action; knowledge that is not translated into action is as bad as ignorance. But perhaps the best result of this needful translation will be the purity of motive and dedication it will foster. The proposed restoration will include a revival of the warrior code that has fallen into disrepute since the edicts of the 1870s forbidding samurai from carrying swords. Reviving this manly code will bolster Japan's national character, and all the economic, political, and social blessings she needs to regain her old grandeur will follow.

But the Leaguers will not enjoy them. Part of Isao's demand to be heard inheres in his insistence that he wants nothing for himself. Eschewing personal gain, he intends to slit his belly right after the rising takes place, regardless of its outcome. His projected sacrifice follows from his puritanism, a belief, by the way, that makes Calvinism look bright and cheerful. People are so corrupt, Isao believes, that they cannot act without sinning. To put down evil for the emperor's sake is evil, because it entails the prideful presumption that the mere individual can help his serene highness, a direct descendant of God. Yet not to act when action is called for is also sinful; to stand by passively while the emperor is being threatened deserves harsh punishment. Isao plans to resolve this paradox by invoking the Japanese virtue of sincerity. Usually equated with youth, sincerity stands for the motive, the idea, or the spirit behind an action. Isao has often seen compromise smirching the purity of his idealism; he cannot escape the painful truth that the noblest of causes becomes tainted once it moves into the drab prose of everyday life. He detaches himself from this defilement by dying before it begins making inroads. In fact, he and his friends devote as much care to dying as they do to wiping out their enemies.

One may complain that all this reeks of mannishness, as opposed to manliness, a virtue that recognizes the life-giving powers of control and restraint. The doomed rebellion only goes so far as it does because its would-be perpetrators are all afraid to denounce it as wasteful and stupid. Another piece of bogus elitism comes in the cool poise with which the Leaguers have planned to die. They believe that both the style and manner of their upcoming deaths assert their superiority; only the truly brave could undergo the agony of seppuku, or self-disembowelment. This pridefulness finds a disturbing parallel in D. H. Lawrence's *Kangaroo*, another description of revolutionary politics that invokes the wisdom of a maligned past and shows men acting in paramilitary groups rather than alone (advisedly, Isao's only independent action outside the kendo ring causes two deaths). *Runaway Horses* and Lawrence's 1923 novel both discredit women; both believe, too, that the European-bred evils of communism and humanism can be best purged by military action. Thus both works rate muscle over negotiation; both dwell at length upon details of rank, responsibility, and chains of command while opting for a militarist society. In both, discussions of goals are accompanied by the consumption of elegant food and drink, and sometimes, even by the touching and jostling that stem from the homosexuality nourishing the two books.

As he did in *Sailor*, Mishima sometimes views militarism as a refuge from the complexities and ambiguities of civilian society. He refers to the "beautiful, sweaty, intricate choreography of death" constituting a military drill in chapter 14. For him, the drill expresses the serene and supreme will of the emperor. But normal civilian routine resists this deathly formality—which may be its salvation. Much of the grip of *Runaway Horses* comes from the book's documentary materials. The revolutionary fervor of the day permeates the action. Ripples from the Bolshevik takeover, which occurred only fifteen years before the time setting of the book's first half, have reached Tokyo; as a result, cells of Marxist activity have been sprouting up in the city. References to the peaceful 1931 revolution that turned Siam into Thailand invoke both the ill-starred Siamese princes from *Spring Snow* and the princess from Bangkok who will stand at the center of *The Temple of Dawn*. But these references also show that public concern over Japan's future has already caused destruction and death. Fresh in the minds of all Japanese at the time of the book was the notorious 15 May 1932 rising, in which Japan's finance minister and prime minister were both killed by fanatical Navy officers.

The failure of this rising colors Honda's attitude to Isao and his fellow Leaguers. As he did in *Spring Snow*, Honda will witness events he condemns rationally but nonetheless finds exciting. His calling the pamphlet that inspires Isao's rebellion, *The League of the Divine Wind,* "a drama of tragic perfection" combines aesthetics, morality, and politics. The moral purity of the men of the League who opposed the Meiji government had a crystalline intensity and beauty. But this very perfection brought on their deaths; today's mixed world of compromise and muddle cannot afford such sincerity. Besides, Honda continues in his long letter to Isao in chapter 10, the Japan of 1932 differs from that of the 1870s, and no surge of will, regardless of its purity or intensity, can transcend history. Better to curb the rush of the blood and achieve your goals over the step-by-step plod of years.

The trouble is that Honda only half believes his own advice. He sees in Isao's courage and resolve a possible last chance to transcend the very prudency he preaches. Thus he quits the bench to defend Isao in court without taking a fee; he cannot forgo the chance to honor the reborn spirit of Kiyo and thus assuage his own survivor's guilt. The immediate effects of his adventure tally with others like it in the tetralogy. "Honda's reputation at the Courthouse seemed not quite as high as it had been," we read in chapter 31. But as rumors about family problems erode his professional standing, his emotions spring to life. He has forsworn reason and appearance for ultimate realities like reincarnation and the emperor's divinity. "He acted as his heart told him to act," says Mishima of him in chapter 31. His boldness also affects the book's form. As Tadeshina reminded us in *Spring Snow*, the keeper of the secrets in opera or romantic comedy is usually secondary; though essential to the plot, he/she has a lesser stake in it than some of the other, usually younger, characters.

Honda will not reveal the long-range effects of interceding for the young until later. But the immediate impact on his soul can be easily imagined. Responding to thousands of letters praising the Leaguers' sincerity, the judge trying Isao renders a guilty verdict with a suspended sentence. Isao can go home after having spent a year in jail waiting to be tried. But he squanders his freedom, killing one of Japan's leading industrialists and then himself three days after his prison release. He has either gone to pieces or followed through perfectly on his earlier resolve to cleanse Japan. In either case, he has seen the purity of his hopes cloud and clot. Honda had already disclaimed his sincerity as a tactical liability because it rejected the moderation and calculation that create helpful testimony. His doubts about Isao's ability to help his own cause on the witness stand were well judged. Isao's radical puritanism could have already unhinged him in view of the betrayal that has been blitzing it. In fact, the ease with which betrayal razes bonds of friendship and blood makes it the norm for human transactions in the novel. The hopes of the Leaguers darken when their unofficial leader, an infantry lieutenant, announces that he cannot take part in the coming raid because he has just been transferred to Manchuria. Prince Toin, who is also sympathetic to the League, later suspects that the lieutenant volunteered to go to Manchuria, thereby betraying the emperor together with the young Leaguers.

The notion that treachery always infects intimates gains force. Iinuma admits that he betrayed Isao to the police because he wanted to save his son's life. But he could be lying. He has already been diminished by the Marquis Matsugae, having taken the marquis's young popsy off his hands and then married her when it suited the marquis. He also idolized the marquis's son, Kiyo. After living in the shadows of two of the most important men he has known, he might well try to stop his son from outshining him, too. The same suicide mission planned to crush Isao would have also given him a luster that Iinuma could never hope to match. Betrayal confuses love with hatred again during Isao's trial; Makiko, the divorcée of thirty who loves him, testifies that he had agreed to abandon the raid after seeing how futile it was. Her words rouse a response in him more convoluted than any he had known in either the kendo ring or the rebel camp. Whereas he feels honored by her having committed perjury to help him, he also sees that her loving lie has discredited him to his fellow Leaguers. But if these friends will scorn him for a traitor, they will not be pushing him onto unfamiliar turf. He has already played the traitor's role. As well he might; treachery is inescapable. To be human is to betray, Mishima believes. Isao had first betrayed his father by visiting Prince Toin after Iinuma, still chafing over the prince's role in Kiyo's undoing, ordered him not to. He betrays Iinuma more grievously by killing the financier Baron Busuke Kurahara. Not only was Iinuma paid to guard Kurahara from such attacks; for years, Kurahara has also been supporting the Academy of Patriotism that Iinuma operates. Certainly, the Iinuma family's main benefactor deserves better than to be killed by someone who has been living off his generosity.

Intriguing moral problems in the novel, like the one created by the baron's death, take resonance from Mishima's sharp instinct for detail. His truckling ways with both Kiyo and the marquis prepared Iinuma to court the patronage of the powerful Kurahara rather than rely on his own powers. Also consistent with his pawn complex is his failure to rise in the secular world. He avoided the hurly-burly of business altogether; nor did he compete for either a teaching or a civil-service job despite his university degree. The "soiled and bent" calling card he gives Honda at their first meeting in nineteen years spells out the futility of his career, perhaps even of his life. Another small but telling touch comes in chapter 29 in the keg of oysters Isao takes to Makiko and her father. This gift from his parents, said to increase sexual potency, comments ironically on the virgin carrying it. Isao had offered to take the oysters to the Kito family because, although he would not admit it, he wanted to see Makiko once more before dying. Yet this self-divided young man also believes that "the most beautiful thing would be to die without seeing her." According to his (and his author's) samurai ethic, enactment of any kind stains the purity of ideal love. The tension caused by the split in his soul reverberates slyly. Whereas he cannot decide whether he wants to see Makiko or not, the sexuality implied in his keg of oysters distorts his confusion by so much that he is cast in a strange new light. The mixed passion bedeviling Isao could easily lurch into sexuality and send him to Makiko's bed. This possibility and the pain it would cause if ever followed through on recall Kiyo and

Satoko, whom Isao and Makiko parody. Again, Mishima will use a fleeting detail to invoke the parody and its possible by-products. Makiko testifies at Isao's trial wearing a kimono with a waterfall stripe. This reminder of Kiyo's dying words joins with the senile wisdom of the rooming-house proprietor to sustain the reincarnation motif undergirding the action; *Runaway Horses* belongs as much to Kiyo as to Isao, the work's deep structure keeps saying.

Its ability to reinforce and thus renew itself includes a system of interchecks. "Why should decay take the color of dawn?" Honda wonders in chapter 23, alluding to the deathly strains interlacing motifs of growth and rebirth in the tetralogy. Good and bad also run through Mishima's self-divided people rather than around them. All of these people both help and hurt the commonweal. An example is Isao's murder victim. Called both "Japan's supreme capitalist" and "the very personification of capitalism," Busuke Kurahawa has a gentle, wondering side his killer overlooks. He lives in an Edwardian villa built at great expense, drives a Lincoln, and reads the London *Times*. This Anglophile and devotee of Edward Gibbon also grows tangerines, which he gives to orphanages and welfare hospitals. The misfortunes of others can make him cry, and the steel nerves that helped earn him a fortune have also made him scorn danger. Though constantly threatened by his foes, he will foil his bodyguards. Even if he were not Iinuma's patron, this impressive, likable man deserves better from Isao. Mishima underscores the point by ending the first half of the novel, in the last paragraph of chapter 20, with the warning to Isao that the baron's death will hurt Iinuma more than anybody. "Go ahead out of a sense of loyalty," the warning concludes, "And you'll find yourself utterly betraying your father."

Isao does not take the warning seriously enough. In the chapter after it is served, he calls Kurahawa "the very source of the evil" plaguing Japan, but without putting forth a shred of supporting evidence. He lacks both the fairness and self-control to perceive the baron clearly, let alone judge him. Also in chapter 21, he nearly brains the friend who told him that the baron has been underwriting the Academy of Patriotism. He prefers to follow his impulses, even after learning that they are misguided. He answers his friend by saying that he wants to "preserve the images" he carries in his mind of both his father and the baron. Forget that these images rest on falsehood; his juvenile drive to heroism must not be blocked. Thus it is no wonder that when he stabs the baron to death, he is given a look of "altogether unfeigned incomprehension." The baron never learns why he has to die. In this novel that features both a judge and a courtroom trial, the condemned man is the only character denied the chance to take the witness stand and defend himself.

The simplistic thinking that causes his death owes as much to Mishima as to Isao. The book's self-correcting moral vision is too weak to serve either justice or sanity. Mishima presents a world ruled by irony and moral complexity. But he merely notes ambiguities rather than reasoning from them. His warrior code underrates the life-abetting virtues of control and balance. The League chooses its members on the basis of style, intellect, and strength of character. Then it sends these young paragons to their deaths. Japan's worst enemies could not have hurt the country more than those pledged to it at the purest ideological level. What sends *Runaway Horses* off course is the rift between the zeal of the Leaguers and the Buddhism that ratifies Honda's belief in Kiyo's rebirth as Isao. In chapter 22, an angry farmer accuses Buddha of having robbed the Japanese of their manly courage. But Buddha also supplies the novel's keystone idea, that of the transmigration of souls. Birth, death, and even selfhood are illusions, Buddhism claims. Our active participation in the same cosmic mind makes the universe a seamless whole. It also confirms reincarnation, a doctrine essential to *Runaway Horses* no matter how much it offends Mishima's fierce warrior mentality.

To his credit, Mishima thought about resolving the clash between the novel's Buddhist and samurai strains. This resolution was to have been performed by Makiko's father, Kensuke Kito, a retired general and poet. But Mishima did not think hard enough. General Kito is not only a visionary and a man of action. This artist-soldier also dramatizes the value of living into old age. Besides enjoying the company of his beautiful, sensitive daughter, he has enhanced his fine reputation by remaining active as a poet. But he appears rarely in the action and says little—in prose or verse. Whatever thematic drive Mishima wanted him to generate runs afoul of casual treatment; Kito remains a minor figure. Another source of value that goes untapped, embodied by his daughter, is the feminine principle.

Women fade into the background of *Runaway Horses*. The "modest and gentle woman" Honda has been married to for seven years barely exists. Besides having had no children, Rie never questions him or asks him to explain himself. When he goes to Tokyo to visit his mother, she does not object. Why should she? His mother is as dim and distant as she is. Nor does he consider for a moment taking Rie with him.

Her insignificance in his life finds a rough parallel in the home of Iinuma and Mine. Apart from being Isao's mother, Mine has little identity. Although she has grown fat, this self-effacing woman is nearly invisible to her husband. The inconsequentiality she shares with Rie chimes with the book's phallocentrism; the lifelines of *Runaway Horses* exclude women. *The League of the Divine Wind* ends with a question posed by a rebel about to commit seppuku to redeem his honor: "Were we to have acted like frail women?" His disciples, the Isao-led Leaguers of 1932, all prefer suicide by dagger than by poison because poison is a "womanish means of putting an end to life." Though true to the warrior code, this slur clashes with the truth enacted by Satoko and Makiko, that, far from being inferior, women serve and sustain life better than men. The tenderness, insight, and bravery of Makiko, called in chapter 13 "the quintessential woman," save Isao's life at the trial. But if Isao's killing himself three days after going free means that he has misprized her gift, Mishima must share the guilt. The irresolution surrounding his portrayals of Satoko and Makiko shows him rattled by intelligent, independent women of good heart. The princess around whom he will build his next novel is as wildly destructive as Etsuko of *Thirst for Love;* he can ignore or malign her as much as he wants without feeling a jot of guilt.

A final objection to *Runaway Horses* relates this insensitivity to the book's art. Honda leaves the action in chapter 8 (p. 61 in the American hardcover [New York: Knopf, 1973] edition) and stays away till chapter 19 (p. 209). The coincidence of his absence with the appearance of the text of *The League of the Divine Wind* and of Isao's hot reaction to it fuels the impression that the novel has not reconciled thought and action. The civilized process and the art of community living that Honda serves stand light years from the youthful recklessness of the leaguers. *Runaway Horses* cracks under the strain caused by its various divisions. This damage extends beyond the novel. As shall be seen, the divisions in the book run so deep that they sabotage the remaining works in the *Sea of Fertility* cycle. The ultranationalism depicted in *Runaway Horses* spurns Western capitalism and communism along with the Buddhism of the East. This rejection of foreign influences springs from a wish to create in Japan a unique culture and character. What this wish begets, though, often resembles destruction more than creation. An unplanned analogue of this sad process shows the consistency and stability that Mishima sought in the doctrine of reincarnation causing an artistic cramp so severe that his tetralogy would never recover from it.

2

The links joining *Runaway Horses* to *The Temple of Dawn* (1970) glitter with promise. In jail, Isao had dreamed of becoming a woman, and after his trial he comtemplated being reborn as one. Then, this aggressively macho hero muttered in his sleep, "Far to the south. Very hot, in the rose sunshine of a southern land." Mishima had already decided to bring Kiyo back to earth as a Thai princess. He had also pondered other key matters of organization. Though self-contained, each work in the tetralogy contains repetitions, complexities, and subtleties that please more in light of its companion pieces. Honda has taken Kiyo's dream diary with him on a business trip to Bangkok at the outset of *Dawn,* as if preparing himself for a miracle or trying to wish one into existence. When the miracle occurs, she has the same name (Chantrapa, or Moonlight) as her father's fiancée, who died thirty-four years before, when the father was attending Tokyo's Peers School. Another echo from Honda's schoolboy past comes in the discovery, in a Tokyo antique shop, of the same emerald ring that a fellow student had been accused of stealing in *Spring Snow*. The taint clinging to the ring still persists. The figures who reappear in *Dawn* from the earlier volumes in the cycle have all gone downhill. Prince Toin cannot make a go of the antique shop where the ring turns up. The ex-*zaibatsu* Baron Shinkawa has dwindled into a garrulous old bore. In his lone appearance, Iinuma, a failed suicide now divorced from Mine, praises

Isao drunkenly and takes money from Honda to revive his now-defunct Academy of Patriotism. Makiko Kito has followed her father in becoming a famous poet. But smirching this honor is her emergence as both a false friend and a peeper; in chapter 27 she watches a couple making love in the next bed. Another notable female from the past, Satoko's nurse Tadeshina, also appears. At ninety-four, wearing makeup applied in the thick style of her youth, she materializes in the litter of broken glass and rusty shards that remain of the Matsugaes' bombed-out Tokyo estate. Yet this ruin discovered amid ruins exudes hope. Though tired and frayed, she feels revived after eating a raw egg, an act symbolizing rebirth. In return for the life-renewing egg, she gives Honda a book containing a mantra that prescribes a cure against snakebite. She also advises Honda to visit Satoko, now the abbess of the same convent where she took her vows.

Taking this advice might have helped Honda. Still nagging at him is his old belief in the futility of human endeavor. Kiyo's death filled no purpose, and his own efforts as defense attorney did not stop Isao from dying just as pointlessly. Honda's belief that history swallows the individual has destroyed the altruism that led him to defend Isao without payment. Since that time, he has only worked for the rich. Yet the fortune he has amassed serving rich clients has left him empty. More fixated on the past than ever, he equates the sun rising over the legendary waters of Benares, India, with the sunburst of Isao's suicide dream. Honda's last recorded moments in India show him inside one of the Ajanta caves near a waterfall and wondering if Kiyo's dying promise to see him again beneath the falls did not refer to this very instant. Several times hence, he will intuit a mystical circuit joining these Ajanta cascades to both those of the Matsugaes' garden in Tokyo, where he met Satoko's predecessor, the old abbess of Gesshu, and the Sanko Falls near Nara, where he saw the three black moles on Isao's left flank that linked Isao to Kiyo. The apparitions at Ajanta and Benares spur him to study in depth the doctrines of reincarnation and the transmigration of souls. His studies fill a big void. Though rich, he sees himself growing old and ugly. Like the law practice that has waned in importance to him and the millions he won on a legal fluke, his marriage still bores him. The transformation he craves can only come from his centricity in the

ongoing drama of Kiyo's rebirth; he must follow the traces left by
Kiyo and Isao.

These traces lead him to Princess Chantrapa (or Moonlight), who
comes to Tokyo as a beautiful nineteen-year-old student. The emerging pattern created by her arrival encourages him. Now called Ying
Chan, the Thai princess is both a third as old as the fifty-seven-year-
old Honda and the same age as Kiyo was during his blazing romance with Satoko (*Dawn* is also the third book of Mishima's *Sea
of Fertility* tetralogy). Now Honda and Ying Chan had first met
eleven or twelve years before, i.e., in 1940, in Bangkok, where the
book opens and where Honda had gone to settle a point of international business law. More needs settling in Bangkok than legal
matters. At forty-six, he is already a year older than Mishima would
be when he took his life, and he feels the effects of time; looking into
a mirror in chapter 10, he sees "the face of a man who had lived too
long." His childless marriage has also directed his yearning for
continuity and closure outside the family. After discovering that the
two Thai princes he knew at Peers School are both out of town, he
manages to gain an audience with the daughter of one of them. But
he is apprehensive. The seven-year-old princess is said to be mad
because she keeps insisting that she is Japanese. She acts just as
Honda heard she might, shrieking and clutching at him while
demanding that he take her back to her real home in Japan. To
support her case, she gives Honda on demand the dates of two
crucial events in the lives of Kiyo and Isao, her presumed earlier
incarnations. Though deeply moved, Honda lets his expectations
cool when he sees the little princess swimming naked and revealing
an upper left torso unmarked by the corroborative three moles. He
takes his puzzlement to India, where his clients have sent him on a
free vacation in exchange for having served them so well. After India,
he stops again at Bangkok on his way home to see the princess, and
it is not till chapter 12 that the book, the only one in the tetralogy to
begin in a foreign country, moves to Japan. Its foreign settings have
conveyed the pervasiveness of reincarnation, a process that transcends national and linguistic borders. Along with Bangkok's Temple of Dawn, the holy place that supplies the novel's title, the
spiritual heritage of both Thailand and India focuses Honda's atten-

tion on the mysteries that his meetings with the little princess quicken in his soul.

Benares, his first stop after leaving Bangkok, makes these mysteries throb and resonate. The scenes at Benares, the juncture of India's five holy rivers and thus India's holiest (and also perhaps filthiest) city comprise a brilliant travelogue. Responding keenly to this meeting point of the sacred and the wretched, Mishima records both the ugliness and the spiritual uplift created by the dogs and the water buffalo soaking alongside the sick and dying people who have come to be healed by the Ganges. Two riverside apparitions burn themselves into Honda's mind—a pinkish white leper nearly stripped of his dark pigmentation and that Hindu embodiment of the life-death-rebirth cycle, a sacred cow, who looks straight at Honda. But in line with the all-inclusiveness central to Hinduism, the humble and the small can also express God. The simple, faded building where Honda first sees Ying Chan impresses him as "too insignificant to qualify as a palace." The stripped and the unadorned convey force again before Honda returns to Japan; when he walks into the cave at Ajanta containing the towering waterfall in chapter 9, he finds it "undecorated, colorless," and presumably void of significance.

The various repetitions marking his association with Ying Chan undercut this uplift. His giving her two rings, in Bangkok in 1940 and in Tokyo in 1952, infers the completeness he hopes to gain through her, the ring symbolizing betrothal. His watching her urinate as a child and his dream of her in chapter 39, sitting on a white peacock and sending down "a shower of fragrant urine" confirm his reaction to her as more than just spiritual. The water motif as an index of his sexual interest in her holds. Later, he will have a pool installed in his Gotemba country house because he wants to see her swimming naked. And when she spends the night at the country house, he puts her in the room adjoining the one he had fitted with a peephole. He also puts the long-missing emerald ring on her finger after she leaves it in its box at the little presentation ceremony he organizes.

Mishima hints that Honda's obscure hopes for redemption through Ying Chan will meet grief. The American occupation army in Japan has prompted an outbreak of low dives frequented by pimps and prostitutes all too eager to service the visiting GIs. Rioting protesters have been overturning cars and throwing Molotov cocktails. Closer to home, Honda's civilized browse in a favorite bookstore in chapter 34 goes rank at the sight of a youth looking at a girlie magazine and masturbating through his pocket. The novel's very first sentence, "It was the rainy season in Bangkok," puts out a bad omen in view of the troubles that broke during showers in *Spring Snow* and *Runaway Horses*. Mishima's determination to sustain the portent recurs at the beginning of part 2, which opens seven years later. The friendly remark made by Honda's neighbor at Gotemba, "You've planted some beautiful cypresses," strikes a deathly note; the cypress is the most popular tree in cemeteries in the West, a fact the world-traveled Mishima had to know.

Unfortunately, much of this poetic foregrounding goes to waste. Lacking the patience, balance, and invention he displayed in *Spring Snow* and in parts of *Runaway Horses*, the Mishima of *Dawn* treats love aestheticially rather than dramatically or morally. Ying Chan's appearance in Japan in 1952 creates a climax that fails to hold. The novel soon falls apart, as if it lacked a story. It never regains the sense of mystery and forward drive created by its opening because, for one reason, given by Miyoshi, "the Thai episode is not well articulated with the rest."[1] Once the action seats itself in Japan, it resists an emotional reading. We do not know why we are following the people; Mishima has not shown anything in them worth dramatizing. In fact, he shows so little interest in them that they come across as his dullest bunch of characters to date, abstractions with names and not identifiable people who change and grow. What is emotional in the book thus leads to abstraction or hysteria. Episodic in the worst sense, *Dawn* consists of a chain of events that lead nowhere.

Edward Seidensticker ascribes the novel's sprawl to Ying Chan:

It is clear that she is of great physical beauty, but she is not enough of a physical presence. . . . The princess is simply not where she should be, at the center of and giving life to the third volume, which is sadly wanting in life.[2]

Support for Seidensticker's disclaimer comes forth in both the inconsistency and the murkiness with which Ying Chan is presented. It is as if Mishima were as puzzled and frightened by her as Honda is. Indeed, character and author have both pinned their hopes on her. For just as Honda's failure to transform himself through her crushes him, so does the inability of Ying Chan to take life both sink the novel and cloud what remained of Mishima's artistic future. This dual failure could have been predicted; once Mishima endows a character with youth and beauty, he becomes too besotted to develop the character's inner qualities; his mind also turns to death. But his attention to plot structure may stay keen. Ying Chan's sudden restoration to the action in part 2 creates some intrigue. Not only does she miss Honda's housewarming party after promising to come; she also spends the night of the party away from Tokyo's Foreign Student Center, her official address in Japan. But she will miss too many social obligations. Her pattern of breaking or failing to show up for dates persists to the point where it creates less intrigue than annoyance and boredom. So remote is she, in fact, that explanations for her absences may reach the reader through a third party, i.e., someone she did *not* have plans with who knows the person, usually Honda, she had disappointed.

Mishima's device of associating her with urine refers cruelly but accurately to the time and effort Honda wastes on her. It can also bring about some witty thematic dovetailing (Yourcenar is right to call *Dawn* "the most difficult [volume in the tetralogy] to judge").[3] After being stood up by the princess in chapter 41 for a dinner date, a shaken, emotionally wounded Honda seeks solace at the apartment of a confidante, slouching through streets "threatened at any moment by heavy showers." His dream of two chapters before, which showed Ying Chan urinating from aloft, is edging into reality. Rain has turned into fragrant showers of piss for the masochist Honda. He will face upward, begging for more. The same confidante who hears him say in chapter 41 that he loves Ying Chan will later take her to bed.

The book offers other excitement. Though Mishima treats his people far too casually, he does justify the princess's cruelty to Honda. Ying Chan may well be punishing Honda for deserting her

twelve years before, even though she claims to have forgotten his visit
(Tadeshina's also saying that she has forgotten this eminent mil-
lionaire-lawyer heightens his desperation). Next, she is insulted and
angry that the two adults, Honda and his confidante Keiko Hisamatsu, her protectors in Tokyo, have been betraying her. Obsessed
by her presumed virginity, the adults conspire to get her deflowered.
As in *Forbidden Colors* and *Spring Snow,* this intergenerational
erotic meddling brings grief. It also extends the book's range of
moral consciousness. The young woman abused by the elders she
has trusted invokes the archetypal Jamesian heroine. How much
does Ying Chan know? and how capable is she of defending herself?
Mishima makes one ask.

The answers he invites invoke the moral darkness found in *The
Turn of the Screw* and *The Wings of the Dove.* If Honda and
Keiko's scheming symbolizes the depravity of the human ties domi-
nating the book, Ying Chan darkens the picture. Her motivation in
becoming Keiko's lover carries a disturbing conviction. Lesbian to
begin with and far from the securities of home, she would be more
inclined to forgive the beautiful Keiko than hangdog Honda. What
is more, Keiko's wit, patience, and feline sensitivity to atmospheres
all ratify Mishima's disclosure that the two women are lovers. The
disclosure also explains the cooling of Keiko's long-standing love
affair with a pleasant American army major. At first, the reader
thought Keiko was avoiding Jack because the American armed forces
gave her back the home they had requisitioned. Jack may have
outlived his usefulness to her after helping her; from what the reader
sees of her, she is ruthless and decisive enough to discard a person
after benefiting from his help. But discarding Jack also means forfeit-
ing the privilege of shopping in the American PX. Keiko understands her priorities. The charms of Ying Chan hastened the
decision of this vital, accomplished woman to drop Jack.

It is here that the novel loses force. The princess has been so busy
breaking dates that she never persuades us of her power to win the
hearts of Keiko and Honda. We do not believe in her charms because
Mishima has not displayed them convincingly. Honda's calling her
in chapter 32 "a universe in herself" and "this black lotus that had
bloomed from the mud of life's flow" endows her with a magic that
remains undramatized. Her death suffers from the same scamped

treatment. As accidental and gratuitous as Seidensticker claims,[4] it is reported in the book's last chapter—a brief epilogue set fifteen years after the preceding action. At a party given at Tokyo's American Embassy, Honda learns that Ying Chan died soon after returning to Bangkok from Japan. Her twin sister, who explains the death in chapter 45, adds that she died from a cobra bite on the thigh. In ways, her death was well adumbrated. The princess dies at twenty, the same age as Kiyo and Isao. The way she dies also makes sense. In chapter 41, Honda kills a snake that had invaded his arbor; then he recalls the mantra from Tadeshina's book that gives the cure for snakebite. By using an emblem of phallic revenge, a cobra bite directed to the thigh, to kill Ying Chan, Mishima is punishing her for violating both natural and supernatural law. But the punishment, a function of homosexual self-contempt, is unduly harsh; nor does it flow from the narrative. Mishima had trouble orchestrating Ying Chan's death; otherwise, he would have integrated it with his plot rather than setting it off at a distance of fifteen years. This treatment strengthens the ongoing impression that he never understood her. He deserts his art, not for having failed to depict the princess, but for having failed to try.

His problems multiply. Because Honda counts so heavily on Ying Chan, he, too, fails to convince the reader of her flesh-and-blood reality; he sees her beauty as something to admire and drool over rather than an expression, ironic or otherwise, of her personality. Part of his blurred vision stems from his past. He has experienced life by observing instead of acting or participating. But what has helped him as a lawyer and a judge undoes him as a man; a career of watching has validated his seeking thrills as a Peeping Tom. Yet his falling in love with Ying Chan takes him beyond voyeurism. No sooner does he cultivate peeping than he outgrows it. Unfortunately, he has no room in which to grow. He does not know what he wants, and Mishima cannot help him. The same rhetorical questions Henry Miller addressed to Mishima's shade in 1972 could have also been put to Honda in 1970:

You were always impaling yourself on the horns of a contradiction, were you not? Your whole life was a dilemma whose only solution was death. . . . Was there nothing then that could truly satisfy you?[5]

Like the Mishima being taunted by Miller, the Honda of *Dawn* exhausts himself circling around problematic monsters rather than attacking them. His indecisiveness in chapter 39 over playing the role of legislator or of violator to Ying Chan shows him already ripening for catastrophe. He loves the princess partly because she contains the soul of Kiyo. A still-greater attraction inheres in the knowledge that she will never return his love; the assurance that she will always spurn him raises her value for him. Believing love incompatible with mutuality, he rejoices when she rejects him. This self-denying man even regards perception and love as preemptive; viewing the beloved is a form of fulfillment that compromises and corrupts ideal love. Yet the princess is a sexual being to him as well as the object of his courtly impulses. He rhapsodizes, in specific, nearly pornographic, detail, about her body, particularly her voluptuous breasts; he even thinks about taking her to bed.

This tormenting ambivalence typifies the twisted interpersonal responses found in the novel. People in *Dawn* may worship others rather than loving them. That the object of their worship can be dead conveys the danger of the process. Iinuma's reverence for Isao led to a suicide attempt whose failure shattered his self-respect. A Mrs. Tsubukihara studies poetry writing with Makiko. Her main passion in life, though, is the son who died in the Pacific War. She has also cast in her dead son's role the writer, Yasushi Imanishi, whose sexual fantasy kingdom, The Land of the Pomegranate, includes a murder theater in which the kingdom's most beautiful inhabitants are tortured and then killed on stage (as in *Confessions of a Mask*). It is fitting that he and Mrs. Tsubukihara should burn to death after sex. Devastation is the logical offspring of the rut of a woman trying to relive a dead past and a man caught up in a future that will never be.

Self-doomed people like this pair resist the purposes of narrative. Though infused with beauty and power, *Dawn* generates little warmth or flow; it suffers from dead spots, and its rhythm falters. Mishima understood these problems. Otherwise, he would not have introduced the regal, worldly-wise Keiko at the start of part 2; he needed her flair to infuse his sagging plot with some human interest along with dramatic drive. But her entrance comes too late. The long treatises in the first half on religion and philosophy and the extended descriptions of Bangkok's canals and temples slow the book so much that a brigade of Keikos could not revive it. Part 2 sags, as well. A work more diligent than spellbinding, *Dawn* should have been trimmed by a third. But even such deep cutting could not balance or refresh this ambitious, unrealized book. The metaphysical issues growing out of the Thai and Indian sections of the book do not knit with the obsessive eroticism that takes over when the action moves to Japan. What is still more embarrassing is the novel's title. Rather than hiding the work's blemishes, Mishima calls attention to them by naming his book *The Temple of Dawn*. Honda does visit Bangkok's Temple of Dawn in chapter 1, but he stays for less than a page and rarely mentions the place again. By contrast, he is more deeply moved by Benares; he stays there longer, visiting the riverside burial ghats at dusk and at dawn; Benares is also described in richer, more poetic detail than the Temple of Dawn. Like the book's other lapses and flaws, its poorly judged title suggests that Mishima may have changed his whole plan for the tetralogy while writing *Dawn*. But very little in the book evokes either those new aims or the methods he had in mind to achieve them.

3

The Mishima of *The Decay of the Angel* is so narrowly geared to disaster and sorrow that he either fails to establish an artistic purpose or he achieves it so well that he loses us. The novel stands as perhaps the bleakest and grimmest creation of an author notorious for his pessimism. This nastiness has hindered discourse (Seidensticker refers to "the remarkably small amount of critical notice which it [the tetralogy] has attracted").[6] Quite understandably, the discourse that does exist usually rivets on the work's depressiveness. Writing in 1987, Yoshio Iwamoto called *The Sea of Fertility* "a fictional account . . . of Japan's ruinous path to modernization." Addressing *Decay* in particular two years earlier, Scott-Stokes saw Mishima's Japan as "dominated by commerce" and as "a place where all human values have collapsed."[7] The by-products of commerce have caused much of this ruination. Coca-Cola advertisements and cellophane wrappers from souvenir shops are strewn everywhere; trash litters the landscape; industrial wastes pollute

Japan's waterways, and the air in chapter 9 is "strangled with gasoline fumes." These depredations have infected nature. At the end of chapter 15, the book's halfway point, Mishima describes clouds splitting, losing shape, and assuming "the ashen hue of death." Later, flowers will stab the sky, and "sharp blades of summer grass" will lance Honda's eyes. Even the sea, the source of life, is savage and malevolent; "stern . . . hard waves with ugly bellies put forth a "manifest vision of death" as they break on the shore in chapter 13.

Because effects take reality from their causes, this malignancy can only spread. The Mishima of *Decay* has surrendered completely to his dark side; a degraded, demented world view infects all. Honda's masochistic dream in *Dawn* of Ying Chan raining down on him fragrant streams of urine while straddling a peacock takes an ugly new turn in *Decay*. The Indian setting of the earlier novel reminds one that the peacock, India's national bird, is a harbinger of peace, hope, and good luck. Thus any association of peacocks with ugliness and waste stands as an attack upon beauty and affirmation. Carrying forward his dream of the pissing princess, the Honda of *Decay* selects as his site for spying on lovers a dark glade that may be "the abode of the Peacock Lord." His friend Keiko Hisamatsu will later be wearing a print dress with a peacock design when she discloses to a young man the forbidden secrets that will turn him into a living death.

This disclosure, which comes in chapter 27, spells out another ugly feature of the book—that, because the characters bring out the worst in each other and usually reach out to inflict pain, any loving act will run to waste. By explaining to young Toru Yasunaga his place in the continuum that began with Kiyoaki Matsugae, the first bearer of the three crucial moles, Keiko defuses the threat he poses to Honda. But this kindness recoils on her. Instead of thanking her for defanging his persecutor, Honda ends his twenty-year friendship with her. How many of these years was Honda looking for an excuse to lash out at her? Is she the victim of his stored-up malice? His hostility to life mounts in direct ratio to his growing resemblance to Mishima. In *Decay,* the differences between narrating and experiencing selves nearly disappear. Although more than thirty years divide Mishima from Honda, both men fear the imminent death that awaits them; neither wants to die harboring regrets. Thus the life portrayed in the book is not something that most people would miss. And the life they would miss least of all is the turbulent inner one.

A scene in chapter 26 that recalls Anton Chekhov reports the upstart Toru cutting down one of Honda's favorite trees. But the tree felling does not symbolize the inevitable supplanting of the old by the young. The process by which the destruction of old trees allows new ones to take hold and push into life symbolizes no romantic decline, as in *The Cherry Orchard;* Japan is not becoming a fragrant, productive garden, and Honda's tree still blooms. Toru only cut it down to do his adoptive father a nasty turn. Just after telling Honda that he felled the tree, he also challenges him to a fight. His explanation that the tree was "old and useless," delivered with a smirk, is another challenge, in view of its implication that Honda, too, is ripe for the ax. But how can the reader sympathize with eighty-year-old Honda, even though Toru is holding the poker in his hand that he had cudgeled Honda with just weeks before? No benign elder, Honda looked forward to seeing his cape myrtle's blossoms because they reminded him of white leprous skin. Mishima also says several times that Honda adopted Toru to begin with because of the wickedness he intuited in the boy. No injustice, his having fallen prey to this malice is what he deserves. Nor does Honda endear himself by revealing that his sole pleasure in life consists of looking forward to Toru's death, an event he expects will occur before the boy's twenty-first birthday, as with Kiyo, Isao, and Ying Chan. Such malevolence is blameworthy. As might be expected, it defeats itself—and in a way Mishima had not anticipated. *Decay* falls apart in its second half; the first half did not work either, but at least it tried for something—to convey the tortured romanticism of an old man heretofore condemned to the nonevent.

Honda's pain fuels the impression, created in *Dawn*, that Mishima abandoned his original intent for the tetralogy. All four works comprising the *Sea of Fertility* cycle embody the enthusiasms, the anguish, and the contradictions of the postwar era. Yet if Toru represents the corruption and iniquity of today, Honda is no torchbearer of the old humanity, if, indeed, Mishima credits its ever having existed in this century. Silent, distant Honda fears being

boring and irrelevant; sadly, he has borne out his own belief, first
stated in *Spring Snow,* in the lack of free will in the historical
process. But his late efforts to change history do not yield the
expected inferences. Though a record of unrelenting travail for him,
the tetralogy describes through him no vision of human goodness
trapped in a sordid world. Honda is a fussy, retiring widower of
seventy-six at the start of *Decay.* But any void created by Rie's death
has been quickly filled in. Keiko is much more of a companion to
him than Rie ever was. She and Honda joke and commiserate
together, they go to Europe, they worry about each other's health;
Keiko even lets him watch her make love to another woman. This
new regimen has changed him. Previously ruled by reason and
caution, he dares to dream. He takes risks. Financially secure but
inwardly empty, he adopts Toru because, through the sixteen-year-
old, he believes he can discover the pattern of reincarnation that has
ruled his adult life.

But his low self-esteem has both fragmented that life and frustrated the formation of patterns. He has divided reality between
those who remember and those who *are* remembered. Beauty and
mind cannot coexist for him in the same person either because
beauty is unconscious, a blind, amoral force. Logically enough, his
fortunes keep falling. Locked in a deathly duel of wits with Toru, he
performs acts to relieve his gloom that only deepen it. The most
dramatic of these comes in his visiting Tokyo's Meiji Gardens for the
first time in twenty years in order to spy on lovers. Prefiguring the
calamity that awaits him is a mirror meeting with another voyeur—
the same rat-eyed man who addressed him as a fellow peeper twenty-
two years before near the Ginza PX. So upset is Honda by this
coincidence that he cannot enjoy the spectacle he has come to see—
a pity because the spectacle costs him so much. Suddenly, the
carnality unfolding less than ten feet from him lurches into violence.
At a moment when he might be expected to consummate sex, the
man Honda is watching stabs the unsuspecting woman spread-
eagled beneath him. Then he flees.

The sound made by the knife that slashes the woman's thigh, that
of "a rasping snake's tongue," both recalls Ying Chan's death and
infers Honda's entrapment; the princess, Mishima wants the reader
to remember, died from a snakebite on her thigh. The recurrence, in

a different vein, of a key event from Honda's past shows that outlets for his renewal, or even escape, have been blocked. Voyeurism brings shame. Literally, his age frustrates his bid for freedom. Because his joints are too calcified and his legs, too weak, he cannot escape the site of the stabbing incident before the police arrive. He is arrested as a suspect. And though he is released, this octogenarian, long associated with the dignity, reserve, and discipline of the law, suffers scandal and disgrace. A reporter for a notorious weekly magazine prints a story about the false arrest that both wrecks Honda's social standing and inspires Toru to get him declared legally incompetent.

One of the sole merits of the thirty-chapter *Decay* inheres in how its structure charts Honda's downfall. In chapter 10, a third of the way through, Honda chances upon the signal station on the Izu Peninsula where Toru reports ship movements. This first meeting between the book's main antagonists cleverly adumbrates the book's title. Honda immediately fastens onto Toru because he sees him as a kindred spirit. An archetype has been thereby wrenched. Honda's fascination with the reckless Kiyo, Isao, and Ying Chan stemmed from the great gulf separating them from him, not from any similarity. Why the wrenching? Toru will remain in phase with creaking, shriveled Honda; the steeliness in him that seizes Honda at first meeting pits and tarnishes as Toru fulfills his destiny as the decaying angel. He even shows signs of his later decay here in chapter 10. Although he appears heroic to Honda while looking down at him from the top of a staircase, he is also wearing a flower that is "brownish and worm-eaten and badly wilted." The bedraggled flower reminds Honda of the decadent angel he had just read about. He is excited; his reading and his life have fused in a pattern whose meaning he longs to probe. This meaning unfolds inexorably. Yourcenar explains how lean, tough Toru will later conform to the fallen angel of Honda's book:

The decaying angel [i.e., Toru] neglects himself, refuses to change his linen and his clothes, and lies in bed all day long . . . throughout the hot summer, in the room stinking of sweat and withered flowers.[8]

This corruption only takes hold after the spirit has started to leave the angel's body. A major step in its advance appears in chapter 20, i.e., ten chapters after Toru meets Honda and ten before the book ends. In chapter 20, Toru cultivates a flair for wounding people. He also decides that, rather than squandering his malice, he will direct it to worthy objects. And he will attack their spirits, not merely their bodies. He later makes good his resolve to damage someone special when he tricks his fiancée into writing a letter full of lies that he later uses to break their engagement. Rather than simply telling Momoko that he does not love her, he breaks with her in a way that impugns her, her family, and her circle of friends. But his plans sometimes miscarry. Honda, the other person whose destruction he has been anticipating, has been changing from within. Waxing and waning simultaneously, he has seen the aches and creaks of his vast age sharpening rather than dulling his mind. The adversities of his years are giving him a clearer and deeper insight into reality. What to do with these new powers of perception? he wonders. He decides to direct them to a project that has occupied him indirectly for the past sixty years. He will visit Satoko Ayakura, Kiyo's former lover, at the Gesshu Temple, where she took her holy vows and also where she has been serving as abbess for many years.

This long-awaited—and long-delayed—visit occurs in chapter 30, the book's finale. Honda sees it as the crowning effort of his life. His upcoming meeting with Satoko—a consummation he both fears and craves—will resolve the most nagging problem of his life; the holy woman's wisdom can either crush or free him. In either case, he will have solved the riddle of Kiyo's reincarnation. To prepare himself for his meeting with Satoko, he insists on walking the last kilometer to the Gesshuji despite the blazing heat. His courage stirs us; he is bound to earn any self-renewal that awaits him. Though condemning his misanthropy, one admires the energy he pours into his pilgrimage. He matters despite his defects. The grand mission he is undertaking at great personal risk incorporates both a morality and a metaphysics.

In his overwrought state, certain features of the temple look familiar, whereas others seem new. Regardless, he perceives them with a new concentration and intensity. And he has fought his way into a suite of rooms inside the sacred Gesshuji, a place "he had thought it impossible to visit." The sexual symbolism describing his passage through the temple's various corridors conveys the grip of the moment. He has attained the core. Perhaps life *does* have meaning; perhaps he *will* be reborn. With a dish of candies nearby, he watches eighty-three-year-old Satoko slide into the room in a white kimono. His expectations rise. Responding from intuitive sources, he observes, "Satoko had changed utterly, and yet he knew at a glance that it was Satoko." Age has not degraded her as it has him. Will she reveal her secret? he wonders, his heart racing. What happens next shatters his hopes. She denies having ever known Kiyoaki Matsugae, in whose memory Honda has come to see her. This shocking disclosure depresses him; he feels betrayed. Her wisdom cannot help him, after all, if, indeed, her unforeseen disclosure is the product of wisdom and not perversity. Is she lying? Or, having banished Kiyo from her memory, has she refined her consciousness to a point beyond his powers of comprehension?

Satoko *has* given him the revelation he came to her for. But his hellish ordeal comes to nothing because of his unreadiness; the revelation bypasses him. Now Mishima has not devastated him and then sadistically withheld any compensating vision that might stem from the devastation. Honda's fate lies in himself, specifically in the lack of faith that has both smudged his view of human purpose and drained his self-trust. This archinfidel can learn nothing from the high priestess of faith. In chapter 25 of *Runaway Horses,* he had visited Kiyo's grave. After praying to Kiyo's spirit, he scanned his dead friend's gravestone for a sign or a message. But the mute gravestone told him nothing. His search for definitive answers meets frustration again at the end of *Decay,* and for the same reason. We must answer life's riddles ourselves; the solutions to our problems lie neither in artifacts nor in formal systems of belief. Honda's final betrayal is one of self. He sees that a lifetime's commitment to destructive habits of mind has calcified his heart. And sustenance cannot be drawn from a stone.

The same retribution that flattens him has buoyed up and refreshed Satoko. Her statement very near the end, "Memory is like a phantom mirror," suggests that she has acquired the control, the grace, and the spiritual refinement to exorcise her youthful sin together with all memory of her co-sinner. She has adopted the means of spiritual salvation along with the ends. The search for an absolute system that defeated Shunsuke of *Forbidden Colors* along with Honda and Mishima himself has ended in triumph for her. She has found God within herself. Hasso Buddhism, the creed on which the Gesshu Temple is based, has facilitated this discovery. Far from confusing the reader, Mishima already ratified Satoko's enigmatic words to Honda in rare intrusion; a footnote in *Spring Snow* (p. 30 n.) calls the linchpin of Hasso Buddhism the belief that "all existence is based on subjective awareness." Satoko has learned to trust her responses. To her, truth lies with the perceiver; it is an activity of the inner self. The proofs and vertifications she lives by dwell in her heart.

All she can do for Honda, she sees finally, is to show him the temple's south garden. At the end of his thwarted life, he faces the burden of starting anew. What will his new start bring? His staggering into the garden, weak and breathless, "as if pulled by strings," describes him as a puppet. He has not yet gained the knowledge that will give him autonomy; at age eighty-one, he seems to lack the inner resources needed to stand free. Faced with his emptiness at the end, he gazes at the empty, "still garden." But the glimmer of a tallying vision might have occurred; Satoko's revelation might have struck home. Yes, the stillness he confronts in the garden's dizzy glare evokes death. Such hopelessness fits with Mishima's description of his intent in the tetralogy, voiced in the note, "About the Author," that follows the book's last page: "The title, *The Sea of Fertility*," Mishima told Donald Keene, "is intended to suggest the arid sea of the moon that belies its name. Or I might say that it superimposes the image of cosmic nihilism on that of the fertile sea." This loveless summary explains the last scene of *Decay*, which shows a confused, frustrated Honda stubbing along on shaky, tired legs; he has seen his expectations dashed. But he is standing erect, however unsteadily, in a garden alive with reds and greens. The wild carnations, celadons, and flaming maples surrounding him all deny the equation of stillness and death. Against odds, Honda could rise to the challenge posed by the garden's thronging fertility and make the new start he desperately needs.

Unfortunately, by the time we reach the brilliant last chapter of *Decay*, our interest in Honda has dropped sharply. The book does not have much life to start with. What follows the first few chapters, though meant to gather in intensity, remains static. As Seidensticker has shown, foremost among Mishima's problems consists of maintaining focus and flow: "It [the book] seems founded upon confusions so considerable as to make us wonder whether Mishima might not have lost interest in or control over his work."[9] This wavering of purpose shows itself most embarrassingly in Mishima's disjointed portrait of Toru. A brilliant orphan of sixteen at the outset, Toru is well suited to his signalman's job. Watching fulfills and gladdens him. He enjoys sending his strikingly beautiful eyes into the distance to catch sight of the ships he guides into port. He searches the skies for glimpses of Venus and Mars. So strong is his visual connection to the world that, in chapter 15, he goes to the movies on his day off. But the objectivity that watching has drilled into him has dried his heart. He lacks a social conscience; he scorns politics and religion; he has no friends. His compulsive washing of his hands conveys an ongoing wish to rid himself of traces of the outside world, particularly human contact. "He lived in a small castle of ice," Mishima says of his radical objectivity. What turns his dispassion into contempt for external reality is his belief that he exists in absolute, rather than relative, terms. He refuses to compare himself to anybody. His progressive alienation ends in the self-reflexive activity of redirecting his awareness to itself; his thinking becomes its own object. The deathly link joining intelligence and cruelty has been forged. Thus he hurts Momoko without giving his confederate in her undoing the satisfaction of learning of his success; earlier, he had twisted Momoko's hair more tightly into a branch where it had accidentally snagged while pretending to free it.

This cartoon villainy defies belief. It also challenges the pattern of reincarnation set by Kiyo and Isao. The problem stems from Mishima's depiction of the degeneration undergone by the archetypal figure over time. If the progressive weakening of the pattern shows cultural dissociation, it also conveys Mishima's disorientation and distraction. Kiyo and Isao both die at twenty; so does Ying Chan, but she may lack the troika of moles that joins her to her predecessors. A real puzzle this, as Mishima intended it to be. Honda claimed to have seen the moles while watching her making love to Keiko at the end of *Dawn;* if his eyes had not failed him in his heated state, then the moles either mutated on her flank between the ages of seven and nineteen or they were there all along but only became

visible during sex. Though Toru's three moles show clearly, he
survives his twenty-first birthday. His pride also blocks him from
living passionately like his three predecessors (the princess's heart
may have been twisted, but it had not chilled). Finally, he departs
from Kiyo, Isao, and Ying Chan by not dreaming. The mental
control and bent for rational analysis that have curbed his dreaming
put him closer to Honda than to his three predecessors. There is
other evidence that the line of descent has changed. Honda, the
guardian of the miracle and the person longest associated with it,
has entered the succession. And why should he not? He has devoted
more energy to it than anyone else. Mishima implies a change in the
pattern by alternating, in his first five chapters, between him and
Toru. The link between the two men strengthens in other ways; Toru
prepares to go to sleep at the end of chapter 3, and Honda *is*
sleeping at the start of chapter 4. His waking up at the end of the
chapter tallies with Toru's being aroused by his alarm clock fifty
miles away in the first sentence of chapter 5. Honda will immediately
intuit his kinship to Toru when they meet in chapter 10 because that
kinship is involuntary and unconscious.

But all too rapidly it falls apart. Honda wakes up at the close of
chapter 4 from one of his many dreams in the book. Toru, with his
arrogance and cynicism, never dreams. An inversion has suddenly
occurred. Honda now joins the impulsive Kiyo, Isao, and Ying
Chan—whereas Toru stands alone. Intriguing enough on their own,
the ambiguities rising from this inversion lack the plotting to sustain
them. Perhaps Mishima was himself the decaying angel whose per-
petual quest for revelation had depleted him and ransacked his art.
To resolve his diffuse, sagging plot, he restores Keiko, who had been
out of view for many chapters. This restoration augurs badly. And
the reader's worst fears are quickly confirmed. Keiko reappears in
Decay for the same reason that she walked midstream into *Dawn;*
Mishima needed her. He uses her to punish Toru for browbeating
Honda.

What he omits to do is to justify Keiko's power over Toru. The
aftermath of the stabbing incident in the Meiji Gardens had solid-
ified Toru's dominance over his disgraced foster father. Keiko seeks
redress for Honda by inviting Toru to a dinner party at which he
soon finds himself to be the only guest. He is outmaneuvered and

outclassed throughout the evening. Explaining that others before him have had the three moles on which he bases his uniqueness, she jars his poise. Her accusation that he is an impostor also includes the cunning inference that, by dying before his twenty-first birthday, he will prove his nobility; on the other hand, his surviving past age twenty will confirm his worthlessness. She argues speciously. Yet she argues from need. She has seen that only his death will end his reign of terror over Honda. But a person of Toru's intelligence should have seen through her casuistry. What is more, it is never made clear why a person as self-possessed and entrenched in his power as Toru should go to pieces upon hearing Keiko's words, even if he believes them. This intrepid, unpitying young man has already razed all obstacles standing between him and total control over the man he hates.

His actions after leaving Keiko observe a tight, if crazy, logic. To convince himself that she was lying, Toru reads Kiyo's now-thread-bare diary; he wants to know that he has always been in charge of his fortunes vis-à-vis Honda. The confirmation he craves is withheld. What he finds in the diary upsets him so much that he poisons himself. But instead of dying, he goes blind; the poison destroys his optic nerves. Here is poetic justice. Not only has evil wrecked itself; the wicked Toru's most beautiful feature and his main tie with the world, his eyes, are annihilated in a single stroke. But for all its inevitability, the stroke is a miscue. Cruel, calculating Toru needs assurances and justifications from Kiyo's diary no more than he needed to listen to Keiko. In order to bring him down, Mishima had to violate Toru's contempt for others and his born ruler's hardness of heart. Scowling, sadistic Toru had to go mushy before his story could end. But Mishima's cheating went beyond falsifying his character. He also omits the passage in Kiyo's diary that drove Toru to take poison. And his whisking Keiko immediately from the action as soon as she addles Toru's mind confirms the suspicion that he could not resolve his plot with the same elements he developed it with.

Toru's behavior after his blinding restores a measure of probability. As has been seen, he slouches in his evil-smelling room, perspiring into the linen and bedclothes he rarely changes. At his side is a local woman advisedly five years his senior. Called "a demented girl" in a detective's report (chapter 16), the unusually ugly Kinue believes that she is beautiful and that men are always chasing her. Her recent attacks of vomiting and her strange new eating habits argue, along with a sudden weight gain, that she is pregnant. But Toru would marry her in any case to spite Honda. Marriage to this bloated lunatic would prove to Honda that his attempts to build and refine Toru's tastes over the years have failed. But this savage justice does not redeem the novel. Scattered, disconcerting, and out of phase with its original concept, *Decay* ends before resolving three important issues—the surgery Honda needs to remove a cancerous growth, the birth of Toru's child with Kinue, and the question of whether Honda will outlive Toru. Perhaps no satisfactory resolutions could occur, anyway, amid the breakdowns in communication that pile up at the end. Kinue goes on speaking nonsense; Iago-like, Toru refuses to speak; Satoko does speak but Honda suspects she is lying.

Nearly a total miss, *Decay* is the work of a bitter, disillusioned man distracted by death. Mishima's extending the time frame of the work to 1975 conveys the pathos of his distraction. No excursion into futurism or political prophecy, the five years that the novel extends past the time of its writing form the only future Mishima would know. His ending the book without resolving three major questions may have been an indirect plea to be reprieved from his self-imposed death sentence; perhaps a miracle would help him supply the resolutions in a sequel to *Decay*. Yet his datelining the book 25 November 1970 after writing its last sentence infers an acceptance of his death mere hours later. The datelining also invites us to view his death and the completion not only of *Decay* but also of *The Sea of Fertility* as a single act. His friends said that he intuited the fiasco his suicide would be. He was also artist enough to perceive the blemishes and flaws in *Decay*. These would have to stand. The creator-showman-scourge who perpetrated them had a date with death. Delaying that date for the sake of editing *Decay* would not have helped the book, anyway. Its cast of angry, frustrated, deluded people reflects a moral defeatism beyond the niceties of stylistic revision. In *The Decay of the Angel*, Mishima wrote the book that was in him during his last year. If it is a shambles, it also reveals a bravery and an honesty that soften the judgment it invokes on aesthetic grounds. Although he would have rejected pity or charity, a flicker of his weary eye might have signaled a wish to be understood. I hope that the flicker included the intuition that any outlay of understanding on our part would be deserved.

Conclusion

Yukio Mishima's writing takes us to Japan. But it also takes us far inside the most opaque and mysterious of all things—a human soul. Mishima writes from deep within himself. Practicing a self-scrutiny on a scale that rivals Nathaniel Hawthorne and Philip Roth, he ventures into places few have glimpsed, and he makes us face the worst they offer. He is candid, too, in his reaction to this worst, even though his candor is sometimes spoiled by posturing or a school-boyish desire to shock. But because this same worst was anchored in his maladjustment, he does not deserve a high place as an artist or thinker. What he does deserve is a considered look. His work has conviction. His books are almost always the ones he wanted to write, and they have human scale. You can see all their faults and remain riveted, anyway.

Compelling us in his best work is an inner dimension of meaning more elusive and primitive than first appears. He knows that we are all frail creatures inhabiting a puzzling, dangerous world, and he searches for his place in that world by using forceful, vivid language; even in translation, the vigor of his prose grips us. Its lyrical and tragical intensity combines a harsh animal edge with vibrancy and formal rigor. This formality serves as a caution. The carnality of his imagination is deceptive. His ability to vary narrative tone and texture can produce smart, sophisticated dialogue. And he is as sensitive to what is hidden, whispered, and inchoate as to the grossly sensual. By modulating the fury and force of his prose, he can create meanings of delicate implication. Much of his magic rises from details that evoke rather than just simply describe emotions. The ecstasy of a woman having sex in chapter 44 of *The Temple of*

Dawn overflows into two realms: her "red-lacquered toes flexed as if she were dancing on a sheet of hot iron, and yet they merely trod the empty twilight." Just as moving as these moments of erotic abandon are the incidental images found elsewhere, like the tiny piece of lint that an infant in *Forbidden Colors* has carried inside its fist since birth.

Mishima's image-making skills infer a steely, spacious mind. The inference has already been made on a broader scale. In 1985, Sandra Lockwood contrasted his sharp individualism with the languid, all-tolerant pluralism of today that neither exerts nor challenges power:

We are confronted by a man who followed his passions, lived out his dreams right to their fatal conclusions when most of us don't even have the courage to discover what we believe in.[1]

Such courage safeguards personal autonomy. How many in the pampered, bureaucratic West care enough about anything to die for it? The single-mindedness of Mishima's dedication humbles most of his readers. Committing oneself absolutely to a cause reveals a purity and intensity few would dare. Mishima's willingness to die rather than to live with what he scorns as tawdriness cannot be dismissed as snobbery or escapism. Too much of human progress rests on the energies of those brave enough to reject the status quo. The rebel who dies physically only to be reborn in the hearts of his followers has recurred often in the world's histories and myths.

It is recurring now. Many of Japan's neonationalists in the late 1980s prize Mishima as a guiding spirit; like him, they want to revive Japan's national character by reinstating pre-Meiji ideals of unity and purity.[2] But these neonationalists comprise a small minority, and Mishima's political appeal will always be limited to fringe groups like them. We can see why. We have to swallow him whole if he is really going to move us; we cannot pick and choose and isolate for approval those pieces of his thought that fit our ethical programming. His intransigence blocks our way. Yes, he stretches our awareness and teaches us to read more carefully. But he does not illuminate important places. His obsession with death has made him slight the moral condition of his people, i.e., their mental health and happiness. Bound neither by reason nor the codes of civilized society, he found his true vocation in death.

He hated where Japan was heading. The United States had given the Japanese a new constitution, eliminated her armed forces, and introduced reforms in education, politics, land tenure, and the law—all to abolish the conditions that presumably fostered the militarism Mishima cherished as vital to his nation's heritage.[3] But wasn't his view of vitality both warped and rearguard? The American occupation of Japan meant more than an infusion of glitz and glare. Admittedly, the popularity of American artifacts introduced into Japan between 1945 and 1955 violated good taste. But it did not make Japan as vulgar and materialistic as Mishima believed. Industrial production was also improved in those years; a healthy balance of payments was achieved and maintained; more consumer goods and more leisure time were created for the masses. Life in Japan under this new prosperity was not as squalid as Mishima claimed.

Thus his literary corpus cannot qualify as a searching criticism of life. His ultranationalism kept him from creating a body of work Japanese in sensibility. The samurai ethic that inspired him also confused and twisted him. His elitism neglects the full range of his culture's myths, voices, and symbols. The way of the warrior provides an ingenious but limiting perspective. It is also an evasion because it is based on a nostalgia for the motifs, materials, and mentality of the past. This nostalgia clouds his whole ontology, not only his politics. Just how far he lost his way can be gauged by comparing him to another nonegalitarian who hated the by-products of mechanized industry. But D. H. Lawrence was a vitalist. *The Rainbow* (1915) and *Lady Chatterley's Lover* (1928) both show the ruin that occurs when the organic tie is snapped between a people and the land it inhabits. Lawrence also favored spontaneity and candor; the sexual dynamic infusing his best work rests on a healthy interchange. Nature to him thronged with gods and goddesses ranging from the Aztec to the Greek pantheon. These gods and goddesses inform reality. His characters attain a flame tip of emotional intensity when they follow their own divine impulses.

Despite all his gifts, Mishima cannot teach humane action. He slights those two benchmarks of man's moral development—freedom and justice. Nor does he explore art's power to debate moral issues. Little about him fosters cooperation or creates hope. Little could. He never reveals anything like a disciplined or concentrated love for his people. And he does not let them try to win *our* love because he removes them from the mild, middling truth of everyday life, where people are not always tragically falling in love or destroying themselves. The people we know are more reasonable and resilient than his hysterical characters. Shunning extremism, they adapt to setback. Things that do not work out for the best will work out for the second best, and people are mostly content.

Not so with Mishima's people. They ignore the warmth and security of family life, the fight for freedom and self-definition, and the rewards of leading a happy, active life. Despite their compulsiveness, they probably also ignore the quest for truth in the shadow of death. Though an exaggeration, Henry Miller's charge that he lacked a sense of humor[4] touches on one of his worst failings. The substance of his books is so stark and grim that the odd spots of freshness smother inside his leaden seriousness. Had he learned to laugh at himself, he might have opened his heart. Had he understood the importance of dispensing simple humanity, he would have discovered vital outlets for his vigorous, lyrical prose. He would have also done justice to his inventiveness; more, he would be remembered as a major writer, one that changes how we see and think.

Notes

Chapter 1: The Point of Action

1. Luis Canales, introduction, *Kaleidoscope Kyoto* [hereinafter cited as *KK*] (April 1985): 141.

2. Graham Greene, "Walter de la Mare's Short Stories," *Collected Essays* (New York: Viking, 1969), p. 141.

3. Henry Scott-Stokes, *The Life and Death of Yukio Mishima* (New York: Farrar, Straus & Giroux, 1974), p. 89; John Nathan, *Mishima: A Biography* (Boston: Little, Brown, 1974), p. 74.

4. Edwin O. Reischauer, *Japan: The Story of a Nation* (New York: Knopf, c. 1970), p. 294.

5. Ivan Morris, *The Nobility of Failure: Tragic Heroes in the History of Japan* (New York: Holt, Rinehart and Winston, 1975), p. 181.

6. Ian Buruma, *Behind the Mask: On Sexual Demons, Sacred Mothers . . . and Other Japanese Cultural Heroes* (New York: Pantheon, 1984), p. xi.

7. Morris, *Nobility of Failure*, pp. 180–216, passim.

8. Ruth Benedict, *The Chrysanthemum and the Sword: Patterns of Japanese Culture* (1946; New York: New American Library, 1974), pp. 47–75.

9. Ibid., p. 315.

10. Yukio Mishima, "An Appeal," *The Japanese Interpreter* 7 (Winter 1971): 74.

11. Yukio Mishima, "Yang-Ming Thought as Revolutionary Philosophy," *The Japanese Interpreter* 7 (Winter 1971): 86–87.

12. Yukio Mishima, "An Ideology for an Age of Languid Peace," *The Japanese Interpreter* 7 (Winter 1971): 79.

13. Alex Shishin, "Thoughts on Mishima," *The Japan Times*, 18 December 1985, p. 14.

14. Nathan, *Mishima*, p. 175.

15. Ibid, p. 210.

16. Mishima wanted to restore the Imperial Way, i.e., reverence for the emperor, by revoking Japan's 1947 constitution, disbanding the houses of the diet, or parliament, and declaring martial law.

17. Robert C. Christopher, *The Japanese Mind: The Goliath Explained* (New York: Linden Press/Simon & Schuster, 1983), p. 120.

18. Reischauer, *Japan*, pp. 334–35.

19. Ian Buruma, "Rambo-San," *New York Review of Books,* 10 October 1985, p. 16.

20. Ibid., p. 15.

21. Christopher, *Japanese Mind,* p. 73.

22. Buruma, "Rambo-San," p. 16.

23. In Sue Townsend, *The Adrian Mole Diaries* (New York: Grove, 1986), p. 168.

24. Morris, *Nobility of Failure,* p. 65.

25. Benedict, *Chrysanthemum and Sword,* pp. 192–93.

26. Kawamura Jiro, "On Mishima's Literature," *Japan Quarterly* 23 (January–March 1976): 87; Gore Vidal, "Mr. Japan," *New York Review of Books,* 17 June 1971, pp. 8–10.

27. Morris, *Nobility of Failure,* p. 214.

28. In Ryusaku Tsunoda, William Theodore de Bary, and Donald Keene, compilers, *Sources of Japanese Tradition,* ed. Theodore de Bary (New York: Columbia University Press, 1964), 2, p. 389.

29. Mamoru Iga, *The Thorn in the Chrysanthemum: Suicide and Economic Success in Japan* (Berkeley, CA: University of California Press, 1986), p. 94.

30. Noguchi Takehiho, "Mishima Yukio and Kita Ikki: The Aesthetics and Politics of Ultranationalism in Japan," trans. Teruko Craig, *Journal of Japanese Studies* 10 (Summer 1984): 439.

31. Masao Miyoshi, *Accomplices of Silence: The Modern Japanese Novel* (Berkeley, CA: University of California Press, 1974), p. 176.

32. "The Maturing of Japan," *The Economist,* 17 August 1985, p. 12.

33. Henry Scott-Stokes, "Lost Samurai: The Withered Soul of Postwar Japan," *Harper's,* October 1985, p. 56.

34. David Pollack, "Action as Fitting Match to Knowledge: Language as Symbol in Mishima's *Kinkakuji* [i.e., *The Temple of the Golden Pavilion*]," *Monumenta Nipponica,* 40 (Winter 1985): 389.

35. Geoffrey Bownas, translator's preface, ed. Yukio Mishima and Geoffrey Bownas, *New Writing in Japan* (Baltimore: Penguin, 1972), p. 11.

Chapter 2: Cables of Discipline

1. Yukio Mishima, introduction, ed. Keizo Aizawa, *Young Samurai: Bodybuilders of Japan* (New York: Grove, 1967), pp. vii–x.

2. Vidal, "Mr. Japan," pp. 9–10. For a rebuttal, see Ivan Morris, "Mishima," *New York Review of Books,* 16 December 1971, p. 42.

3. Yukio Mishima, "A Famous Japanese Judges the U.S. Giant," trans. Donald Keene, *Life,* 11 September 1964, p. 83.

4. Scott-Stokes, *Life and Death,* p. 65.

5. Gwenn Boardman Petersen, *The Moon in the Water: Understanding Tanizaki, Kawabata, and Mishima* (Honolulu: University Press of Hawaii, c. 1979), pp. 283, 232–33.

6. Noriko Mizuta Lippit, *Reality and Fiction in Modern Japanese Literature* (White Plains, NY: M. E. Sharpe, 1980), p. 185.

7. Robert Jay Lifton, Shuichi Kato, and Michael R. Reich, *Six Lives Six Deaths: Portraits from Modern Japan* (New Haven: Yale University Press, 1979), p. 269.

8. Luis Canales, "Mishima Yukio: A Romantic Pyramid of Modern Japanese Literature," *KK* (April 1985): 10.

9. Marguerite Yourcenar, *Mishima: A Vision of the Void*, trans. Albert Manguel in collaboration with the author (1980; New York: Farrar, Straus & Giroux, 1986), p. 100.

10. Martin Seymour-Smith, *Who's Who in Twentieth Century Literature* (New York: McGraw-Hill, 1976), p. 243; Ian Buruma, " 'Rabu' Conquers All," *New York Review of Books*, 26 September 1985, p. 38; Buruma, "Rambo-San," p. 15; Scott-Stokes, "Lost Samurai," pp. 56, 60.

11. See Eikoh Hosoe, *Barakei: Ordeal by Roses* (1963; New York: Aperture, 1985).

12. In Mark Holborn, afterword, Eikoh Hosoe, *Barakei*, n.p.

13. Scott-Stokes, *Life and Death*, p. 291.

14. Jiro, "On Mishima's Literature," p. 86.

15. Scott-Stokes, "Lost Samurai," p. 60.

16. See Scott-Stokes, *Life and Death*, pp. 302, 258–59.

17. "Comments on His Death," *KK* (April 1985): 26.

18. Lifton, Kato, and Reich, *Six Lives*; Robert Jay Lifton, *The Broken Connection: On Death and the Continuity of Life* (New York: Simon & Schuster, 1979), p. 262; Petersen, *Moon in Water*, p. 201; Hisaaki Yamanouchi, *The Search for Authenticity in Modern Japanese Literature* (Cambridge: Cambridge University Press, 1978), p. 137.

19. Buruma, "Rambo-San," p. 15; Scott-Stokes, "Lost Samurai," p. 61.

20. "Mishima as an Actor," *KK* (April 1985): 23.

21. Buruma, "Rambo-San," p. 17.

22. Ibid., p. 15.

23. Pollack, "Action as Fitting Match," p. 398; see n. 35, above.

Chapter 3: A Boy's Own Stories

1. Petersen, *Moon in Water*, p. 201.

2. Henry Miller, *Reflections on the Death of Mishima* (Santa Barbara, CA: Capra, 1972), p. 32.

3. Nathan, *Mishima*, p. 90

4. Donald Keene, *Landscapes and Portraits: Appreciations of Japanese Culture* (Tokyo: Kodansha International, 1971), p. 206.

5. Nathan, *Mishima*, p. 95.

6. Miyoshi, *Accomplices*, p. 152.

7. Ibid., p. 150 n.

8. See Richard Plant, *The Pink Triangle: The Nazi War Against Homosexuals* (New York: New Republic/Holt, 1986).

9. Keene, *Landscapes and Portraits*, p. 205.
10. Miyoshi, *Accomplices*, p. 150.
11. Keene, *Landscapes and Portraits*, p. 209.
12. Nathan, *Mishima*, p. 95.
13. Yourcenar, *Mishima*, p. 16; Scott-Stokes, *Life and Death*, p. 56.
14. Yourcenar, *Mishima*, p. 8.
15. Scott-Stokes, *Life and Death*, p. 128.
16. Keene, *Landscapes and Portraits*, pp. 210–11.

Chapter 4: Narcissus Bound

1. Yourcenar, *Mishima*, p. 32.
2. Anatole Broyard, "About Books: Sadder Music and Stronger Poetics," *New York Times Book Review*, 27 April 1986, p. 15.
3. Yamanouchi, *Search for Authenticity*, p. 152.
4. Yourcenar, *Mishima*, p. 33; Miyoshi, *Accomplices*, p. 158.

Chapter 5: Sundowners

1. Petersen, *Moon in Water*, pp. 217–18.
2. Nancy Wilson Ross, introduction, *The Temple of the Golden Pavilion*, by Yukio Mishima, trans. Ivan Morris (New York: Putnam's/Wideview/Perigree, n.d.), p. v; Yoshio Iwamoto, "Beneath Mishima's Masks," *Insight*, 23 March 1987, p. 71.
3. Ross, introduction, p. xviii.
4. Keene, *Landscapes and Portraits*, p. 214.
5. Miyoshi, *Accomplices*, p. 169.
6. Ibid.
7. Pollack, "Action as Fitting Match," p. 395.
8. Miyoshi, *Accomplices*, p. 165.

Chapter 6: Breaking the Rules

1. Miyoshi, *Accomplices*, p. 170; Petersen, *Moon in Water*, p. 278.
2. Scott-Stokes, *Life and Death*, p. 159; Nathan, *Mishima*, p. 192.
3. Edmund White, "Too good to be true, at least too good to be interesting," *New York Times Book Review*, 24 June 1973, p. 3.

Chapter 7: Tragedy at the Crossroads

1. Yourcenar, *Mishima*, p. 57.

Chapter 8: Echoes from a Waterfall

1. Miyoshi, *Accomplices*, p. 173.
2. Edward Seidensticker, *This Country, Japan* (Tokyo: Kodansha International, 1979), p. 144.
3. Yourcenar, *Mishima*, p. 75.

4. Seidensticker, *Japan,* p. 141.
5. Miller, *Reflections,* p. 38.
6. Seidensticker, *Japan,* p. 139.
7. Iwamoto, "Beneath Mishima's Masks," p. 71; Scott-Stokes, "Lost Samurai," p. 57.
8. Yourcenar, *Mishima,* p. 91.
9. Seidensticker, *Japan,* p. 141.

Conclusion

1. Sandra Lockwood, "A Literary Exhibit Not to Be Missed," *KK* (April, 1985): 25.
2. Ian Buruma, "A New Japanese Nationalism," *New York Times Magazine,* 12 April 1987, pp. 22–27, 29, 38.
3. See Theodore Cohen, *Remaking Japan: The American Occupation as New Deal* (New York: Free, 1987).
4. Miller, *Reflections,* p. 23.

Bibliography

Principal Works by Yukio Mishima

Confessions of a Mask. 1949. Trans. Meredith Weatherby. New York: New Directions, 1958.

Thirst for Love. 1950. Trans. Alfred H. Marks. New York: Knopf, 1969.

Forbidden Colors. 1951. Trans. Alfred H. Marks. New York: Knopf, 1968.

The Sound of Waves. 1954. Trans. Meredith Weatherby. New York: Knopf, 1956.

The Temple of the Golden Pavilion. 1956. Trans. Ivan Morris. New York: Knopf, 1959.

Five Modern No Plays. Trans. Donald Keene. New York: Knopf, 1957.

After the Banquet. 1960. Trans. Donald Keene. New York: Knopf, 1963.

The Sailor Who Fell from Grace with the Sea. 1963. Trans. John Nathan. New York: Knopf, 1965.

Tropical Tree. Trans. Kenneth Strong. *Japanese Quarterly* 11 (1964): 174–210.

Madame de Sade. 1965. Trans. Donald Keene. New York: Grove, 1967.

Death in Midsummer and Other Stories. 1966. Trans. Edward G. Seidensticker. New York: New Directions, 1966.

The Way of the Samurai. 1967. Trans. Kathryn Sparling. New York: Basic Books, 1977.

Sun and Steel. 1968. Trans. John Bester. Toyko: Kodansha International, 1970.

Spring Snow. 1968. Trans. Michael Gallagher. New York: Knopf, 1972.

Runaway Horses. 1969. Trans. Michael Gallagher. New York: Knopf, 1973.

The Temple of Dawn. 1970. Trans. E. Dale Saunders and Cecilia Segawa Seigle. New York: Knopf, 1973.

The Decay of the Angel. 1970. Trans. Edward G. Seidensticker. New York: Knopf, 1974.

Selected Books and Articles on Yukio Mishima

Buruma, Ian. *Behind the Mask: On Sexual Demons, Sacred Mothers . . . and Other Japanese Cultural Heroes*. New York: Pantheon, 1984.

————. "A New Japanese Nationalism." *New York Times Magazine* 12 April 1987, pp. 22–27, 29, 38.

Hosoe, Eikoh. *Barakei: Ordeal by Roses* [photographs of Yukio Mishima]. 1963; New York: Aperture, 1985.

Iga, Mamoru. *The Thorn in the Chrysanthemum: Suicide and Economic Success in Japan*. Berkeley, CA: University of California Press, 1986.

Iwamoto, Yoshio. "Beneath Mishima's Masks." *Insight,* 23 March 1987, p. 71.

Jiro, Kawamura. "On Mishima's Literature." *Japan Quarterly,* (January–March 1976): 86–87.

Kaleidoscope Kyoto, 13 (April 1985) [special Mishima issue].

Keene, Donald. *Dawn to the West: Japanese Literature of the Modern Era: Poetry, Drama, Criticism*. New York: Holt, Rinehart and Winston, c. 1984.

————. *Landscapes and Portraits: Appreciations of Japanese Culture*. Tokyo: Kodansha International, 1971, pp. 204–5.

Lifton, Robert Jay. *The Broken Connection: On Death and the Continuity of Life*. New York: Simon and Schuster, 1979, pp. 262–80.

————, Suichi Kato, and Michael R. Reich. "Mishima Yukio—The Man Who Loved Death." *Six Lives Six Deaths*. New Haven: Yale University Press, 1979, pp. 231–74.

Lippit, Noriko Mizuta. *Reality and Fiction in Modern Japanese Literature*. White Plains, NY: M. E. Sharpe, 1980, pp. 181–90.

Miller, Henry. *Reflections on the Death of Mishima*. Santa Barbara: Capra, 1972.

Miyoshi, Masao. *Accomplices of Silence: The Modern Japanese Novel*. Berkeley, CA: University of California Press, 1974, pp. 141–80.

Morris, Ivan. *The Nobility of Failure: Tragic Heroes in the History of Japan*. New York: Holt, Rinehart and Winston, 1975.

Nathan, John. *Mishima: A Biography*. Boston: Little, Brown, 1974.

Noguchi, Takehiho. "Mishima Yukio and Kita Ikki: The Aesthetics and Politics of Ultranationalism in Japan." Trans. Teruko Craig. *Journal of Japanese Studies* 10 (Summer 1984): 437–54.

Petersen, Gwenn Boardman. *The Moon in the Water: Understanding Tanizaki, Kawabata, and Mishima*. Honolulu: University Press of Hawaii, 1979, pp. 201–336.

Pollack, David. "Action as Fitting Match to Knowledge: Language and Symbol in Mishima's *Kinkakuji* [i.e., *The Temple of the Golden Pavilion*]." *Monumenta Nipponica* 40 (Winter 1985): 387–98.

Scott-Stokes, Henry. *The Life and Death of Yukio Mishima*. New York: Farrar, Straus, & Giroux, 1974.

Seidensticker, Edward G. *This Country, Japan*. Tokyo: Kodansha International, 1979, pp. 129–48.

Ueda, Makoto. *Modern Japanese Writers and the Nature of Literature*. Stanford, CA: Stanford University Press, 1976, pp. 219–59.

Wagenaar, Dick, and Yoshio Iwamoto. "Yukio Mishima: Dialectics of Mind and Body." *Contemporary Literature* 16 (Winter 1975). 41–60.

Yamanouchi, Hisaaki. *The Search for Authenticity in Modern Japanese Literature.* Cambridge: Cambridge University Press, 1978, pp. 137–52.

Yourcenar, Marguerite. *Mishima: A Vision of the Void.* Trans. Albert Manguel in collaboration with the author. 1980; New York: Farrar, Straus, & Giroux, 1986.

Index